PLANNING
FOR SCHOOL
BUILDINGS

PRENTICE-HALL EDUCATION SERIES

Dan Cooper, Editor

PLANNING

JAMES D. MacCONNELL

Associate Professor, School of Education, and Director of the School Planning Laboratory, Stanford University

FOR SCHOOL

BUILDINGS

PRENTICE-HALL, INC.

Englewood Cliffs, N. J. · 1957

PRINTED IN THE UNITED STATES OF AMERICA

67944

PREFACE

Planning for School Buildings discusses (1) school planning problems and their solution; (2) skilled and lay personnel involved in the planning; (3) timing of the planning; (4) organizational patterns of programming; and (5) economies in school building. This book will be useful as a basic text in school planning courses at the college and university level as well as a guide for school personnel —particularly school board members and their superintendents— architects, engineers, and other planners of school buildings.

Planning for School Buildings is the culmination of many years' work and was made possible with the assistance of my colleagues at Stanford University and elsewhere throughout the United States. The names mentioned below indicate the high caliber of assistance I received during this undertaking: Dr. William R. Odell, Professor of Education, Stanford University; Dr. Jon S. Peters and Dr. Raymond C. Schneider, Consultants in the School Planning Laboratory at Stanford University; Dr. J. Russell Kent, Acting Assistant Professor of Education, Stanford University; Dr. Keith Goldhammer, Associate Professor of Education, University of Oregon; Dr. O. Kenneth O'Fallon, Associate Professor of Education, Kansas State College; and Dr. Paul W. Seagers, Professor of Education, Indiana University.

Many valuable suggestions were made by school planning personnel from State Departments of Education throughout the United States. Extensive contributions came from Mr. Paul L. Rivers, Chief of the Division of School Planning, California State Department of Education, and Dr. Ray L. Hamon, Chief, School Housing Section, Office of Education, United States Department of Health, Education, and Welfare.

Advice and counsel of immeasurable value were received from many superintendents of schools regarding the communicability and level of understanding which their respective boards of education felt would be most beneficial to those who are facing school building problems first hand. Important among this group were: Paul W. Briggs, Bay City (Michigan) Public Schools; R. Guild Gray, Clark County (Nevada) School District; George D. Miner, Richmond (California) School Districts; Walter M. Ostenberg, Salina (Kansas) School District; Nolan D. Pulliam, Stockton (California) Unified School District; Sheldon Rankin, Walnut Creek (California) School District; and William M. Staerkel, Beatrice (Nebraska) School District.

Much of the technical information used in portions of *Planning for School Buildings* was supplied by the following professional people: John Carl Warnecke, Mario J. Ciampi, and John Lyon Reid, San Francisco; L. F. Richards, Santa Clara; John A. Shaver, Salina; and Harold Hovind, Seattle—all of whom are architects; Dames and Moore, foundation engineers; Lawrence Halprin, landscape architect; G. M. Simonson, mechanical-electrical engineer; and Lawrence Livingston, Jr., city and regional planner—all of San Francisco. William E. Spangle, Jr., Chief, San Mateo County Master Plan Project; and Faber Birren, color consultant, New York City. Robert R. Lydecker of San Francisco prepared the illustrations at the beginning of each chapter.

JAMES D. MACCONNELL

TABLE OF CONTENTS

PART 1: PLANNING IN EMBRYO

General Population Trends. United States Population. Inadequacy of School Facilities. Planning a Program for School Plant Construction. Determining the Needs. The Survey. The Cooperative Survey. Subcommittees. Population Survey. Predicting

vii

PLANNING
FOR SCHOOL
BUILDINGS

INTRODUCTION

Planning and building a school today is a very complex undertaking. Large numbers of federal, state, and local agencies, and a multitude of specialized individuals are involved both before and after the local governing board announces its intent to erect or rehabilitate a school plant. The time is past when the concerted efforts of a school board and local builders could bring about the completion of an adequate school plant within a short time.

Education has been and is recognized to be a social continuum beginning with social needs and ending with social needs. This fact is most true in a society such as ours which depends, for its existence, upon the positive contribution of every member in it.

In kindergarten children learn to live and work together, learn to do for themselves and with others, learn to use tools, begin skills, and play safely. They do all of this as individuals; and gradually understanding that they are parts in a social organization. The elementary school is a place further developing the beginnings made in kinder-

1

garten and the learning of subject skills. Out of activities allowing for new learnings and the maturing of things learned comes the fixing of facts, the formation of habits of thinking and creating, and the building of character and appreciations. Junior high school learning is characterized by exploration and integration. New experiences highlight the importance of the junior high school. Things learned in elementary school further develop. It is here that intellectual and social experiences are placed in the context of usage. The junior high school catches the young adolescent at a stage in life where it is practical to help him discover himself and where he can start planning for the future. Opportunities for exploration in fundamental areas as well as in such special areas as art, music, home living, mechanical arts, and physical education determine the program.

Exploration begun in junior high or upper intermediate school continues through high school. It is here that conscious effort is made to pull together experiences to develop an individual having the general understandings important to total citizenship. Special aptitudes, attitudes, abilities, interests, and understandings are uncovered; planning begins for their use in building special competencies. In many instances, formal education stops at this point in the social continuum; high school should have built a base for the pupil beginning adult life.

The junior college as an extension of secondary education and as a beginning of higher education extends public education and social guidance. General knowledge, skills, and appreciations are basic to junior college offerings. Experiences building competencies for an effectively functioning individual, the member of a family, a community, a nation, and a world are developed. Complete training for those stopping formal education is consciously undertaken. Such training aims at the achievement of occupational, civic, and personal adequacy at the adult level. Exploration, in terms of the self, continues in the junior college. Prerequisite course offerings, work in the liberal arts, scientific, engineering, and professional fields are given for those who plan to go to college. This community college also provides for the cultural and vocational needs of adults living in the area.

An educational program which recognizes its importance as a developer of individual and social competency in a changing society must be adaptable to and must, in fact, encourage change. It must consolidate the best of the old with the best of the new. Such change is made difficult by stereotyped conventional school plants. The excitement of creative, developing education demands that buildings exceed convention.

Comparison of present-day school plants with those of even two or three decades past reveals an underlying difference in philosophy as to what the plant is and what it should do. Formerly the plant was considered to be "the place where school was kept"—now it is a place for school. Early American school buildings were designed to provide spaces where a few sat to be instructed—now school plants are conceived to be activity areas where all children and youth go to participate in exercises resulting in understandings, attitudes, skills, ideals, and appreciations enabling them to live as intelligent social beings. Educational experiences are real today where they were vicarious a few short years ago.

The process of extending education to all the children and youth of all the people at secondary as well as elementary levels has helped to develop a new concept of the school plant. Special outdoor spaces such as football fields, shops which allow for automobile and large machine repair, music rooms for large vocal and instrumental groups, science facilities which make possible the use of live specimens or the growing of plants and animals, food service areas for all who attend school, and community service areas, are but a few outgrowths of the new basic philosophy which has resulted in a different kind of school plant. Recognition of the importance of good lighting, adequate ventilation, and proper sanitation, pleasant color, and proper placement of related building areas to the learning situation has also had a part in bringing about differences. The necessity of using different materials to hold costs within limits of the ability to pay and the development of new materials to better serve needs has also promoted the building of "modern" school plants.

The educational activities of today's children and youth are sheltered with grace, developed through participation, enlivened with beauty and appreciation, and created with enthusiasm when housed in present-day buildings. The spacious informal atmosphere of the modern well-planned building provides an environment encouraging the kind of enjoyable informal or semi-formal activity causing both students and teachers to go beyond minimum requirements. Individual enterprise on the part of pupils, and individual supervision and instruction by teachers, are made easy because of flexible classrooms and special areas. Varied approaches to teaching become easy and pleasant.

The modern school helps the instruction process by providing a clean, simple, light, colorful, and beautiful place in which children and youth work with colorful, attractive, materials. Appreciation of beauty develops from living in and with it. The building and its furnishings encourage and help youth do things. People in a community are encouraged through the young people; youth as a result of its school activity takes a simple aesthetic approach to living. Parents enthusiastically send their children to school. Schools have ceased to be "institutions," and have become homes of learning.

The responsibilities of planning for and building a school plant fall on many people with specialized understandings and skills. At one time the local school administrator was looked upon by the board of education and the community as one who would, in addition to his regular job (which included a cross section of educational competencies), carry major responsibilities in the school building program. With expanded enrollments, added to a full-time job of guiding the increasingly complex educational destiny of the school system, he no longer can assume this burden. Today he is a coordinator of educational and technical specialists and must keep abreast of the vast number of responsibilities that are being assumed by the schools. Society is now asking more of its schools than it ever has before, and those who are familiar with the curricular demands on the school plant are being asked to participate in planning for the necessary facilities.

Because most communities have too little school construction to employ the services of a full-time specialist, they frequently depend on outside consultants to assist their own staff members with the technical phases of *planning for* and *planning the* school plant. The school administrator, with the assistance of his staff members responsible for planning, must then become acquainted with the responsibilities and competencies of the various available educational and technical team members. He must be skillful in coordinating *their* services.

The school administrator must be aware of accepted practices of determining population growth and trends, making existing building evaluations, and planning procedures for acquiring new buildings and sites. His knowledge of sources of information, the roles of the various state, college and university, and independent specialists, and evaluation procedures can determine the difference between the success and failure of his administration.

All those involved in the planning must become acquainted with their proper roles and function as team workers. Smooth efficient teamwork should result not only in a functional school plant that represents the best thinking of the group but also in a feeling of oneness that can only invite future association of a similar nature as additional building needs become evident.

This book concerns itself with the techniques and procedures for organizing lay, educational, and technical teams to be involved in planning and building school plants. It points to the competencies needed for optimum performance. It gives examples of results obtained in a variety of situations in which group planning was followed. It discusses problems presented by the educational team members under the guidance of the school administrators, and the solutions achieved in working cooperatively with the technical team headed by the architect.

This book has been written to guide those responsible for the planning of schools and to assist school administrators and architects or those who are studying in these fields as they approach the complicated and extremely important area of planning for and constructing school buildings.

The well-conceived, well-constructed school plant should create an environment conducive to the successful performance of the most important task of the schools—the education of the children and youth of America.

PLANNING IN EMBRYO

CHAPTER 1

DETERMINING AND SATISFYING LOCAL SCHOOL PLANT NEEDS

There has probably been more school construction since the end of World War II than during any other period in American history. Some of it has been highly satisfactory in terms of serving present-day educational needs, yet some of it has been an expensive duplication of the mistakes of the past. General school building deficiencies and the means whereby local school districts can investigate their own unique and specific needs and establish a planning organization to meet these requirements are discussed in this chapter. It is essential that cooperative planning techniques be used

9

so that new and better replacement facilities can be planned to serve the specific needs and purposes of the community.

GENERAL POPULATION TRENDS

America's problem of continuing to improve its public school system has been intensified by the rapid and constant growth of its school population, resulting in serious inadequacies in school facilities and a lack of qualified teachers. The marked increase in the population of the United States during the last decade has brought about a corresponding increase in school enrollment.

UNITED STATES POPULATION

The 1950 United States census confounded the experts, most of whom had agreed that the nation was approaching a period of static if not declining population. One of the foremost population experts wrote as recently as 1947, ". . . future population will be 144.7 millions in 1950 and 155.1 millions in 1960. . . . If these assumptions prove reasonable, the population will increase between 1940 and 1950 by more than 12 millions, or at a rate of over nine per cent."[1]

Actually, the 1950 census returns show that the continental United States had a population of 150,697,361, an increase of 14.5 per cent over that of 1940.[2] This percentage gain was consistent with the gains made between other census periods. An examination of the following table shows, however, the gain experienced during the thirties. This is significant since the high rate of increase preceding 1930 was due to a considerable amount of immigration. For example, from 1900 to 1910 immigration was responsible for 3,823,694 of the total gain in population of 15,977,691. The growth rate since 1940, then, represents primarily the increase of native population.

[1] Frederick Dewhurst & Associates, *America's Needs and Resources* (New York: Twentieth Century Fund, 1947), p. 36.

[2] Bureau of the Census, 1950 Census of Population, Vol. 1, "Number of Inhabitants, U.S." (Washington, D.C.: Government Printing Office, 1952), pp. 1-3.

TABLE 1

POPULATION OF THE UNITED STATES

Census Period	Population	Per Cent Increase
1956	167,440,000*	11.1**
1950	150,697,361	14.5
1940	131,669,275	7.2
1930	122,775,046	16.1
1920	105,710,620	14.9
1910	91,972,266	21.0
1900	75,994,575	20.7
1890	62,947,714	25.5
1880	50,155,783	30.1
1870	38,558,371	22.6
1860	31,443,321	35.6
1850	23,191,876	35.9

° "Estimate of the Population of the United States," U.S. Bureau of the Census Series P25, No. 136, (April, 1956).
°° Estimated for 5.25 year period.

The pronounced upswing in the pattern of population growth which has occurred since 1940 in the United States has been complicated further by the problems of movement within and between the several states. This is not a new circumstance. Since the early days of the industrial revolution in this country there has been a movement from rural areas to urban, industrialized sections. More recently a new development has occurred. This is a movement from urban areas to surrounding suburban communities, made possible by the development of the private automobile. Culminating in the last decade, the resulting freedom of movement permitting much greater choice of a home site, combined with the pressures of a mounting population and a swifter pace of economic development, has brought about a virtual revolution in community population patterns. In 1940 less than one-fifth of the nation's total population was located in areas surrounding large cities, but between 1940 and 1950 such areas contributed nearly half of the country's population increase. A release by the Census Bureau stated:

> Population growth in the United States during the last ten years was very largely growth within the standard metropolitan areas . . . (and) nearly half of the population increase of the entire country took place in the outlying parts of the 168 metropolitan areas.[3]

[3] 1950 Census of Population, Preliminary Reports, Series PC-3, No. 3 (November 5, 1950).

The national Education Association, in noting the profound effect that this great population movement has had upon the nation's schools, pointed out that:

> During the seven year period 1940 to 1947 over 13 million people moved from one county to another within their respective states and over 12 million crossed state lines. The Bureau of the Census concludes that, "probably never before in the history of the United States has there been internal population movement of such magnitude."[4]

INADEQUACY OF SCHOOL FACILITIES

In the depression years of the thirties, the construction of school buildings was delayed for lack of funds. With the advent of World War II manpower and materials had to be funneled into the war effort, resulting in the further postponement of the erection of school buildings. With the return of full employment and the beginning of war, young people married early and started families. The nation had what is termed an "explosive" growth of population which was characterized by an enormous increase in the number of children. A dramatic reversal of the previous population trend was experienced. For the first time in the history of the United States, the rate of population rose sharply. Population doubled the growth experienced in the previous decade.

The baby crop surpassed the four million mark for the first time in 1954 and again in 1955. Consequently, school construction not only failed to keep pace with the need for new facilities during these times but kept falling progressively farther behind. Among the causes for this failure were competition for materials and manpower and a continuing inflation of prices.

The findings of the Federal Facilities Survey are impressive in that they show that earlier estimates of total classroom needs were much too conservative. In 1952, it was estimated that some 312,000 classrooms were needed in 43 states to house 8,881,360 pupils at a cost of approximately $10,600,000,000. It is variously estimated that the cost of required new construction will range from $11 billion to $34 billion by 1960.[5]

[4] NEA Research Bulletin, "Schools and the 1950 Census," Vol. XXIX, No. 4 (December, 1951), p. 151.

[5] Charles A. Ouattlebaum, Federal Aid to School Construction (Washington, D.C.: U.S. Government Printing Office, 1954), p. 4.

As citizen groups studied the problems, regrets inevitably arose. In many cases it was difficult to enlarge existing schools because the sites were too small. To buy adjoining property—which could have been purchased cheaply a few years before—was often too costly a step. Furthermore, many of the older buildings were so constructed that it was not practical to expand them, and to add rooms would not only have been prohibitive in expense but would have resulted in unsatisfactory makeshifts and overcrowded sites. Moreover, educational techniques and philosophy had changed in recent years, and many old school buildings could not economically be adapted to the new concepts.

These problems presented an object lesson: school buildings must be planned—and planning must be long-range in character. It is necessary, as a matter of economy and good sense, to build for children who will come to school five, ten, twenty, and even thirty years from now.

PLANNING A PROGRAM FOR SCHOOL PLANT CONSTRUCTION

Although the decision to build new school plants must be made by a Board of Education with the assistance of the school superintendent and his co-workers, the process involves a long period of study, research, and planning before reasonably competent decisions can be made. Some of the decisions, too, are a matter of preferences and conditions which must be carefully weighed.

First, it is necessary for the school system to decide upon the nature of the educational program its community wants. This involves finding out how many children must be housed and taught over a given period of time; where those children live; in what grades they must be placed; how many pupils each school must accommodate; what is the nature of the program of learning activities for each school. To guide the architect further in his planning, it is necessary to prepare a precise description of the teaching methods that will be used. From these data it is then possible to outline the functional school plant needed and desired by the people of the district.

Second, if any existing facilities can fit into this desired plan they must be incorporated as a matter of dollars-and-cents economy. The existing school plant, therefore, must be carefully appraised to enable as much of it as possible to be utilized in the future program. Some of the existing facilities, while not now in harmony with future requirements, probably can be adapted to meet those needs. Such adaptation, when not too costly, must be made part of the planning.

Third, when this background of work is accomplished it is possible to set up a schedule for the step-by-step construction of a school plant that will ultimately be as adequate as circumstances permit. The 27th Yearbook of the American Association of School Administrators lists the major steps in the development of a long-range construction program. Building an adequate educational plant is a community enterprise of large proportions. These steps give some idea of the very broad scope and lengthy sequence involved in such an effort:

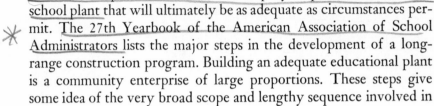

1. Becoming aware of school housing needs.
2. Appointing an educational consultant.
3. Appointing an architect.
4. Setting up planning committees of staff members.
5. Determining exact needs by surveys.
6. Determining the financial program.
7. Selecting bond attorneys.
8. Preparing bond issue (if necessary) and submitting it to voters.
9. Making credit data on the school district available to prospective bond purchasers.
10. Determining types of furniture and equipment.
11. Submitting educational specifications to architect.
12. School staff meeting with architect for give-and-take conferences to guide him in preparing preliminary drawings.
13. Board of Education approving preliminary drawings.
14. Preparing final drawings and specifications.
15. Checking and approving final drawings and specifications.
16. Calling for bids on construction and equipment.
17. Accepting low (or preferred) bid when proper performance bond has been supplied.
18. Securing legal approval of contract documents.
19. Executing contract documents, including agreement on payment schedule.
20. Arranging for supplementary supervising of construction, by owner.

21. Starting construction.
22. Awarding contract for furniture and equipment not covered by general contract.
23. Reporting progress at successive stages—foundations, first floor, building enclosed, building completed.
24. Inspecting construction.
25. Accepting building.
26. Completing contract.
27. Equipping building with furniture, apparatus, machines.
28. Occupying building.[6]

Some of these steps are hardly more than formalities. Others, the fifth, for example, requires the cooperative work of many people over a period of many months.

DETERMINING THE NEEDS

School housing needs become most emphatically felt, perhaps, as parents enroll their children in school. At this point the lack of space may have become a crisis. Far too often, in recent years, schools have had to make multiple use of classrooms by instituting half-day and staggered sessions. Even triple sessions have come into use. The results, of course, are disturbing congestion; overcrowded locker rooms, laboratories, and gymnasiums; traffic in hallways and on stairs that is far too heavy; and discipline problems that become frequent and difficult—to mention but a few factors which result in the reduction of educational benefits to children.

Enrollment, however, merely indicates the present school-year population. When planning construction for the future, it is necessary to know how many pupils must be housed by the school district in the years ahead. Naturally, it is impossible to foretell *exactly* how many children must be accommodated five or ten years from now, but an effort must be made to establish the approximate number. If the estimate is too small, schools will be overcrowded; if too large, expensive classrooms will stand empty, in mute but costly evidence of unnecessary spending. It is recognized by most communities that a reasonable margin for error must be allowed.

[6] American Association of School Administrators, *American School Buildings*, 27th Yearbook (Washington, D.C.: The Association, 1949), pp. 321-22.

Some related questions are:

1. Where must the schools be located in order best to accommodate these children?

2. How many elementary, junior high, and high schools will be needed?

3. How large must each one be?

4. What educational objectives (and specifications) are desired by the parents of the district?

5. To service such a program most effectively, how must the schools be designed?

These are big questions. Obviously, answers to them can come only after thorough study and discussion which involves teachers, community representatives, administrators, and experts in various related fields.

The questions which now arise are: Who will do this? Who will make the area studies, the surveys which are basic to the long-range planning of a school system? Who will work out the statement of educational objectives which will be the philosophy at the heart of all this far-reaching effort? Who will prepare the educational specifications—the activating instrument?

THE SURVEY

The process of making a systematic determination of a community's school plant needs is termed *the survey*. There are a multitude of ways in which surveys may be and are being conducted. In *Planning Together for Better School Buildings*[7] three successful methods —the independent, the cooperative, and the combinations of each— are described. Each method has its advantages and disadvantages.

The school system sponsoring an independent school survey may have it done under the direction of a separate organization. This may consist of a small group of education consultants or experts working full time on the project. Sometimes this group may consist entirely of specialists in survey techniques brought in from outside the system. Sometimes the group is made up of people from within the system, with the superintendent or a layman from the commu-

[7] "Planning Together for Better School Buildings," Bulletin No. 2, published by Lee M. Thurston, Supt. of Public Instruction (Lansing, Michigan, 1950).

nity as director. The members of the survey group do the bulk of the work, though at times they may call on teachers, principals, and supervisors for assistance in locating information or interpreting the data accumulated prior to or during the study.

The survey group plans the study, gathers and interprets the data, and derives from them certain conclusions and recommendations. When the survey is completed the staff presents the results in a report to the school authorities for examination, approval, and adoption.

The following table illustrates how an independent survey group related new and converted school building needs to a conservative as well as a more liberal school population projection.

TABLE 2

SUMMARY OF IMMEDIATE SCHOOL NEEDS FOR CONSTRUCTION, ALL CLARK COUNTY
NEVADA ATTENDANCE AREAS

(All figures approximate—based on best available estimates of current
building and land costs)

Attendance Area #1

Construct new high school plant, Virgin Valley	$ 350,000	
Improvements at Logandale and Overton	50,000	$400,000

Attendance Area #2

Administrative offices	50,000	
Remodeling at Las Vegas High	100,000	
Industrial Arts at Rancho High	100,000	250,000

Minimum projections, without conversions

1. Elementary school construction	$1,910,000	
Junior high school construction	4,700,000	6,610,000

Minimum projections, with conversions

2. Elementary school construction	3,360,000	
Junior high school construction	3,470,000	6,830,000

Mid-projection, without conversions

3. Elementary school construction	3,960,000	
Junior high school construction	6,850,000	10,810,000

Mid-projection, with conversions

4. Elementary school construction	5,360,000	
Junior high school construction	5,170,000	10,530,000

Attendance Area #3

Construct a Music, Drama, & Arts Building	$ 400,000	$400,000

Attendance Area #4

Construct two new elementary schools	700,000	
Additions to Basic High School	200,000	900,000

	Minimum Projection without Conversions*	Minimum Projection with Conversions	Adjusted Mid-projection without Conversions	Adjusted Mid-projection with Conversions
Total buildings	1–$8,560,000	2–$ 8,780,000	3–$12,760,000	4–$12,480,000
5% contingency	1– 428,000	2– 439,000	3– 638,000	4– 624,000
Subtotal	1–$8,988,000	2–$ 9,219,000	3–$13,398,000	4–$13,104,000
Arch. and engineer ..	1– 404,460	2– 414,855	3– 602,910	4– 589,680
Subtotal	1–$9,392,460	2–$ 9,633,855	3–$14,000,910	4–$13,693,680
Site acquisition	300 acres @ $2,000 per acre–$600,000			
Total	1–$9,932,460	2–$10,233,855	3–$14,600,910	4–$14,293,680

Note: It is anticipated that federal funds will be available to assist materially in paying for the construction of the facilities planned for in Attendance Area #3. Since the amount that will be available is not known at this time, the entire amount necessary to finance school buildings is shown above.

* Buildings to be remodeled to house a different program.

Some of the advantages of the independent survey are: (1) the task may be accomplished in minimal time with little interference in the routine school program already existent; (2) if the staff of the survey group is thoroughly competent, a considerable amount of expert judgment is made available to the school district.

The cooperative method of conducting a school survey takes far more time than the independent method and, under certain circumstances, may be less efficient. But this method has one great advantage and that is the excellent public relations it may build for the school system. This cooperative process is undertaken by giving spokesmen of the local population an opportunity to make their ideas a part of the final school program. As a result the community acquires an awareness of what the key educational problems of the community are, which usually results in a deepened interest in its schools. Thus, meetings of the survey committee should be open to the public. They should be held at frequent intervals and for the convenience of all who wish to attend should take place in different areas of the community.

This advantage of the cooperative method also accrues to the use of consultants because the recommendations of the various committees are the inferences from data gathered by the many representatives of the community—they are the results of community cooperation and interest. Inefficiency and time-loss, the disadvantages of the cooperative method, are usually prevented under the expert guidance of such a consultant.

In most instances the superintendent initiates the survey and guides its progress. However, other school personnel and community groups may assist. In a cooperative survey all groups are given equal opportunity to gather data, discuss interpretations, and make recommendations. These recommendations are considered in turn, and the board and superintendent examine the data in order that they may make any broad policy decisions deemed advisable to the district.

A third method is the employment of a consultant who advises the Board of Education and superintendent on matters in which he has demonstrated superior competencies. Such a consultant is usually an educator who has specialized in the field of school planning and, in addition to having a broad knowledge of the environmental needs of school children, recognizes the need for specialists in the profession and sees to it that they are called upon where their services are needed.

It is still necessary to allot a sufficient period of time for those making the study to make a careful analysis of the local area; otherwise the survey and its conclusions may be superficial. If this precaution is taken, the consultant may render a community valuable service. He will set up the survey procedures; he will instruct the various fact-finding committees and study groups in the use of survey techniques and explain the methods by which they may arrive at valid findings. He directs the survey and in the end interprets the findings to the school officials and interested community lay-groups.

THE COOPERATIVE SURVEY

Since the cooperative survey is the survey most commonly used and abused throughout the United States today, a more complete discussion of organizational patterns is presented. If the cooperative method of making a survey is decided upon, a survey committee should be selected that will represent the entire community. This is particularly true in small communities where this type of study has been most popular. Since it is a total community venture, every effort must be made to see that the opinion of a cross section of the total community population is obtained and carefully considered before a final solution for the problem is reached.

During the survey, members of the survey committee should keep in mind key points, such as:

Objectives
Information needed to attain objectives
Methods to be used in collecting information
Sources of available help
Duties to be assigned
Time schedules
Method of reporting
Type of final report
Distribution of report.

SUBCOMMITTEES

A variety of tasks can be delegated to subcommittees. Subcommittees make it possible to share the burden. Groups are organized to gather data and develop recommendations in various fields. For example, one subcommittee is given the job of gathering information on population trends in the school district. Another group is appointed to develop a statement of educational objectives and specifications for the community. Still another subcommittee is set up to handle publicity, and so on.

Ways of working with local organizations are decided upon. Channels of communication are clearly structured in order that the findings and recommendations of women's clubs, service clubs, parents' groups, and so forth, can reach the survey committee promptly and be handled with tact and efficiency.

Without competent leadership these lay groups can often become sources of great confusion and misinformation. Small pressure groups evolve and are soon on their own irrelevant problems. In order to avoid this situation, consultants from various fields are necessary to the planning effort. The sequence of utilizing specialists in planning school facilities is most important and yet is given insufficient consideration by professional educators and lay groups planning an educational program.

Methods are standardized for making use of specific consultative services. From time to time, consultants from various fields are necessary to the planning effort. The sequence of utilizing specialists in planning school facilities is probably one of the most important things and yet is given insufficient consideration in planning an educational program.

In spite of the fact that there are a number of areas that must be considered before the architect, foundation analyst, and structural and mechanical engineers become active, their being called into the picture when the studies are being made often results in a much better educational plant at a financial saving. The same procedure applies to the legal counsel, budget advisor, and others—who must come into the planning at an early date if their contribution is to be efficacious.

The survey committee should set up a policy for utilizing the publications on school planning which are available from local and state agencies, such as the Chamber of Commerce, Bell Telephone Company, college and university service bureaus, the U.S. Census Bureau, and so forth. These agencies can be very helpful to the various subcommittees seeking data.

The survey committee divides the work to be done into a number of sections and delegates responsibility for the effort in each division to a subcommittee. Common practice is to appoint a qualified member of the top committee as chairman of each subcommittee, and although the ultimate goal is to determine school plant needs, usually it is necessary to study many areas before adequate information for decision-making is available.

The survey committee, for example, may designate classifications and form a subcommittee for each one. The areas of responsibility for the subcommittees may be:

1. School curriculum
2. School plant
3. School finances
4. School population trends
5. Tax structure
6. School personnel
7. School transportation
8. Economic development of the area
9. Community trade area boundaries
10. Recreational facilities
11. Health

Space does not permit a complete discussion as to just what would be studied by the committee in each classification. The items will vary with each community; however, some of the most probable topics are listed below in the areas of curriculum and school finances:

Curriculum
1. Are the present school plants meeting the curriculum needs?
2. What subjects are being offered that were not available when the school plants were constructed?
3. If rehabilitation were to be decided upon, would the available spaces and their location still be inadequate?
4. What additional out-of-school, curricular demands are being cared for, such as adult education classes?

Finances
1. What portion of the tax dollar is for schools?
2. What choices are available in raising money for additional school plants?
3. Discussions of false economies in school construction.
4. A study of comparative building costs with other school districts.

The survey committee may then ask for volunteers from the community to staff these working groups. The appeal can be broadcast through newspapers, radio, television, publicity, and mass meetings. As each committee is formed it prepares a statement of its project and works on it until completion.

Curriculum

Each school district is responsible for organizing its own curriculum. This is a necessary freedom: schools over the state and nation differ in size, needs, and resources, to mention only a few of an endless list of differentia. No two school populations are identical. Nor can any two schools be served by the same program; needs distinguish. A curriculum must be planned to fit the unique needs of a school's pupils. The curriculum must change with its students.

Minimum standards of educational achievement are usually set for school districts by state curriculum committees. A uniformity of learning is forced through the use of textbooks recommended by state commissions. However, no state prescribes a rigid course of study which would proscribe individual course contents and teaching methods.

In the junior high schools of California, for example, such individuality is practiced in the educational program. The general pattern is the same for all schools: most offer English, social studies, mathematics, science, physical education, practical arts, and fine arts. However, the emphasis in these fundamental subjects differs. Furthermore, a variety of the electives is provided to suit the varying needs and interests of boys and girls from different communities, different cultural backgrounds, and of different social, psychological, and economic needs.

Buildings are needed to enhance the educative process. Space must be adequate, lighting proper, necessary books, laboratory equipment, audio-visual aids available, recreational equipment plentiful, and transportation facilities provided. These elements vary to suit the particular educational objectives of each school program.

A modern school program might be described as one which is based on the psychological principles of growth and development and the learning process. The California Framework Committee states that "learning is not a process of passive absorption" but rather "a process of growth through active participation."[8] An individual learns best through direct experiences which are supplemented by books and other instructional materials. His impulses, desires, and interests are basic factors in the motivation and direction of his learning. As a pupil realizes purposes that are meaningful to him, he learns. Facts are useful as tools in critical thinking, not as ends in themselves; generalizations and abstract concepts are more fully grasped when derived from concrete experiences. Learning is more effective when the pupil draws conclusions from his own experiences, while he is working at purposes that are meaningful to him and adequate to his maturity.

A good design for a school is one that has been derived from a successful interpretation of such educational specifications. Facets of the physical structure that grows from the design stand as evidence of the achievement of such interpretation:

Thus the varied activities a modern school offers require unique facilities in a building. Different activities, for example, raise different space requirements. The adequacy with which these space requirements are filled will determine the success of the activities. Each building—each room—must be planned in careful detail in terms of the educational program. Rooms planned for specific pur-

---

[8] "A Framework for Public Education In California," California Framework Committee, *California Elementary School Journal*, Vol. XVII (1949), p. 228.

poses must be of proper size, shape, and capacity to fit those purposes.

School programs based on these principles differ in numerous ways from traditional programs. The modern school uses tables and chairs which can be grouped informally, instead of desks and seats screwed to the floor. Such flexible grouping is indispensable to a curriculum which includes music, construction activities, and dramatic play, and which sociometrically divides groups for some classes. Fixed furniture is an obstacle to the varying use of space necessary in such a classroom. Furthermore, the modern teacher is not a taskmaster, but a guide and counselor. His pupils are not kept rigid and in silence in their seats, but are permitted to act socially, to move about and consult with others in the normal activity of learning. A limit to the hum and buzz of their work is set but discipline problems dwindle when the pupil is interested and engaged.

The modern school also offers various materials to satisfy specific and individual learning needs: wood, clay, paint, tools, visual aids, a variety of textbooks, reference works, and recreational books all attractively arranged for ready use. Instruction with such materials is not rigidly set to grades but is adjusted to the individual's needs and abilities: another reason why children need to work in flexible social groups.

In such schools the day is not a succession of question-answer recitations. School time is broken into periods during which children study, participate in discussions and a variety of activities under the guidance of the teacher. References to divers books, an exchange of ideas, and a growing interest in learning about new things characterize this period. The goals are not simply the acquisition of factual information but the development of happy, effective, well-adjusted individuals who continue to learn into adult life.

The school program provides for frequent contact between parent and teacher to insure mutual understanding of the child. These contacts are brought about by parent-teacher conferences as well as by group meetings where parents and teachers discuss ways of creating better learning situations for the children. Furthermore, the community itself serves as an educator. Pertinent materials—plants, animals, and a wide variety of other things—are brought into the classroom by the children. It is these associations with what they are already familiar that make information about new things more meaningful. These contacts also make it possible for them to know more about things that they had known little about.

The school is a part of the community, and the program requires a school plant that will accommodate the educational needs of the community. As our country becomes more industrialized, many school plants that had adequately served agricultural areas are now out of date. Agricultural areas require vocational education facilities that will accommodate farm shops, and adult education programs that are popular in rural areas. Secondary plants built in regions where chemistry is the major industry, such as in Midland, Michigan, usually have to accommodate a more extensive science program. Many school districts are finding it necessary to rehabilitate their facilities to accommodate the new demands.

One of the chief concerns of the architect planning a school is that of grouping rooms according to the activities they will be used for. Related activities should be placed in rooms which are close to and within easy access of each other. Movement between such rooms and groups of rooms should be direct and convenient.

It is important, too, to plan units that are flexible and expandable. Multiple use is economical use. Hence it is wise to plan spaces so that they can be used for a variety of activities.

The educational specifications, referred to in more detail in Chapters V, VI, VII, VIII, IX, and X, do not replace the architect. They furnish answers to questions concerned with subsidiary functions, such as the following:

1. Who will use the building?
   a. What is the expected enrollment of regular pupils?
   b. What other groups will use the building?
2. What will be the size of regular classes?
3. What will be the size of various special classes?
4. What will be the plan of class organization?
5. How large will the groups using the building outside of regular class schedules be?
6. How many groups on the average will be meeting?
7. Will there be shops or laboratories, in addition to academic classes, in the building?
8. Which of these classes can share space with other classes?

9. Will specially designed facilities be necessary for any part of the program; e.g., for kindergarten, or special education groups?
10. What equipment and furniture will each room require?
11. Will audio-visual facilities be needed?
12. What storage facilities will be necessary?
13. What communication facilities will be required—telephones, bells, loud-speakers, and so forth?
14. Will library facilities be needed?
15. Will a stage be needed?

The architect's task is to integrate these demands into a design.

POPULATION SURVEY

To determine who will use the building is not an easy task. It is not simply a matter of looking in an almanac, at a census report, or into a city directory to discover the number of children likely to attend school next semester, next year, or five or ten years from now. To compile figures on population growth is a complicated task requiring research skill with technical procedures.

The first step in a school population survey is to determine the boundaries of the area to be studied, to ascertain the limits of the school district, and to assemble information on the location of business districts, special service centers, such as the offices of doctors and dentists, hospitals, banks, and on residential areas and new suburbs being settled.

Good maps are needed. They may be obtained from:

1. State and County Highway Commissioners' offices.
2. Aerial survey, State and County Engineers' offices.
3. County School Superintendent's offices.
4. U.S. Department of the Interior—Geological Surveys.
5. County and U.S. Agricultural offices.
6. Private utility companies and utility corporations.
7. Local and County Planning Commissioners' offices.
8. Commercial map companies.
9. Local graphic service agencies.
10. Local real estate offices—tract development offices.
11. Local architects and civil engineers.
12. Assessor's office

From dot maps showing new home construction it is possible to determine the location of the potential school population in a district.

The subcommittee working on school population trends should prepare dot maps showing children in the district for the primary

FIGURE 1. Dot map showing distribution of high school pupils within the school district (*Courtesy Bay City Public Schools, Bay City, Michigan*).

grades Kindergarten-6 (enrollment, public school and nonpublic school), secondary grades 7-12 (enrollment, public school and non-public school), and of out-of-school children and youth (16 to 20).

In addition to the number of children, it is important for the subcommittee to know how the land of the district will be settled. This will facilitate the prediction of population and indicate the direction of the community's growth—where children will most probably live in the future.

The "land use" maps should be marked to show:

1. Developed residential areas.
2. Proposed residential areas.
3. Under-developed lands suitable for residential areas.
4. Residential building in last ten years (to show location of new neighborhoods or expansion of old ones).
5. Commercial areas.
6. Light industrial areas.
7. Heavy industrial areas.
8. Vacant lots.
9. Agricultural lands.
10. Highways, railroads, waterways.
11. Recreational areas.
12. Airports.
13. Lakes, swamps, forests.
14. Cemeteries.
15. Untilled areas.
16. Aircraft flyways and flight patterns at airports.[9]

Maps should show the location of present schools and proposed school sites and indicate the attendance areas of the following:

1. Elementary (Kindergarten-6) and (Kindergarten-8).
2. Intermediate (7-9).
3. Secondary (7-12), (9-12), (10-14).

The enrollments of existing schools, public and private, should also be noted.

PREDICTING PUPIL POPULATION

From 1800 until recently, the direction of population movement has been from the rural areas to the urban areas. During the 1940-

[9] School of Education, University of Michigan, *Making An Area Study* (Ann Arbor: University of Michigan).

1950 decade the general population movement was toward the industrial centers. The Pacific Coast states had an increase in residency of about 50 per cent.

Usually there is about a two-year lapse between the time that it is decided by the local board of education that a school plant should be provided and the time when the new facilities are completed. During this period a number of time-consuming activities take place. Among them should be: land acquisition, voting of bonds, legal clearance of site and bond documents, preparation of educational specifications, preparation of plans by the architect, letting contracts, and construction of the plant. Due to the increased birth rate during the past few years, most school districts have experienced growth. This growth varies from a slow, normal increase in some districts to a rapid increase in others that has resulted in the overcrowding of some school plants from the day they came into use. There is every indication that higher enrollments at all levels of education will continue for some time to come.

The population in a given area is altered by three factors—birth, death, migration. People move into a district, or out of it, as job

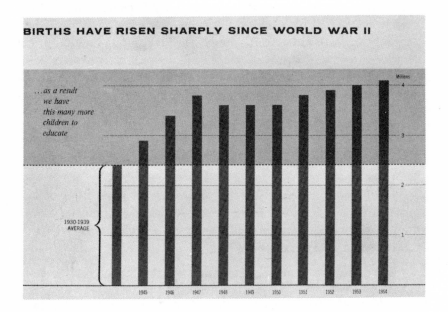

FIGURE 2. Ford Study of birth rates (*from* Teachers for Tomorrow, *Fund for the Advancement of Education, Bulletin No. 2, 1955*).

opportunities vary, or as people are influenced by information on employment potentials for the area due to industrial expansion plans or other changes that will affect employment. Available housing, shopping, recreational, and educational facilities are important factors in determining the total number of families that will be attracted to the area. Each school district, in making forecasts of total as well as school population trends, must contend with unique factors. An administrator may have to consider unprecedented conditions.

The school population of a district varies with the number of local children who move out and the number of outside children who move in, with the number of local children who reach school age, with the number of pupils who die or who leave school. Pupils transferring, from private and parochial schools to public schools, and from one public school to another within a district must also be considered. All these movements keep pupil population shifting and makes forecasting difficult.

A number of methods of predicting population have been devised. Most of them apply to school population situations. Most techniques have some features that apply to predicting future school enrollments. It is impossible to say which one is best. In fact, no single method should be relied upon entirely because most of them have been devised for a specific purpose; for example, the analogy method was worked out to predict school population in urban centers and has not proven successful in strictly bedroom communities. Methods should be selected which promise to fit best the factors unique to each community. Some usual methods of prediction follow:

Forecasting by Analysis

This method of predicting the future school population of any school involves the use of all the accumulated facts obtainable about the past growth of that particular school's population. Dr. Thomas C. Holy describes this method:

> Take the actual numbers of births in the school district between 1940 through 1946. Those born in the years 1934 to 1940 would be six years old in the years 1940 to 1946 and should, therefore, be enrolled in the schools during those years for which actual enrollments are now known. For each of these years calculate the per cent of survivorship between the number of births

and the enrollment in the first grade for the known years which in this case would be 1940 to 1946. Take the average of the percentages for the known years and apply it to the actual numbers of births which occurred during 1940 to 1946 to get the estimated enrollments in the first grade for the years 1946 to 1952 during which time those children born between 1940 and 1946 would enter school.

Calculate the percentage of survivorship from grade one to grade two and so on and apply these to the known figures to get estimates in the years immediately ahead. Children born during 1940 to 1946 will affect the total school enrollment twelve years beyond the latest date of entry, that is, to the year 1964. . . . Incidentally, our checks to date show our estimates to be a little high.[10]

The following grade progressions show how this method has been applied in a specific school survey.

TABLE 3

BEATRICE, NEBRASKA GRADE PROGRESSIONS (IN PER CENT)[11]

(Grades 1-6)

Year	Grade 1-2	Grade 2-3	Grade 3-4	Grade 4-5	Grade 5-6
1949-50	91.6	106.8	100.6	96.0	88.2
1950-51	112.6	101.2	91.1	98.1	100.0
1951-52	91.1	97.9	95.8	96.5	96.7
1952-53	89.0	98.8	91.8	98.7	100.7
1953-54	95.8	99.3	94.2	100.0	95.5
Total 5-year	480.1	504.0	473.5	489.3	481.1
Average	96.0	100.8	94.7	97.9	96.2

PROJECTED ENROLLMENTS—BEATRICE SCHOOLS
Calculations Made September 8, 1954

Year	K	1	2	3	4	5	6	Total Elem.
1954-55	219	200	207	162	144	160	163	1,255
1955-56	197	180	192	209	153	141	154	1,226
1956-57	225	205	173	194	198	150	136	1,281
1957-58	194	177	197	174	184	194	144	1,264
1958-59	203	185	170	199	165	180	187	1,289
1959-60	205	187	178	171	188	162	173	1,264
1960-61	205	187	180	179	162	184	156	1,253
1961-62	205	187	180	181	170	159	177	1,259
1962-63	205	187	180	181	171	166	153	1,243
1963-64	205	187	180	181	171	167	160	1,251
1964-65	205	187	180	181	171	167	161	1,252

[10] Dr. Thomas C. Holy, "What Future Needs are Revealed by School Population Studies?" *The Education Digest* (May, 1947, 9:24-26).

[11] William R. Odell and James D. MacConnell, *Beatrice Faces the Future* (Stanford, California: October, 1954), pp. 10-11.

Forecasting School Enrollment from Total Population

This method assumes that an observable ratio between total population and school enrollment has existed in the past and will hold good for the future.

This method is usually applied by getting an average of the per cents which total school enrollments were of the Federal census figures for each of the previous two or three decades and applying that average to the future estimated total population of the school district. This estimated total population, particularly in the larger communities, can generally be secured from city planning commissions and similar planning bodies.[12]

Prediction Based Wholly on Past Census Data   *no*

This method assumes that the average percentage rate of growth true in the past will hold for the future; that the general population will show a total constant numerical increase from one census year to the next; and that the percentage rate of growth will vary from decade to decade.

The method involves plotting a curve showing how the percentage increase has changed in the past and extending the curve to show future percentage increases.

This method . . . is done by plotting on a chart actual enrollments for past years and from these data projecting the growth curve of the future. In so doing, the curve is generally "smoothed" so that it is projected as a straight line. Experience has shown that this is not a very reliable method of forecasting.[13]

Method of Analogy   *no*

This method consists of studying the growth of various larger cities from a period at which their population equaled the present population of the city building the school, and deducing its probable future population from these studies.

Forecasting by analogy . . . involves making use of the per cents of total population attending schools in comparable com-

[12] *American School Buildings*, American Association of School Administrators, 27th Yearbook (School Planning Laboratory, Stanford University, Stanford, California), p. 55.
[13] *Ibid.*

munities, and applying these to the district under consideration. Because of the many variables which affect school enrollment even in so-called comparable communities, this has not been found to be a reliable method.[14]

Multiple Factor Method

This method assumes that a number of social and economic factors condition population growth, that a prediction based on a number of such elements is more reliable than one based on a single index, and that factors which have had a positive correlation with increases of population in the past will continue to affect population in the future. Some of the factors considered are:

1. Total population shown by U.S. Census.
2. Public school enrollment grades 1-8.
3. Water meter service connections.
4. Gas meter service connections.
5. Telephone stations.
6. Names in city directory.
7. Death certificates.
8. Birth certificates.
9. Assessed valuation of property.
10. Bank deposits.
11. Building permits.
12. Postal receipts.
13. Families.
14. Dwellings.
15. High school enrollment.

The mean of the increase over a period of years for certain of the factors is used as a basis for predicting future population. Only factors whose average increment of increase fall within one standard deviation of the mean increments of all the factors employed are used.[15]

Bell Telephone Company's Method of Index Analysis

This method is considered one of the most accurate. When its findings can be obtained from the company, they should be used.

[14] C. C. Hauser, "How Accurately Can Engineers Predict Future Population Growths of Cities?" *American City* (September, 1928), 39:124-6.
[15] *Ibid.*, p. 8.

They are of special help to small districts which cannot spare funds or workers for extensive population studies.

Present estimates:

Estimates of present population of Telephone Company are based upon what they call the "family unit." To get this information, the city is subdivided into working areas. Within each area workers make a house to house check to determine the number of family units in the area and the status of the families living there. It is explained that one big problem is that of "hidden families." By this is meant that when the workers ask, "How many families live here?" many times the answer is "Only one" when actually a married son and his family, a married daughter, or both, may live there, but are considered by the one giving information as "part of the family." Many types of checks are used to find hidden families. The Telephone Company has established a factor of 3.42 persons in each family; therefore, with the number of families known, they can estimate the present population of a city with great accuracy.

Future estimates:

In making estimates of future population, the Telephone Company first determines its objectives: i.e., the years which it wishes to estimate. Next, the birth and death data for past years in the city are analyzed, and from this analysis a new birth rate is established. Using a known census figure as a base (the present population) the net birth figures are added to this known figure and the net death figures are taken from it. To this are added the net increases, if any, resulting from in-migration and out-migration, . . . (which) is based upon an analysis of industrial, commercial, and agricultural reports and data, and any other available pertinent data. This migratory factor is the most difficult of all to obtain with any degree of accuracy.[16]

The "Law of Growth" Principle—Pearl-Reed Logistic Curve

This method is subject to errors, however, in view of its projecting a constant or constantly declining rate of increase. Actually, even in rapidly increasing communities the rate of increase is subject to much variation. The logistic curve, being essentially an arithmetic computation, cannot take into consideration many local variables which produce fluctuations in the rate of growth. No arithmetic calculation, in fact, can project changes in population

[16] Elden B. Busby, "A Study of Population Trends and School Building Needs in the City of Fort Worth, Texas" (Not published) (October, 1948), pp. 97-8.

trends. The main use of the logistic curve is as a rough check applied to other methods.

This method assumes that if a population is expanding freely over unoccupied country, the percentage rate of increase remains the same. In a limited area, though, the rate diminishes as the population increases, leveling off as an upper limit is neared. The method is subject to general errors. Its most valid use is as a rough check applied to other methods.[17]

Projecting Natural Increase

A method of estimating *current population*, which can be adapted either to a county area or to a city:

1. Civilian population (latest census),
2. *Plus* persons in armed forces as of the above date,
3. *Gives* total population including persons away in the armed services as of the above date,
4. *Plus* natural increase (resident births over deaths),
5. *And* net migration to estimate date (statistics on elementary school enrollment can be used for the purpose of estimating net migration),
6. *Gives* total population on estimate date (including persons away in armed forces).

Estimates of future population, then, can be determined by projecting natural increases and net migration.

Another, but more complicated method, uses the same types of data as above, but requires official U.S. census data by age groups. Data from any more recent census that was tabulated by age may be used. The method is more accurate than the one above. Details can be secured from the U.S. Bureau of Census.

Combination Method

It is always possible, of course, to secure projections based on several of these different methods. In forecasting population, one is trying to arrive at an approximate figure. The pertinent variables

[17] W. A. Spurr and D. R. Arnold, "A Short-Cut Method of Fitting a Logistic Curve," *Journal of the American Statistical Association* (March, 1948), pp. 127-34.

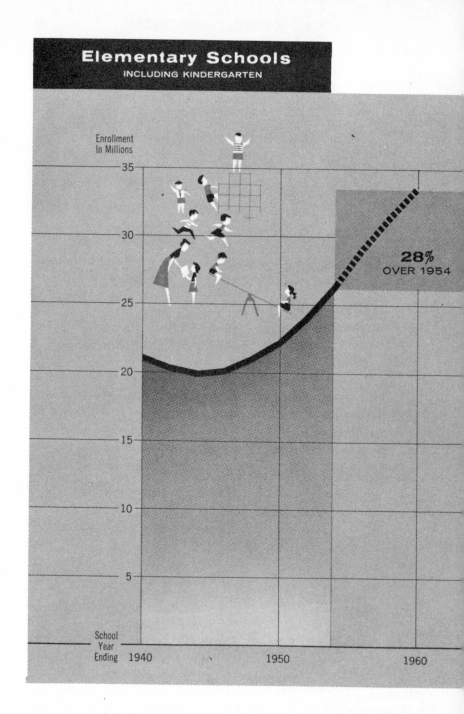

FIGURE 3. School enrollments are rising (*from* Teachers for Tomorrow, *Fund for*

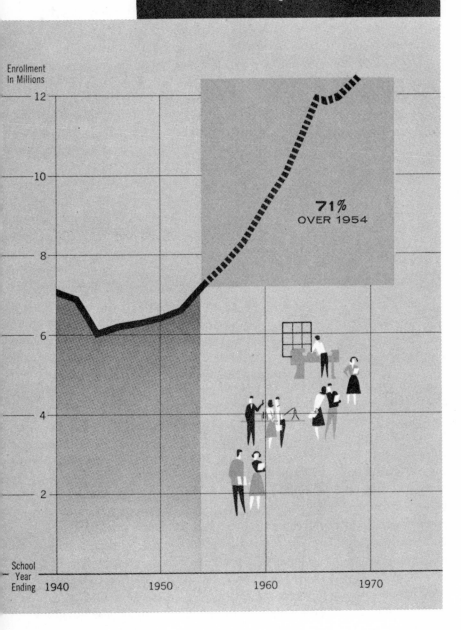

Enrollment In Millions

71%
OVER 1954

School Year Ending   1940   1950   1960   1970

the Advancement of Education, Bulletin No. 2, 1955).

make it difficult, if not impossible, to do this by a mechanical projection. Observation of developments within a community that affect population changes, combined with the use of several, different, mechanical, projection techniques, should provide the administrator with a sound basis upon which he can make his decisions.

While gathering data for population forecasts, personal data on the school population should be collected. Not only must the number of pupils be ascertained, but who they are and what they plan to do when they graduate or drop out of school.

Personal data consists of:

1. Place of birth.
2. Age.
3. Parents' education.
4. Parents' employment.
5. Home: whether owned or rented; number of rooms; number of people living in it.
6. Pupils' vocational interests.
7. Why (for students who have dropped out) they have quit school.

SOME GENERAL PRINCIPLES ON FORECASTING SCHOOL POPULATION

Usually the trends for total population, school enrollment, and the number of births are related. This relationship can be shown by plotting all three on the same graph. The data should go back for fifteen or twenty years, and be plotted by years. However, in fast growing communities the population figures for past five years usually give a more accurate picture of future trends. Over a short period of time the percentage of the population attending school generally remains fairly constant. If school enrollment is inconsistent with total population, compare the birth data with school enrollment figures. Where such ratios are unstable or unusually high or low, other variables that are potentially related factors must be sought. A key to the determination of potential causes for variation can possibly be found in the relationship of births to first-grade enrollment six years later. Babies born in any particular year usually enter kindergarten in the fifth year after birth, and then enter first grade the following year. Peak periods can be shown on a graph of school enrollment over the previous twenty years. When birth rates are rising, larger enrollment in lower grades can be anticipated after six years. Where first-grade enrollments are larger than the number of births recorded for the area six years previously, it is apparent that immigration into the district is a current phenomenon. Where the enrollments are smaller, it is apparent that if the decrease is greater than could be anticipated by normal causes, the district is experiencing a general loss of population.

To get accurate predictions it is necessary to determine the number of births each year for each elementary school district. Districts which do not have these data can secure them in one of two ways: (1) by a continuous counting of births or (2) by an annual census conducted by school personnel for their own districts.

An illustration[18] of a school population projection based upon land-use saturation studies[19] and housing development follows:

TABLE 4

POTENTIAL HOLDING POWER OF THE ELEMENTARY SCHOOLS IN
RICHMOND, CALIFORNIA, PLANNING AREAS

Planning Area	Enrollment 1955	Forecast E 1960	Forecast 1965	Forecast 1970	Ultimate Enrollment
South Richmond	7,356	6,500	6,600	6,680	7,425
Central Richmond ...	4,241	4,400	4,600	4,640	4,880
El Cerrito	5,782	5,800	5,900	5,950	6,615
Wildcat Canyon		1,000	1,800	2,055	4,110
Total Richmond Elementary School District	17,379	17,700	18,900	19,325	23,030
San Pablo*				3,780	4,200
El Sobrante				6,530	10,050
North Shore	6,600	8,800	11,000	1,515	2,330
Pinole				2,200	3,000
Total Entire Area ...	23,979	26,500	29,900	33,350	42,610
Total Outside of Richmond	6,600	8,800	11,000	14,025	19,580

* Includes only a part of present San Pablo Elementary School District.

[18] W. R. Odell, J. D. MacConnell, K. Goldhammer, Scanning New Horizons in School Enrollments for the Richmond Area (Stanford, California: School Planning Laboratory, School of Education, Stanford University, Stanford, California, 1955).

[19] Land-use saturation studies are studies that base the projection on ultimate saturation of the land. In other words, in Table 3, although the forecast for South Richmond in 1970 is 6,680, when all the land is built on they would have an enrollment of 7,425. During early developments, many slopes that are expensive to build on are left vacant, but as land becomes scarce, these areas are usually improved by terracing or designing side-hill homes that will accommodate themselves to a contour of this type. Many times, also, a large land owner will refuse to sell his land to subdividers, and it may take a couple of generations to get it into buildings. If planning is not done for the ultimate use of this land, school housing problems are quite certain to result.

The corrected figure for annual births will give an estimate for kindergarten five years ahead and an estimated first grade enrollment six years in the future. Future school records will show not only enrollment figures but drop-outs, retardations and the per cent who finish high school. School population estimates should include the number of school children in areas which will eventually be included in the school district. Since school enrollment is modified by the expansion or reduction of industries in the school district, the district should maintain a constant check upon economic trends within the community.

Large numbers of new homes might be under construction in the suburbs of a district. If this is so, surveys should be made of:

1. The number of new homes.
2. The number of children per home.
3. Their ages.

The data from these surveys can then be combined to give a new, reliable correction figure to compare with previous enrollment estimates.

Before school sites are bought—even before starting building plans —it is wise to re-check former enrollment estimates.

PLANNING THE IDEAL CONSTRUCTION PROGRAM

When the curriculum subcommittee has worked out a statement of educational objectives and from this statement developed a detailed set of educational specifications, and, concurrently, the population trends subcommittee has prepared a forecast of the school's population, then, knowing _what_ is to be taught and _how many pupils_, and _where_ those pupils live, it will be possible for the school plant subcommittee to plan adequate, functional facilities that will fully meet all requirements. It will decide on the total number of buildings that will be needed for the school plant—including the location of each structure, the kind of site each should have, the grades each should house, as well as the pupil capacity of each building.

Planning at this stage should be as ideal as possible. Our purpose

is to develop an *ideal* construction program—one which fully sat-
isfies the set of educational specifications. The planning group vis-
ualizes a building that will meet the community's needs in ideal
fashion.

SCHEDULING THE PROGRAM
OF DEVELOPMENT

The next logical step in the long-range planning program is to
establish a schedule of procedure. This is a series of "next steps"
leading to the construction of the school building.

A number of general factors must be borne in mind as this work
schedule is developed:

1. The educational needs of the pupils and adults of the district.
2. The financial ability of the district to pay for work as it is
   done.
3. The chronological order of the building schedule should be
   flexible:
   a. To permit departures from the construction schedule if
      unforeseen destruction of school facilities occurs by fire or
      other causes.
   b. To permit adjustment to unforeseen changes in educational
      organization.
   c. To adapt to changes in population due to the unexpected
      influx of large industrial plants, the sale of large estates or
      tracts for housing development purposes, and so forth.

THE SURVEY COMMITTEE REVIEWS
SUBCOMMITTEE REPORTS

After a survey committee receives the reports of the various subcommittees it makes a thorough study of them. It is at this juncture
that the consultant makes his contribution. He interprets the data;
and his ability to translate such data into the terms of the committees
and of the community requires deep insight and "know-how" in the
area of social interpretation. The top committee evaluates the subcommittee recommendations, discarding the impractical, com-
promising conflicts, and paring down and revising recommendations
which are beyond achievement, and develops a final series of recom-

mendations. An illustration of a typical consultant's report on a total building program is appended to this chapter.

EVALUATING THE EXISTING SCHOOL PLANT

After the master plan for an ideal building program is formulated, it is possible to evaluate existing facilities to test their adequacy in terms of the ideal school layout. In any community many of the school buildings must and should continue to be used. Thus, as a matter of economy, careful evaluation of the existing school structures is necessary previous to the construction of the new school plant. If existent buildings can fulfill needs of the new program, or may be adapted to these needs, the cost of new construction can be saved. However, hidden costs often result in excessive expenditure when any major rehabilitation is undertaken. The recommendations of a competent structural engineer should be sought before such a project is undertaken.

An evaluation of existing facilities should answer these questions:

1. Which buildings are hopelessly inadequate for the new program, and should be abandoned at once?
2. Which buildings should be adapted for limited use?
3. What improvements are necessary to make these buildings function in the new program?
4. Which buildings should be retained without changes as satisfying the ideal school plan?
5. What major alterations, expansions, and rehabilitation should be made on the existing plant's facilities?
6. What land should be acquired for site expansion?

The final evaluation of existing school facilities should reveal how adequate the plant is in terms of the phases of the community's approved educational program. The evaluation should also review the condition of the present buildings, picture overcrowding (if and where it exists), and enumerate the inadequacy of the plant. The evaluation provides a figure, so to speak, which can be subtracted from the sum representing the ideal school plant. The difference, of course, is an expression of the need for more adequate, better located sites, and the need for further construction.

SCHOOL	DATE OF CONSTRUCTION	TYPE OF CONSTRUCTION	FIRE-RESISTANT QUALITIES	SANITARY FACILITIES	AUDITORIUM	GYMNASIUM	TEACHERS' WORK ROOM	KITCHEN	HOT LUNCH PROGRAM	SPECIAL ROOMS	ACOUSTICS	BASEMENT ROOMS
Central	1935	Brick	Fire-Resistant	Adequate	Study-Hall Combination	Yes	Yes	Yes	No	Ind Arts Art. Home-Making Music. Science	Average	Yes
Hawthorne	1910	Brick and Stone	Semi-Fire-Resistant	Inadequate	No	No	No	No	No	None	Average	Yes
Lowell Addition in	1909 1935	Brick and Stone	Semi-Fire-Resistant	Inadequate	Study-Hall Combination	Yes	Yes	Yes	No	Boy Scout	Average	Yes
Lincoln	1911	Stone	Semi-Fire Resistant	Inadequate	Large Classroom Auditorium-Gymnasium Combination		No	Yes	Yes Not School Sponsored	None	Poor	Yes
Paxson	1922	Brick	Fire-Resistant	Adequate	Yes	Yes	Yes	No	No	Library	Poor	Yes
Willard	1922	Brick	Fire-Resistant	Adequate	Yes	Yes	Yes	No	No	Library	Poor	Yes
Whittier	1922	Brick	Fire-Resistant	Adequate	Yes	Yes	Yes	No	No	Library	Poor	Yes
Roosevelt	1905	Stone and Wood	Combustible	Inadequate	Fixed Seats	Music Combination-Low Ceiling. Very Inadequate	No	No	No	Sick Room	Poor	No
Prescott	1890	No longer in service										
Addition in	1951	Brick and Concrete	Fire-Resistant	Adequate	Auditorium-Gymnasium Combination		Yes	Yes	No	Nurse's Room	Good	No
Washington	1950	Brick and Concrete	Fire-Resistant	Adequate	Auditorium-Gymnasium Combination		Yes	Yes	No	Nurse's Room	Good	No
Jefferson	1950	Brick and Concrete	Fire-Resistant	Adequate	Auditorium-Gymnasium Combination		Yes	Yes	No	Nurse's Room	Good	No
Franklin	1916-1951	Brick	Fire-Resistant	Adequate	Auditorium-Gymnasium Combination		Yes	Yes	No	Lunch Room	Good	Yes, in Old Building
Missoula County High School Rebuilt in	1932 1941 1921	Brick and Concrete	Fire-Resistant	Adequate	Yes	Boys' - Yes	Yes	Yes	Yes	Library. Music. Study Hall	Average	No
East Wing Annex		Brick and Frame	Semi-Fire-Resistant	Inadequate		Girls' - Inadequate				Shops	Poor	Yes

FIGURE 4. An education evaluation of existing school facilities at Missoula, Montana.

43

BIBLIOGRAPHY

Alexander, Robert E., "The Planning Process Behind the Blueprint," *The American School and University*. Twentieth Annual Edition. New York: American School Publishing Corporation, 1948. Pp. 202-15.

American Association of School Administrators. *American School Buildings*, Twenty-seventh Yearbook. Washington, D.C.: The Association, 1949. Pp. 321-22.

Bureau of the Census, 1950 Census of Population, Vol. 1, "Number of Inhabitants, U.S.," Government Printing Office, Washington, D.C., 1952. Pp. 1-3.

Bureau of the Census, 1950 Census of Population, Preliminary Reports, Series PC-3, No. 3, November 5, 1950.

Bureau of the Census #110, Illustrative Projection of the Population by States: 1960-1965, February 20, 1955.

Bureau of the Census, Statistical Abstract of the U.S. 1954. Seventy-fifth Anniversary Edition. Washington, D.C.: Government Printing Office, 1954, XVI, 1056 pp. (includes projections of population to 1975).

Busby, Elden B., "A Study of Population Trends and School Building Needs in the City of Fort Worth, Texas." (Not published.) October, 1948. Pp. 97-8.

California Framework Committee, "A Framework for Public Education in California," *California Elementary School Journal*, 17:228, 1949.

Dewhurst, Frederick, & Associates, *America's Needs and Resources*. Twentieth Century Fund, New York, 1947. P. 36.

Hauser, C. C., "How Accurately Can Engineers Predict Future Population Growths of Cities?" *American City*, 39:124-6, September, 1928.

Holy, Thomas C., "What Future Needs are Revealed by School Population Studies?" *The Education Digest*, 9:24-26, May, 1947.

MacConnell, James D., and William R. Odell, *Missoula Plans its Educational Future*. Stanford: Stanford University Press, 1952. Pp. 32-33. (A survey report.)

Making an Area Study. School of Education, University of Michigan. Ann Arbor: University of Michigan.

N.E.A. Research Bulletin, "Schools and the 1950 Census," Vol. XXIX, No. 4, December, 1951. P. 151.

New York State Education Department, *Room to Learn: A Guide for Community Participation in Planning for School Building Needs*, Albany, The Department, 1949. P. 27.

Odell, William R., and James D. MacConnell, *Beatrice Faces the Future*. Stanford, California, October, 1954. Pp. 10-11. (A survey report.)

Odell, W. R., J. D. MacConnell, K. Goldhammer, *Scanning New Horizons in School Enrollments for the Richmond Area*. Stanford, California, February, 1955. (A survey report.)

Ouattlebaum, Charles A., *Federal Aid to School Construction*. Washington, D.C.: U.S. Government Printing Office, 1954. P. 4.

"Planning Together for Better School Buildings," Bulletin No. 2, published by Lee M. Thurston, Superintendent of Public Instruction. Lansing, Michigan, 1950.

Proceedings. Sixteenth Annual Conference for Administrative Officers of Public and Private Schools. Chicago: University of Chicago Press, 1947. Pp. 80-87.

Schmidt, Robert C., "A Method of Projecting the Population Census Tracts," Journal of the American Institute of Planners, 20(2):102, Spring, 1954.

Sellen, R. W. and Ruder, C. B., "The Preplanning Survey," *American School Board Journal*, March, 1952. P. 52.

Spurr, W. A. and D. R. Arnold, "A Short-Cut Method of Fitting a Logistic Curve," *Journal of the American Statistical Association*, March, 1948. Pp. 127-34.

Strevell, Wallace H., "Techniques of Estimating Future Enrollments," *The American School Board Journal*, 124:3, March, 1952. Pp. 35-38.

Sumption, M. R., "Technics of Setting Up a Citizens Advisory Group," *The Nation's Schools*, 48:71-72, October, 1951.

Teachers for Tomorrow, Bulletin No. 2, Fund for the Advancement of Education, New York, International Press, 1955, P. 9.

Urban Patterns. University of Chicago Community Inventory for 1950, 1954. 30 pp. plus tables.

AN ILLUSTRATION OF
A BUILDING EVALUATION

Washington School
Howard Avenue and Anite Road
Burlingame, California

PLANT DATA

I. *Facilities*
   a. kindergarten
   b. twelve classrooms
   c. principal's office
   d. auditorium
   e. cafeteria
   f. library
   g. teachers' room
   h. health room
   i. general-purpose room

II. *Construction dates*
   a. main building—1915
   b. east and west annexes—1932
   c. auditorium reconstruction and new
   d. classroom unit—1948

III. *Types of construction*
   a. main building—two-story frame, cement plaster on wood sheathing
   b. annexes—one-story frame, cement plaster on wood sheathing

IV. *Site*
   1.58 acres

V. *Capacity*
   a. kindergarten—50 pupils
   b. grades 1-6—300 to 360 pupils

VI. *Enrollment as of October 31, 1953*
   a. kindergarten—63
   b. grades 1-6—326

Washington School is located, as are all Burlingame's older schools, on a site which does not meet the minimum recommendations for site size. The site is 1.58 acres, providing approximately 42,000 square feet of playground space. Blacktop predominates as a playground surface, although a tanbark area is provided under a jungle gym consisting of a horizontal ladder, horizontal bars, a slide, and a merry-go-round. Two basketball courts and three practice backboards are available.

The main building and west annex have finished fir flooring throughout, with the exception of the auditorium, which has a maple floor, and the cafeteria, floored with red asphalt tile. Ceilings and walls are plaster on wood lath, except in the auditorium and in the new addition in both of which acoustical plaster on metal lath is used. Lighting is provided by incandescent fixtures in all classrooms. The main building is heated by air from gas-fired boilers, the east and west annexes by unit gas heaters, and the new classroom addition by radiant floor panels.

Community use of Washington School is scheduled twice weekly, once semi-monthly and twice monthly.

Lavatory facilities throughout the school are adequate, but no facilities for students are located on the second floor of the main building, and no hot water is provided in the lavatories.

The principal's office and health room are satisfactory for their purpose. Planned removal of an electric kiln from the latter space will improve its area.

The auditorium is adequate, having nearly 3,000 square feet of seating area; folding chairs are used. In addition, there are 150 permanent seats in a balcony.

Cafeteria facilities are located on the lower floor of the main building, are 2,200 square feet in area, and have tables and chairs seating 180 pupils. The cafeteria is attractive, with red asphalt tile flooring, yellow walls, and a white ceiling.

At the time the survey was made, a former classroom in the main building was being converted into a combination library, store room, and teachers' work room.

A teachers' room, with lavatory facilities, is located on the second floor.

A general-purpose room, of 1,100 square feet, used for tumbling exercises, music, and meetings, is located on the lower floor of the main building behind the cafeteria.

Typical classrooms in the main building and in the east and west annexes have between 800 and 900 square feet of floor space, dark stained floors (east annex rooms have linoleum), colored walls, white ceilings, dark stained woodwork, and unilateral fenestration. The two classrooms in the new unit more than meet the recommended standards for classroom size, being respectively of 1,150 and 1,275 square feet. Both of these rooms have asphalt tile floors, light green walls, white ceilings, and bilateral fenestration, with side window and clerestory light sources. Sinks are provided in each of these rooms.

The chalkboard and tackboard installation throughout the school is considered adequate.

A structural survey of the buildings in 1935 indicated the need for certain alterations and reconstruction. This work has been accomplished at various intervals and the entire plant is now considered to be structurally safe.

Specific classroom characteristics are denoted on the following page.

Improvements which would produce a more satisfactory educational environment are:

1. To refinish the soft wood flooring in a light, natural shade or to cover the flooring with a suitable material, preferably light-colored asphalt tile.
2. To recondition the lavatories in the main building so as to make them more attractive and improve their sanitation.
3. To increase the water heating facilities in the kitchen.
4. To provide hot water in the lavatories.
5. To install lavatory facilities for students on the second floor of the main building.
6. To refinish the dark woodwork in the classrooms with a light color of proper reflectance value.
7. To refinish dark desk tops with a light, natural finish.
8. To redecorate and refinish the kindergarten room.
9. To investigate the auditorium floor's structural strength to determine its feasibility as a gymnasium.

WASHINGTON SCHOOL, BURLINGAME, CALIFORNIA

Room	Use	Approx. Area	Lighting in Ft. Candles High	Low	Glare Control	No. Pupil Stations	Furniture Type	Condition
West Annex	K	790	100	14	Pebbleglass & roller shades	32	Tables & chairs	Fair
1	4	910	150	25	Bamboo roller shades	25	Adjustable tandem	Fair
3	2	825	120	18	Bamboo roller shades	32	Desks & chairs	Good
4	4	770	130	14	Bamboo roller shades	24	Adjustable tandem	Fair
5	6	790	67	18	Bamboo roller shades	30	Adjustable tandem	Fair
6	6	875	25	14	Bamboo roller shades	30	Adjustable tandem	Fair
7	5	875	30	16	Bamboo roller shades	22	Adjustable tandem	Fair
8	5	875	110	20	Bamboo roller shades	21	Adjustable tandem	Fair
East Annex Left	1	790	110	30	Roller shades	30	Desks & chairs	Fair
East Annex Right	1	790	100	22	Roller shades	27	Desks & chairs	Fair
West Annex	3	875	100	20	Roller shades	29	Adjustable tandem	Good
New Annex	3	1,155	58	25	Porch shades	33	Desks & chairs	Fair
New Annex	3	1,275	35	19	Porch shades	30	Adjustable tandem	Good

49

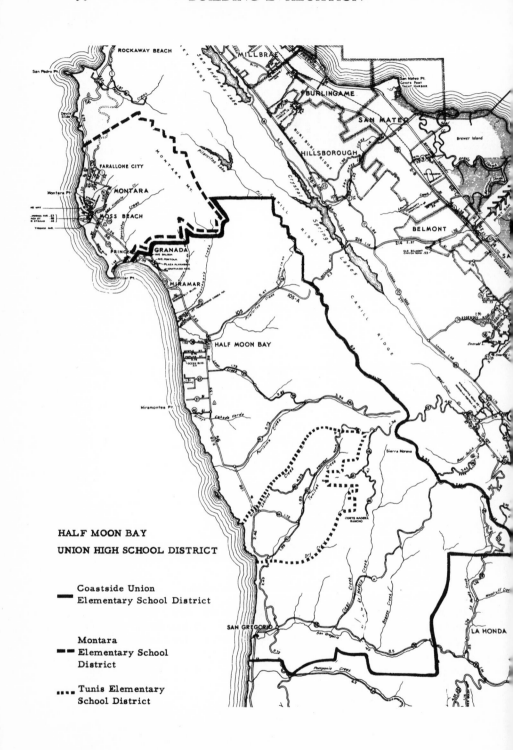

HALF MOON BAY
UNION HIGH SCHOOL DISTRICT

━━━ Coastside Union
Elementary School District

▬ ▬ Montara
Elementary School
District

•••• Tunis Elementary
School District

AN ILLUSTRATION OF A SCHOOL DISTRICT SURVEY REPORT*

Preface and Acknowledgments

Public education is important business. Not only do the public schools involve large outlays of a community's wealth, but the program of the schools is designed to perpetuate the values that are basic to our

* A report presented to the Boards of Education of the Coastside Union Elementary School District and the Half Moon Bay Union High School District by W. R. Odell, J. D. MacConnell, and K. Goldhammer, April, 1955.

American way of life. It is certainly a truism that the public schools reach into every home of the community and relate both to the present and the future well-being of every community.

The basic policies which affect the schools, consequently, must be made by the people of a community after they have thoroughly studied and analyzed all the factors that are involved. It is the role of the educational consultant to help the community in its study—to reveal the pertinent factors, to analyze the implications of the trends affecting the schools, to show the consequences of different policies upon the educational program. But the basic decisions must be made by the people and their elected representatives.

The writers wish to acknowledge the great assistance that has been rendered to them in making this study by Mr. Curtis Beacock and Mr. Ellis Benson, the administrators of the Coastside Union Elementary Schools and the Half Moon Bay Union High School, respectively. Assistance has also been secured from the San Mateo County Planning Commission and the San Mateo County Health Department staffs. The State Department of Education and the office of the San Mateo County Superintendent of Schools have been consulted. The assistance of all of these persons and agencies is gratefully acknowledged.

Perspective

The first school district to serve the Half Moon Bay area was organized in 1859 and was known as District 2. Strangely enough, today the Coastside Union Elementary School District serves almost the same territory as the original district, although in the intervening years there has been a long history of the division into many smaller districts which flourished for a period and then united again with Half Moon Bay in order to provide for their children the advantages of a broader and more efficient educational program.

The Half Moon Bay Union High School District was formed on May 22, 1909, by a vote of the Montara, Miramar, Half Moon Bay, Pilarcitas, Higgins, Tunis, and Seaside districts. The vote was favorable, thus leaving the Purissima district as an island within the Union High School District. On June 2, 1913, Purissima voted to be annexed to the Union High School District. When it was first organized, the Half Moon Bay Union High School District had approximately 50 students. It was not until the late nineteen-thirties that the enrollment exceeded 100 and the need for larger plant facilities than originally provided became apparent. The district today comprises the territory which is a part of the Coastside Union, Montara, and Tunis Elementary School districts.

Miramar consolidated with Half Moon Bay Elementary School District in 1941, to form the Coastside Union Elementary School District. At the time of the consolidation, Miramar had five pupils in the elementary school. Higgins and Pilarcitas districts consolidated in 1943, Pilarcitas having eight pupils while Higgins had only five. San Gregorio became a lapsed district in 1947 and was joined to Coastside; and Purissima, having only ten pupils, was annexed in 1948. Bell and Seaside both voted to join the Coastside Union Elementary School in 1951, bringing about 30 additional children into the district.

It is interesting to note the degree to which the complicated interdistrict problems are slowly being resolved in the area. Tunis now remains the only extremely small school district in the area, having less than ten pupils in October 1954. For the October 1954, Report Month, 692 elementary school youngsters (grades kindergarten through eight) were enrolled in the districts contributing to the Half Moon Bay Union High School. Of these, 561 were in the Coastside Elementary Schools, 122 were in the Montara Elementary School, and 9 were in the Tunis Elementary School. A part of the problem for the school districts involved is the fact that although the high school enrolled 58 ninth graders and 45 twelfth graders in 1954, at the same time there were 60 youngsters enrolled in the eighth grade in the area and 89 pupils enrolled in the first grade. Every grade in the elementary schools of the area exceeded the number of youngsters enrolled in any grade of the high school.

Present Enrollments

There is no certain method known for the forecasting of future populations or future school enrollments. Every forecast is based upon certain assumptions, and if the method is sound, the forecasts will be true only if all of the assumptions remain operative. The methods used in making the forecasts that follow have been popular in educational analysis for many years and are well tested. They assume, however, that the trends now affecting the enrollments of the schools in the area of the Half Moon Bay Union High School District will remain operative during the next decade. It is necessary for a school district to keep a yearly check upon all forecasts in order constantly to evaluate their accuracy in the light of new trends.

Table 1 presents the elementary school enrollments of all the districts which form the Half Moon Bay Union High School District, as of October 1954. At this time 688 elementary school youngsters were enrolled, 606 of them being in grades one through eight. Of these youngsters 81 per cent were in the Coastside Union Elementary School District, 18 per cent were in the Montara Elementary School District, and a little more than 1 per cent were in the Tunis Elementary School District. The dominant growth in the area can be expected in the Coastside Union and the Montara Elementary School Districts. Progression ratios show, however, that Coastside is by far the most rapidly growing district of the three. As subdivisions are developed further south from San Francisco, it is anticipated that they will affect the Montara Elementary School prior to the Coastside, but, as will be shown subsequently, there appears at present to be more building activities in the Coastside territory. It will, undoubtedly, be many years before the Tunis Elementary School will have much of an increase.

TABLE 1

ELEMENTARY SCHOOL ENROLLMENTS IN THE HALF MOON BAY
UNION HIGH SCHOOL DISTRICT, OCTOBER 1954

1	2	3	4	5
Grade	Coastside Union	Montara	Tunis	Total
K	68	14	0	82
1	76	11	2	89
2	75	12	1	88
3	62	11	3	76
4	66	10	0	76
5	66	16	2	84
6	55	18	0	73
7	47	13	0	60
8	42	17	1	60
K-8 Total	557	122	9	688
1-8 Total	489	108	9	606

The trend in school enrollment in the Coastside Union Elementary School District is shown in Table 2. In 1949, there were 305 youngsters enrolled in the Coastside Union Elementary School District. By 1954, at the end of the second report month, 557 youngsters were enrolled, for a gain of 82 per cent. Some of these youngsters, however, were brought into the district by annexation, and it is calculated that the net gain by natural causes and immigration (that is, by other than annexation) amounted to approximately 66 per cent.

TABLE 2

COASTSIDE UNION ELEMENTARY SCHOOL DISTRICT ENROLLMENTS
1948-54

1	2	3	4	5	6	7	8
Grade	1948	1949	1950	1951	1952	1953	1954
K	42	38	45	47	57	66	68
1	43	63	59	60	58	67	76
2	44	57	61	52	64	78	75
3	33	35	38	53	68	63	62
4	25	29	48	38	51	61	66
5	34	27	30	38	43	47	66
6	32	32	35	37	44	45	55
7	24	30	38	32	45	41	47
8	28	30	39	42	34	43	42
Total K-8	305	341	393	400	464	501	557
Total 1-8	263	303	348	352	407	435	489

It is interesting to note that during the past six years the annual rate of increase has amounted to about 10.7 per cent. The range has been from 1.8 per cent to 16.0 per cent, which typifies a fairly stable pattern of growth over the period. Were this rate to continue during the next five years, by 1960 there would be approximately 1,030 youngsters enrolled in the Coastside Union Schools. This is slightly larger than the Survey Team anticipates.

The pattern of growth for the Half Moon Bay Union High School is shown in Table 3. In 1948 there were 142 youngsters enrolled in the high school, and the enrollment dropped to 136 in 1950. The figure rose to 154 in 1951 and continued at approximately 150 through 1953. Between 1953 and 1954 there was a 15 per cent increase in enrollment, making a total of 173 youngsters enrolled. Since 1948, then, there has been a 21.8 per cent increase in enrollment. The loss and stabilizing of enrollments during some of these years is readily explained by the fact that the youngsters attending high school during these years were born when the birth rate in the United States was very low. The enrollment rise since 1952 is the reflection of years when the birth rate began to rise—and of course, the children born during the largest birth rate years are only now starting to enter high school.

TABLE 3

HALF MOON BAY UNION HIGH SCHOOL ENROLLMENTS
1948-54

1	2	3	4	5	6	7	8
Grade	1948	1949	1950	1951	1952	1953	1954
9	40	44	36	57	34	39	58
10	38	36	39	36	50	36	43
11	36	34	33	32	34	46	27
12	28	26	28	29	30	29	45
Total	142	140	136	154	148	150	173

San Mateo County Resident Births

Probably one of the surest guides to forecasting school enrollments is the resident birth statistics. Unfortunately, accurate counts of resident births by school districts are not recorded, and it would be an almost impossible task to sort out the county records over a long period of time in order to isolate local births. The next best index, consequently, is the county births as a whole, assuming that in the local district, a constant ratio of local births to county births maintains. Table 4 presents the number of resident births in San Mateo County since 1943, with the Survey Team's estimate for 1954. It is readily seen that in 1954, it is estimated that there were three times as many children born in San Mateo County as there were born in 1943. Each year there has been a steady increase, which is no doubt due to increased population within the county as well as to the maintenance of a fairly stable birth rate.

TABLE 4

SAN MATEO COUNTY RESIDENT BIRTHS
1943-54

Year	Number of Resident Births
1943	2,882
1944	2,960
1945	3,338
1946	4,090
1947	4,766
1948	4,976
1949	5,478
1950	6,041
1951	6,686
1952	7,123
1953	7,959
1954	8,500 (Estimate)

There is no particular reason to presume that either the birth rate or the flow of people into the county will significantly decrease. The best estimates of population trends in California indicate that birth rates will remain high. During the past few years they have continued to increase, but even if they level off, the fact that there are continually larger populations in California will mean that there will be increased numbers of children born within the state. California's rapid increase in population is reflected to a high degree in San Mateo County, and the growth will, no doubt, continue.

Housing Developments

Another indication of enrollment trends is housing developments within the school district. Records in the San Mateo County Planning Commission offices were checked, and it appears as though there were approximately 36 new homes built in the Half Moon Bay Union High School District in 1953, and 44 new homes were constructed during 1954. The largest percentage of these were built in Half Moon Bay and the area within the boundaries of the Coastside Union Elementary School District.

This gain to the Elementary School District is reflected in Table 5, which shows that during these two years 68 youngsters moved out of the district, but 89 (beyond the first grade) moved in, for a net gain of 21 children, which constituted approximately 25 per cent of the gain in enrollment.

It is difficult to determine exactly what the situation was in the high school, but a careful check would indicate that more children moved in than moved out, since many of the drop-outs are from families which do not leave the community.

It is readily apparent that subdivisions are steadily moving south along the Skyline and Highway Number 1 from San Francisco. Large sub-

TABLE 5

DROP-OUTS AND NEW ENROLLEES
(GRADES 1-8) COASTSIDE UNION ELEMENTARY SCHOOL

1	2	3	4
		June 1954 to October 1954	
Grade	Drop-outs	New Enrollees	Net Gain
8	—	3	1
7	2	5	2
6	3	8	5
5	3	4	−3
4	7	7	3
3	4	9	5
2	4	5	−2
1	7		
Total	30	41	11
		June 1953 to October 1953	
8		3	−3
7	6	3	−1
6	4	9	5
5	4	8	2
4	6	8	0
3	8	9	2
2	7	8	5
1	3		
Total	38	48	10

divisions either completed or in process of construction are on the edge of the Montara Elementary School District, and with the completion of the improvements to Highway Number 1, Half Moon Bay, itself, is less than a half-hour's drive to San Francisco. Aerial photographs of the area, included herewith, readily show that there are many desirable locations for new developments in the vicinity of Half Moon Bay, some of which can utilize land not now under cultivation. No one can say when these developments will take place—and it is, indeed, possible although unlikely that they may never materialize—but this community and its schools could be involved in a serious situation if the people failed adequately to plan for the future.

Enrollment Forecasts

The most important problem facing the community today is the potential size of the enrollments in the schools. Tables 6 and 7 present a fairly realistic forecast of the enrollments of the Coastside Union Elementary Schools and the Half Moon Bay Union High School, from the present to 1965. In studying these figures, the reader should bear in mind that the margin of error increases with each year beyond the present, for although a number of factors were considered in making these forecasts, there was no basis for determining when or if present trends would change in the course of the period indicated. There is more reason to believe, however, that these figures are a low rather than a high estimate. It should also be assumed that each of the figures is a round number, with the true number lying within a short range of it. The totals are probably more accurate than the figures for individual grades.

Table 6 indicates that the enrollment is likely to increase to approximately 960 by 1960 in the Coastside Union Elementary School District and that it is apt to be in the neighborhood of 1,400 by 1965. This means that by 1960 the district should anticipate about a 70 per cent increase in enrollment, but the rate of increase may well accelerate after 1960 as a result of the development of new subdivisions in the area. If the district maintains a constant check upon enrollment trends, there is no particular reason at the present to plan beyond 1960. If new subdivisions develop more rapidly than anticipated, the district can then be forewarned and speed up its timetable for additional construction.

TABLE 6

FORECAST OF ENROLLMENT 1955-65
COASTSIDE UNION ELEMENTARY SCHOOL DISTRICT

1	2	3	4	5	6	7	8	9	10	11	12
Grade	1955	1956	1957	1958	1959	1960	1961	1962	1963	1964	1965
K	79	88	93	104	108	113	120	125	130	135	140
1	81	95	105	112	125	130	136	144	150	156	162
2	89	95	91	100	107	120	153	160	170	177	184
3	72	85	91	91	100	107	115	147	154	163	170
4	66	72	85	91	93	100	107	115	147	154	163
5	73	73	73	86	93	94	102	109	117	150	157
6	74	82	82	82	97	105	106	115	123	132	169
7	58	78	86	86	86	102	110	111	120	129	139
8	50	61	83	91	91	91	108	117	118	127	137
Total K-8	642	729	789	843	900	962	1,057	1,143	1,229	1,323	1,421
Total 1-8	563	641	696	739	792	849	937	1,018	1,099	1,188	1,281

The Half Moon Bay Union High School, according to Table 7, is likely to have over 300 youngsters enrolled by 1960 and approximately 450 youngsters by 1965. One is impelled to hazard the assumption that these may be minimum figures, for along with ascertainable natural increases caused by larger elementary school enrollments, indications are that economic conditions will tend to foster improvement in the high school's holding power, thus augmenting high school enrollments even further than generally anticipated. By 1960, the high school will have increased by approximately 90 per cent over the 1954 enrollment. It is interesting to note that the figures indicate practically no increase in enrollment for next year, but a fairly constant rise in enrollment from that point on. At this time it appears that the only thing that could produce a leveling off or decline in high school enrollments would be a war, which would call many teen-agers either into the armed services or into war industries.

TABLE 7

FORECAST OF ENROLLMENTS 1955-65
HALF MOON BAY UNION HIGH SCHOOL

1	2	3	4	5	6	7	8	9	10	11	12
Grade	1955	1956	1957	1958	1959	1960	1961	1962	1963	1964	1965
9	57	61	73	93	97	96	97	112	123	127	138
10	57	56	60	72	92	96	95	96	111	122	126
11	37	50	49	52	63	80	84	83	84	97	106
12	24	33	45	44	46	56	71	75	74	75	86
Total	175	200	227	261	298	328	347	366	392	421	456

Facilities and Needs

The core of the problem, as it affects the community at this time, is the determination of school building needs which will result from the potential increases in population. It is readily apparent that housing for an educational program must be maintained, with facilities that are adequate for the nature of the program and for the number of children that will be involved. It is also important to note that there has been considerable research on the optimum class size, and although the evidence is not conclusive, there is a significant amount of data to suggest that the characteristic program found in elementary schools today requires a classroom of less than 30 pupils for best results. Most educators, however, would prefer to see elementary school classrooms that did not exceed 25 youngsters.

It is a little more difficult to determine the optimum size of high school classes, although the same general principles seem to apply. Some classes, naturally, can be larger than others, depending upon the nature of the instructional techniques employed, the skills involved, the activities in which the pupils are engaged, and the amount of individual attention that is required.

Assuming that this community would like to maintain its elementary school classrooms at about the 30 pupil level, by 1960, as indicated in Table 8, the Coastside Union Elementary School District will need approximately 30 classrooms. Kindergarten classrooms are considered to have a capacity of 50 pupils, since most kindergartens operate on half-day sessions. Since Coastside will probably have for some time to come a kindergarten enrollment that is steadily increasing, the ratio has been determined as one classroom to an absolute maximum of 60 pupils. If the enrollment forecast for 1960 is borne out, Coastside should double its present plant capacity by that date.

TABLE 8

MINIMUM CLASSROOM NEEDS
COASTSIDE UNION ELEMENTARY SCHOOL DISTRICT

1	2	3	4	5
Year	1-8	K	Total	Deficit
1954	16*	2**	18	2***
1955	18	2	20	4
1956	22	2	24	8
1957	23	2	25	9
1958	25	2	27	11
1959	26	2	28	12
1960	28	2	30	14
1961	31	2	33	17
1962	33	3	36	20
1963	37	3	40	24
1964	40	3	43	27
1965	43	3	46	30

* Based on 30 pupils per classroom.
** Based on maximum of 60 pupils per classroom. It should be noted that provision for more than 50 pupils per classroom is considered sub-standard.
*** Based on present 14 classrooms for grades 1-8 with capacity for 444 children and one kindergarten room with maximum capacity of 60 pupils.

It is a little more difficult to determine exact high school classroom needs, since a larger number of factors affect a high school program than an elementary school program. It is characteristic to speak of "teacher stations" in a high school, since gymnasiums, shops, libraries and other special facilities engage pupils for a part of their daily schedule and a teacher must be in charge of the pupils while they are engaged in all activities. A sliding scale, depending upon the total enrollment, is usually employed, and it is generally considered that in a school of less than 500 pupils a ratio of one teacher station to every 22 pupils is desirable, with a minimum of ten stations for any school in excess of 100 pupils.

On this basis, the Half Moon Bay Union High School should have approximately 15 stations by 1960, or one more than is currently provided. By 1965, if these forecasts are correct, 20 teacher stations will be required.

TABLE 9

HALF MOON BAY UNION HIGH SCHOOL
MINIMUM TEACHER STATIONS REQUIRED*

1954	10	1960	15
1955	10	1961	16
1956	10	1962	17
1957	10	1963	18
1958	12	1964	19
1959	14	1965	20

* These are approximations for the number is actually dependent upon the nature of the program involved.

Present Facilities

The significance of these needs for additional capital outlays for the districts is, of course, dependent upon the extent and adequacy of present facilities. Since the three buildings serving the Coastside Union Elementary School District and the Half Moon Bay Union High School District are fairly modern and in a satisfactory state of repair, their continued use for a period beyond that involved in this forecast is a foregone conclusion.

Coastside Union Elementary School District at the present time is operating two schools, a K-8 unit, containing 15 classrooms at Half Moon Bay, and a 1-3 unit at King's Mountain containing one classroom, although taught by two teachers.

The school at Half Moon Bay was constructed originally in 1940, and a new classroom wing was constructed in 1949. The rooms are somewhat smaller than generally desired for elementary school purposes today, although most of them may be considered the minimum that is acceptable for a 30 pupil classroom. Any classroom that exceeds 30 pupils in this unit is overcrowded and, presumably, could result in a corresponding reduction in educational advantages to the

Half Moon Bay Elementary School Unit I.

Half Moon Bay Elementary School Unit II.

children who are involved. It is estimated that this unit has a maximum capacity of 60 (although preferably 50) kindergarten children and 412 children of grades one through eight. Service facilities for this building are inadequate. There is a significant insufficiency of toilet and lavatory facilities, involving large waiting lines during recess periods, which undesirably cuts into the time for organized and free play which the children should have in order to return to their classrooms refreshed and relaxed. Storage facilities are extremely inadequate for a school unit of this size, which should also have a larger health room. The superintendent's office is also inadequate for the management of a school program as large as that in which the Coastside Union School District is involved.

The King's Mountain Elementary School has one room which is standard for a maximum capacity of 32 children. At present this room is grossly overcrowded as a result of the three-grade span that is taught within it. An inefficient educational program is the result. There is no health room or teachers' work room in the building, and both of these facilities are badly needed. Present lavatory facilities are inadequate, but plumbing has been stubbed in for a sufficient number of units to rectify this situation.

Were the enrollments within the elementary school district to remain the same, a significant amount of construction would still have to take place in order to rectify inadequacies that now exist. The Coastside Union Elementary School at Half Moon Bay does not have a library or a multi-purpose room. These are essential for every elementary school of this size. Next year, the elementary school should have about 520 pupils in grades one through eight—and this is at least three classrooms larger than the maximum capacity of the school, although four class-rooms would have to be constructed in order to overcome the over-crowding that will result in some rooms. The teachers' work room should be converted into a part of the health room so that boys and girls, when ill or resting, can have separate and private facilities, and so that the nurse can go about her duties even though children are being kept quiet in the health unit. This will mean that a new teacher's work room will be required. As previously indicated, the volume of business and responsibilities channeled through the superintendent's office re-quires a much larger and more functional office space. With all of these additions, the school would still lack many special facilities (music, shop, homemaking, arts and crafts rooms) that are particularly neces-sary for a good seventh and eighth grade program.

King's Mountain Elementary School.

Regardless of any other consideration, the King's Mountain School requires immediately a new classroom, a health unit and teachers' work room, and the provision of those toilet and lavatory facilities for which the plumbing is already stubbed in.

Half Moon Bay Union High School District was originally constructed in 1939 and additions have been made to the building since. At the present time, the high school provides 14 teacher stations, which have a maximum capacity of approximately 300 pupils. This should not be construed that the building has more stations or space currently than is needed. A small high school has to provide space for an inclusive educational program which does not get maximum use. The present size of the building could not be lessened without resulting restrictions to the secondary school program.

The 14 stations include seven classrooms for academic and commercial subjects, one homemaking unit (with a capacity for 15 girls), one all-purpose shop suite, one band and choral music suite, a library, an arts and crafts room, and a gymnasium with a stage and dressing room facilities. The fourteenth station is actually provided away from the school site. It is an agricultural shop, classroom, and farm, which is

Half Moon Bay Union High School.

several miles away from the building. The pupils are transported to this unit for class by school bus.

Currently, the building is adequate for the enrollment and for the educational program that is provided in it. By 1960, however, it will be crowded beyond capacity and the school district will have to consider the addition of approximately six more teacher stations—which should be adequate to about 1965.

Evaluation of School Sites

At present the elementary school district owns four sites and the high school district owns one site, in addition to which it rents a farm for agricultural instruction. Because the high school site and the main elementary site are contiguous and jointly used, they will be discussed together last.

King's Mountain Site.

King's Mountain Site is located near the Skyline Road and south of the King's Mountain Road. It contains 3.05 acres. The terrain is uneven and presents some difficulties for adequate utilization. The site, however, is probably adequate for the size of the school that will be developed on it. It would appear that 100 pupils in primary grades (K-3) could be satisfactorily maintained here. The natural setting is beautiful, but no effort has as yet been made to beautify the grounds, the major portion of which are asphalted. Some attractive plantings should be considered as soon as possible.

San Gregorio Site is located a few miles off Highway Number 1 at San Gregorio and contains 3.25 acres. This site should be retained by the district as it would provide a satisfactory site for a maximum of 100 primary youngsters. Ultimately, it may be necessary to have a full elementary school on this site and more land will have to be obtained. The district should have ample warning, however, of population shifts if the forecasts presented here are maintained by yearly analysis.

El Granada Site is well located for elementary school purposes on the southern end of the El Granada subdivision. It contains 7.7 acres and is probably adequate for a K-6 program of up to 300 pupils. The only apparent disadvantage is its proximity to the highway, but a high bank which can be adequately fenced will provide a sufficient safety barrier. To eliminate highway noises, the building should be constructed on the point furthest from the highway. If the El Granada subdivision is fully developed, a school for 300 pupils will not be adequate. Careful consideration should be given to the problem of expanding the site. It would be most desirable to have a site of not less than ten acres at this point.

Half Moon Bay Site is the major school site in the area. The high school district owns 11 acres, while the elementary school district owns approximately six acres. The acreage owned by the high school district is adequate for the present high school enrollment, but not for the capacity of the building—the minimum site required for a high school enrollment of 300 pupils being 13 acres. The elementary school enrollment, at the present time, requires a site of not less than ten acres. By 1960, the elementary school enrollment would justify a site of 15 acres.

For a combined unit, the site is physically inadequate and it cannot be justified from an educational perspective. There are already more youngsters on this site than should be housed here, and it must be recognized that the utilization requirements of a site for elementary school and for high school purposes are incompatible. The elementary school children deserve an opportunity for free play on playgrounds designed for their physical development—and this is also true for the high school pupils. In addition, as inevitably occurs in combined units, the educational program of the elementary school suffers from types of high

El Granada Site.

school uses of the site, and the high school program is restricted by elementary school uses of the site.

The site is already overcrowded, making it unfeasible for any further building developments upon it. It is an absolute certainty that to provide a satisfactory high school program, the high school will eventually if not rather soon have to be located on a different site.

Recommendations

General

1. The Survey Team did not undertake a complete study or analysis of school district organization in the Half Moon Bay area. Some analysis of the efficiency, effectiveness and the ability of the school districts of the area to solve their particular problems was inevitable. The existence of very small school districts in the area constitutes a problem for the future development of satisfactory educational programs, and there can

be little doubt but that a more efficient, integrated school district organization would pay rich educational dividends to the community. Consequently, the Survey Team recommends that the governing boards of the school districts involved give very serious attention to the problems of school district reorganization or unification of the entire area in order to determine if some program working toward such unification is feasible and desirable. It should also be noted that other small districts, either elementary or high school, on the fringes of the area, may wish to be included in such unification. It would certainly be desirable at least to study the recommendations of the County Reorganization Committee in this connection.

2. As a result of the findings of the Survey Team, who have checked

Half Moon Bay Union High School and Half Moon Bay Elementary School.

their data with the State Department of Education, there can be little question but that the present site of the Half Moon Bay Union High School and Elementary School is not adequate for the activities and educational program involved in a 12-year school span and the present size of the enrollment housed upon it. Unless a sizable addition of land is made to the present site, no further construction or enrollments should be considered on this site. But even if the site were enlarged, the undesirable features of combining an elementary school and a high school program on the same site will still exist. If the first alternative presented below is not feasible at the present time, the governing boards involved should continue to meet jointly from time to time to consider their basic problems and to study the eventual solution to this particular problem.

Recommended Alternatives for Action

1. *The Union High School Building should be sold to the elementary school district and used to house grades six, seven, and eight. This would necessitate the development as rapidly as possible of a new high school plant on a new site.*

For the high school district, this proposal would mean the selection of a new site, preferably in or close to the town of Half Moon Bay, and the erection at this time of a first unit of sufficient size to house the secondary school program through 1960. This would mean a plant capacity of at least 300 pupils and would involve an approximate cost of $450,000.

This proposal would provide adequate space for the elementary school district's sixth, seventh, and eighth grades through 1960, but beyond that date some additions to the building may be necessary. In 1955, there will probably be approximately 380 youngsters enrolled in grades one through five, 40 of whom will probably be at the King's Mountain School. Those at Half Moon Bay could probably be housed in 13 classrooms, permitting one room to be converted to a library. By 1960, grades one through five will have approximately 440 pupils, at least 400 of whom will be located outside of the King's Mountain area. This enrollment, excluding that at King's Mountain School, will require 17 classrooms. As this need develops, it will be desirable to develop a K-5 unit at El Granada. Although the first unit at El Granada should house only the primary grades, eventually the building should be expanded at least to a six-room unit.

Since this proposal would provide the gymnasium for the elementary school, it is likely that a multi-purpose room would not be needed at the present time. As the upper grades enrollment increases, however, it may be desirable to construct one as an addition to the present elementary school building.

As previously noted, the situation at King's Mountain is not justifiable, and a one-room addition, with added service facilities as discussed above, is needed immediately. It is estimated that additions here will cost about $25,000.

2. *In the event that the districts do not wish to solve the basic problems involving the existing site at this time, the elementary school district should develop the site at El Granada immediately.* If it is possible at this time to increase the size of the site, it would be desirable to do so, since the influx of people to this area may necessitate a school which eventually will have multiple sections of each grade. It is estimated that at the present time, four classrooms should be built at El Granada. The approximate cost of this unit should be in the neighborhood of $125,000. Serious consideration, if funds can be secured, should be given to the construction of a multi-purpose room at Half Moon Bay Elementary School and the addition of other service facilities as suggested previously. The King's Mountain addition is also a necessity, and it is estimated that the total immediate construction needs of the school district involve approximately $200,000.

It should be borne in mind that although this program will greatly relieve the crowded conditions in the elementary school at the present time, it does not give a sufficient amount of space to rectify the restricted educational program for the seventh and eighth grade pupils.

Other Alternatives

There are other alternatives which are also possible but because they would involve temporary expedients rather than long-term solutions to the basic problems, *they are not recommended.*

1. A six-year high school program, involving the seventh through the twelfth grades, could be developed. The boards would have to investigate the legal requirements involved therein. But it would still be only a few years before a new high school site would have to be developed to house greatly augmented enrollments. The existing building would be filled, relatively soon, to capacity, and some construction would be necessary—construction which, under the circumstances, the State Department of Education is very likely to oppose. This may be a desirable avenue to follow if the high school is relocated, but it is not feasible on the present site.

2. An addition to the site at Half Moon Bay could be acquired, although at some expense, and elementary school classrooms could be added. This would be only a temporary measure, however, and the basic problems of this site and of the school districts involved would still remain to be solved. It is possible, too, that consideration could be given to the acquisition and development of a new site within Half Moon Bay, but it would appear at this time to be better planning as a result of new housing developments in El Granada to start a building on that site.

3. Double sessions could also be contemplated, but this would solve nothing, and it would appear to be a very poor solution, even though

temporary, when the bonding capacity of the district remains available for adding much needed classrooms. The district would in no fashion be justified in providing the minimum educational program which would then be necessary.

Financial Considerations

A summary of financial data for the two school districts is presented in Tables 10 and 11. Neither district can be considered as wealthy, although it certainly appears as though both have the financial ability necessary to solve their educational problems—if not immediately at least over a relatively short period of time.

TABLE 10

COASTSIDE UNION ELEMENTARY SCHOOL DISTRICT
FINANCIAL INFORMATION 1942-55

1	2	3	4	5	6	7	8
Year	Average Daily Attendance	Total Current Expense	Expense per Average Daily Attendance	Capital Outlay	Total Assessed Value	Assessed Value per Average Daily Attendance	Tax Rate
1942-43	138	$ 14,383	$104	$ 5	$1,122,995	$ 8,138	$ .6949
1943-44	151	13,896	92	57	1,130,835	7,489	.3773
1944-45	166	18,521	112	1,762	1,673,735	10,083	.3597
1945-46	184	21,824	119	2,044	1,641,715	8,922	.5206
1946-47	239	28,325	119	328	1,784,320	7,466	.6521
1947-48	262	38,931	149	6,843	1,922,978	7,340	.6113
1948-49	287	55,870	195	99,844	2,687,105	9,363	.9096
1949-50	335	63,316	189	11,935	2,824,815	8,429	.9100
1950-51	362	67,909	187	14,207	2,806,391	7,751	1.6700
1951-52	367	83,354	227	24,953	2,980,632	8,119	1.5300
1952-53	417	108,053	259	15,969	5,057,743	12,128	1.3500
1953-54	470	117,302	249	24,624	4,984,844	10,605	1.2420
1954-55	550 (Est.)				4,879,027	8,870	1.5470

TABLE 11

HALF MOON BAY UNION HIGH SCHOOL FINANCIAL INFORMATION

1	2	3	4	5	6	7	8
Year	Daily Attendance Average	Current Expense Total	Average Daily Attendance Expense per	Capital Outlay	Total Assessed Value	Assessed Value per Average Daily Attendance	Tax Rate
1942-43	105	$29,324	$279	$ 1,186	$2,816,040	$26,819	·$
1943-44	89	29,385	330	1,461	2,808,010	31,551	
1944-45	90	31,099	346	1,397	2,902,960	32,255	
1945-46	98	34,422	351	640	2,928,325	29,881	
1946-47	115	39,902	347	3,532	3,048,110	26,505	
1947-48	135	46,583	345	14,664	3,267,030	24,200	
1948-49	135	51,490	381	12,574	4,005,580	29,671	
1949-50	134	57,307	427	4,701	4,172,047	31,134	.7700
1950-51	132	60,815	460	4,210	4,190,241	31,742	1.0700
1951-52	151	75,779	501	10,165	4,410,112	29,205	1.0800
1952-53	149	86,737	582	6,416	6,505,118	43,657	1.0500
1953-54	142	97,294	685	7,844	6,452,014	45,436	1.0450
1954-55	170 (Est.)				6,354,942	37,381	1.0720

Last bond election June 28, 1938—$80,000 to run for 20 years at 3¼%.

Tables 12 and 13 present current bond data for the two districts. It is seen that the elementary school district has a bonding capacity at present of approximately $170,000, with redemptions on present bonds at the rate of $7,000 per year until 1958, and then at $4,000 per year until 1968.

TABLE 12

COASTSIDE UNION ELEMENTARY SCHOOL DISTRICT—BOND INFORMATION
(INCLUDING ANNEXED DISTRICTS)

1	2	3	4	5	6	7
			Bond	Interest	Bond	Remaining
	Bonding	Bonds	Redemption	on	Tax	Bonding
Year	Capacity	Outstanding	Rate	Bonds	Rate	Capacity
1949-50	$163,175	$109,000*	$7,000	$4,177.50	.370	$ 54,175
1950-51	162,015	102,000	7,000	4,072.50	.380	60,015
1951-52	171,733	95,000	7,000	3,386.25	.330	76,733
1952-53	252,887	88,000	7,000	3,262.50	.170	164,887
1953-54	249,242	81,000	7,000	2,955.00	.290	168,242
1954-55	243,951	74,000	7,000	2,775.00	.177	169,951

*First issue of July 1, 1946 ($30,000) rate 2%, as of June 1, 1954, outstanding $15,000.
Date of last redemption schedule—July 1, 1958.
Redemption rate $3,000.
Second issue of June 1, 1948 ($90,000) rate 3¾%, as of June 1, 1954, outstanding $66,000.
Date of last redemption June 1, 1968.
Redemption rate $4,000 per year.

TABLE 13

HALF MOON BAY UNION HIGH SCHOOL—BOND INFORMATION

1	2	3	4	5	6	7
			Bond	Interest	Bond	Remaining
	Bonding	Bonds	Redemption	on	Tax	Bonding
Year	Capacity	Outstanding	Rate	Bonds	Rate	Capacity
1949-50	$208,602	$36,000*	$4,000	$1,235	.110	$172,602
1950-51	209,512	32,000	4,000	1,105	.120	177,512
1951-52	220,505	28,000	4,000	975	.100	192,505
1952-53	325,255	24,000	4,000	845	.070	301,255
1953-54	322,600	20,000	4,000	715	.070	302,600
1954-55	317,747	16,000	4,000	650**	.069	301,747

* Issue of July 1, 1938. Effective rate of interest 3¼%.
Date of final maturity July 1, 1958 (original amout $80,000).
** Estimate.

The high school district has a bonding capacity of $300,000 at present. The redemption rate on existing bonds is $4,000 per year until 1958, when current outstanding indebtedness will be completely repaid.

Table 14 indicates the approximate investments in buildings and sites that will be necessary for whatever course of action the boards and the community decide upon. If the first recommended alternative is selected, a new high school site and plant will have to be acquired. Approximately $450,000 should be sufficient for the site and the facilities that will be required. The additions needed at King's Mountain will cost approximately $25,000 and before 1960 the unit at El Granada will have to be started, involving an expenditure of approximately $125,000. It will also be desirable to make the necessary additions of service facilities at the Half Moon Bay Elementary School, which will involve an investment of approximately $25,000. The total cost to the districts over the next five years will probably be in the neighborhood of $625,000. For the Coastside Union Elementary School District, this may indicate the necessity for its entering into a state-aided construction program.

The second recommended alternative would involve the same construction at King's Mountain, the addition of a multi-purpose room and service facilities at Half Moon Bay Elementary School (approximate cost $50,000), and probably the construction of at least five or six rooms at El Granada, for a total cost of approximately $225,000. A minimum amount of state aid may also be required for this program.

The first of the alternatives that are not recommended would involve an approximate addition of site and classrooms to the high school of $200,000. The Half Moon Bay Elementary School would need the addition of multi-purpose room and service facilities, while the King's Mountain and El Granada construction would also be necessary. The elementary school would probably not have to enter into the state aid program in this instance.

The second non-recommended alternative would involve a heavy investment at the Half Moon Bay Elementary School, both in site and additional construction. Minimal construction at King's Mountain and El Granada would still be necessary.

The double shift program could involve before 1960 at least the same investment as that provided in the second recommended alternative. By the time the building is started at El Granada, however, the bonding capacity should increase to the point where the district should be able to finance it without state aid.

TABLE 14

ESTIMATED CAPITAL INVESTMENTS TO 1960

1	2	3	4	5	6
Alternatives	High School	King's Mountain Elementary	Half Moon Bay Elementary	El Granada Elementary	Total
Recommended					
Alternative 1	$450,000	$25,000	$ 25,000	$125,000	$625,000
Alternative 2		25,000	50,000	150,000	225,000
Not recommended					
Alternative 1	200,000	25,000	50,000	125,000	400,000
Alternative 2		25,000	175,000	125,000	325,000
Alternative 3		25,000	50,000	150,000	225,000

Conclusions

The Survey Team has consulted various other authorities in behalf of the school districts that have requested this study, and all competent advice that has been received points to the same conclusions—namely, that the area will have a much larger population within the next decade, and the influx of people will result in greatly increased school enrollments. The maintenance of our American way of life is predicated upon the development of a highly educated citizenry. Faced with the complexities of modern living, it would be poor economy, indeed, to neglect or to provide inadequately for the education of American children. The greatest resource of our country is its well-educated and highly productive people. The future prosperity of this region is dependent upon the maintenance of a citizenry who are able constantly to enhance the wealth of the state and the community.

The people of the Half Moon Bay area are to be congratulated for the careful study which they are making of their educational programs and facilities. Their future will be bright to the extent that they find the most desirable solutions to their problems, but to fail to plan now for the future may mean that ultimately the basic costs necessary for their children will have increased many times.

CHAPTER 2

THE SPECIALIST'S ROLE IN SCHOOL PLANNING

The pioneering-era one-room schoolhouse has passed from most areas of the United States. Planning such schools was no particular problem; volunteers built the plant in a single day, providing only space, windows, doors, heating, and crude furniture.

Today such planning involves a number of problems stemming from the complexities of providing an adequate yet economical educational environment for children. The capital investment, the demands of modern building codes, the maturing approaches to education, the individual needs of pupils and the total involvement of their community make extensive planning essential.

75

COOPERATIVE SCHOOL PLANNING

School planning is an endeavor that requires the "teamwork" of various groups, each with its own specialty. A number of professional, technical, and lay people are involved, and the extent of their cooperative consideration of problems encountered will frequently determine the difference between the planning's success or failure. Only by working together on construction problems can they insure adequate schools: functional, economical, integral parts of their communities.

FIGURE 5. A school planning team considering a college site problem. The group includes three architects, three land appraisers, three educator consultants, two lawyers, the business manager, an engineer, a board member, and the college president (*Courtesy San Mateo Junior College, San Mateo, Calif.*).

This chapter will discuss the roles of these specialists. Heuristically, the functionaries have been divided into an educational team and a technical team. Each group operates as a unit coordinating its activities with the other team.

THE EDUCATIONAL TEAM

The educational team consists of the governing board of the school system, the superintendent of schools, the professional education staff, the noncertificated or classified school staff, the educational consultant, the financial, legal and insurance advisors, and members of the community. Although the latter group is not a part of the educational team per se, it makes available the resources of individuals who aid in the evolvement of the planning's educational specifications. The primary goal of this planning is to suggest functional facilities to satisfy the educational program of the community.

In addition to this general activity, members of the educational team fill specific roles involving long-range investigations, forecasting, and planning. The roles as characterized in the following sections are typical of these specific functions.

THE GOVERNING BOARD

The governing board, often designated as the school board, the board of education, or the school trustees is the representative group of the lay individuals of a community responsible for the operation of the educational system in consistency with the objectives of the community and the limitations imposed by legal obligations. This group of three to twenty individuals has legislative, executive, and judicial powers. Nonetheless, the governing board does not possess authoritarian and uncontrolled power. It functions within a framework of state law and local regulation.

The board is an agent of the state managing local districts. The board represents the public and its interest. It keeps the public informed of the community's educational program; it solicits the public's financial support to supplement the program; it translates the objectives of the community into educational goals, formulating local policy.

A portion of the board's executive function is delegated to a professional educator, such as a superintendent of schools. The teaching of children and the operation of the schools is done by both professional and nonprofessional personnel, operating under the governing board's system of rules and regulations. The board appraises its agents and the services in terms of the community's objectives. Through these agents the governing board provides its most important function, maintaining the physical facilities essential to a satisfactory educational program.

School planning differs from the general nature of the board's activities in so far as a more concrete program of action is developed. A master building plan is a program operating over a period of years. The specific needs of the future can only be estimated, necessitating a flexible program. Thus the governing board continuously reappraises the building plan.

Planning is necessary for ordered activity. It is the responsibility of the governing board to see that such planning is done in a manner consistent with the school district's needs and resources. The selection of the appropriate planning organization will thus be of major importance. In a large district a section of the administrative staff might act as organizers with consultants being called upon for assistance in specific details of the over-all program. In a smaller district it is feasible to rely on outside assistance from university staffs, architectural organizations, independent consulting services, or county and state educational staffs.

A school building survey guides the governing board in its capacity of making ultimate decisions. The governing board, then, assigns responsibilities for school planning, participates cooperatively with the planning agency in the development of the program, and guides itself by the studies of specialists.

THE SCHOOL SUPERINTENDENT

The school superintendent is usually the executive officer of the governing board; he reports directly to the board, and the directives of the board are addressed either to him or through him to other members of the school staff. The superintendent is the professional leader of the certificated personnel of the school system, the coordinator of all personnel involved in the manifold aspects of the educational program. He is concerned with the educational and business functions of the school district. He evaluates the program and is the via media of the governing board.

His personal involvement in all of these functions is determined by the size of the school district. He has the choice of either performing or delegating the responsibilities of his professional assignment.

As the coordinator of the educational efforts of a school district the superintendent of schools has a major function in school planning. In smaller districts he assumes entire responsibility for such planning; in others he works with specialists. As professional advisor to the governing board he aids it in determining educational needs, including the school's physical facilities. His planning is long-range; he is the governing board's closest advisor. After a planning program has been initiated, the superintendent works with all individuals involved, members of the school staff, outside agencies, and members of the community.

There have been occasions when outside consultants have been retained to justify a program determined by the school district's superintendent or the governing board. It is essential in such instances that the superintendent make available to the planning agency all data pertinent to the building problem. He must explain his translation of educational objectives into building requirements. He must emphasize his district's characteristics to indicate the appropriateness of his planning. Candor, cooperation, and a common purpose in the relationships between the governing board, superintendent, and the planning group will clarify a school program and justify it in terms of a communal effort.

The effective superintendent is involved with all agencies or individuals participating in school planning. He coordinates the efforts of the educational team, works closely with the members of the technical team, and does all possible to insure mutual cooperation.

Some of the specific activities of the superintendent in school planning are listed below. He should:

1. Guide the board's policy making.
2. Help to develop an educational program to meet the needs of the community.

3. Supervise research on the present buildings and educational program, considering future educational needs.
4. Coordinate staff study of the educational program.
5. Translate planning into a constructive program of education.
6. Advise the board in the securing of a competent architect to coordinate the planning, engineering, and construction.
7. Recommend the employment of educational specialists, from both within and without the local school system, to aid the architect and board of education in determining educational and building needs.
8. Give the architect the facts of the educational program; assisting in the transferring of educational specifications to building needs.
9. Present the project's budget for approval by both the board and architect.
10. Assist the architect in determining competent building bids.
11. Insure that time, energy, and money are not wasted.
12. Represent the board in all stages of planning and construction.
13. Record each step and phase of the school planning procedure for the school's permanent record.
14. Help the board interpret the building program to the community.
15. Develop a program to use the buildings to their maximum capacity.

THE PROFESSIONAL STAFF

The professional staff, employed by the governing board and working under the supervision of the superintendent, differs from district to district. In smaller districts, the superintendent and staff members operate individually; in larger districts staff members will have specialized assignments. Some of these assignments include supervising instruction, managing business, developing curricula, providing special services, administering individual schools, counseling students, instructing, supervising (extracurricular) activities, transporting pupils, operating and maintaining physical facilities, procuring supplies and equipment, directing special programs, evaluating programs, coordinating community-school relations, and planning long-range educational objectives and enduring facilities.

All members of the professional staff have valuable contributions to make to school planning. In an efficient school organization the administrative staff utilizes the capacities of all educational personnel to forward the instructural program and to plan the school's physical accommodations. Experience has shown that much effective planning has been done by teachers and other members of the professional staff. These individuals are more aware of the school's practical needs than are remote committees or impersonal consultants. They may be given the opportunity to work with other members of the professional staff, with planning consultants, and members of the technical team.

THE NONCERTIFICATED OR CLASSIFIED STAFF

Included in the noncertificated or classified staff are all of those individuals, without professional training in education and its related fields, having important functions in the effective operation of a school system. Central staff office managers, controllers, purchasing agents, bookkeepers, secretaries, clerks, supervisors of buildings and grounds, warehousemen, and maintenance workers have specific functions in the school system. The same is true for such noncertificated, school staff members as secretaries, clerks, custodians, gardeners, cafeteria workers, bus drivers, and locker-room attendants.

The noncertificated staff of the school system is essential to the school's operation; opinions and suggestions based on their experience can concretely contribute to effective planning. These are the individuals who have first-hand working knowledge of the school plant. They are the people who have observed waste motion and inefficiency—traceable to weaknesses in design, crude arrangement, and inept facilities. If a school plant is to be efficient *all* employees responsible for the plant and its activities should be consulted by the planning committees.

THE EDUCATIONAL CONSULTANT

The educational consultant may be from the faculty of a college or a university, a member of an architect's staff, in private practice, on the staff of a county superintendent of schools, or a state superintendent of public instruction. He is tactful and a coordinator. He has a background in education, and available to him are its specialists. Educational consultants are characteristically experts outside the school system called upon to aid the professional staff and the governing board in the study of problems of organization, administration, finance, facility planning, improvement of instruction, program evaluation, the public information program, personnel, district problems and combinations of these problems. Their contributions involve findings, conclusions, recommendations, and programs of a long-range nature.

Educational consultants are essential to the school system if the board or professional staff lacks the time or experience to deal with any problem. The consultant's value is as a recognized authority in a specialized field of education. The major functions of such an authority in school planning are:

1. To advise in the planning of buildings for health and safety.
2. To direct or assist in divers school surveys.
3. To examine educational specifications for school facilities.
4. To appraise the total program's efficiency.
5. To coordinate the contributions of the individuals and committees involved in planning.

There are two areas of school planning in which the consultant works: (1) the determination of the general requirements for school facilities and (2) the development of educational specifications to aid the educational and technical teams in insuring the functional character of specific facilities.

In determining general requirements consultants are concerned with the following: (1) anticipated enrollments; (2) space requirements; (3) surveys of existent facilities; (4) financial analyses; (5) school sites and the effects of population distribution upon their selection; (6) district organizations; (7) legal restrictions imposed by and possible assistance stemming from county and state agencies.

The consultant will make periodic and summary reports, both oral and written, containing specific recommendations. The presentations will be to the staff, to the governing board, and in public meetings, and will be printed for distribution in the community.

Consultants are often retained after the completion of their final reports. Becoming involved in continuous problem analysis, seeing the board and architect through a building program, interpreting the long-range plan to the community at large, they render assistance during the months preceding a bond election for new school construction. Furthermore, consultants' staffs might be made up of graduate students, thus training students for educational work.

FINANCIAL, LEGAL, AND INSURANCE ADVISORS

Most school systems, at one time or another, call upon financial, legal, or insurance specialists. This advice is often available from county or state officials, or from expert agencies.

Financial advisors will analyze the cost of a building program, anticipate regular and special apportionments or subventions from county, state, or federal governments, and list all available sources of revenue.

The legal advisor will familiarize the school board with the lawful procedures of site acquisition, title assurance, contracts, bonding, bidding, specifications and their descriptions, building codes, elections, and bond issues. He will keep the governing board informed of all current and any anticipated legal complications in the building program, and will represent the interests of the board in any conflicts with civil authorities over sewers, utilities, streets, or other public services.

The insurance advisors of the school district will assist the governing board in planning insurance economies for new construction, in contractual bonding, compensation, liability, and general coverage. They will reappraise the district's insurance program at the completion of new plants, and in their conferences with the board recommend the total insurance coverage for the school district.

MEMBERS OF THE COMMUNITY

Involvement of lay individuals and groups in a planning program serves two important purposes. (1) Members of the community ultimately determine the educational program. Their support makes a desirable program possible. Their demands determine the extent of the school plant. (2) The participation of the community in school planning often leads to its understanding of the objectives of education.

The resources of the community must be tapped if its educational system is to satisfy. Parents are unavoidably interested in the school environment in which their children will live. Businessmen are seeking contracts from the the school board. Thus, real estate brokers can help in site selection; engineers can serve on technical committees; most people will lend assistance in accordance with their talents and special training. Their function is as advisors and consultants to protect the public's interest in education. They do not perform technical services, but protect their heirs.

PUPILS

A school is basically for the education of children. A major portion of a child's day is passed in school; securing his suggestions might benefit him in many ways. (1) Children anticipate new things with a great deal of pleasure; helping to plan their own school might be a maturing experience in their lives. (2) School planning activities can be an integral part of their study, proving of educational value. (3) By aiding with the planning of the building children will feel responsible for its care. (4) The child's perspective will help to plan surroundings of maximum efficiency and utility to him.

THE TECHNICAL TEAM

The technical team includes an architect, a structural engineer, a mechanical engineer, a civil engineer, an electrical engineer, an illuminating engineer, an acoustical engineer, a foundation engineer, a color consultant, a landscape architect, and local and state government agencies. The architect is the center of the group. With the exception of the government agencies, the professional experts listed above can be regarded either as members of the architect's staff, as entities in their own right, or as subcontractors for the architect. The latter arrangement is most usual, and is satisfactory to the majority of engineers.

Professionally, the members of the technical team perform the same functions in school construction as in any other assignment.

However, the significance of their roles is likely to be different in school planning. The requirements of a school plant are frequently less clearly defined than are those for a comparable structure planned for a commercial firm. Building codes for schoolhouse construction are different from those for private institutions. School planning involves more individuals than a nonpublic project of similar magnitude. Thus a school building program requires the involvement of the technical team in educational theory and in the community's ambitions, increasing its responsibilities.

The Architect

The architect designs and supervises the construction of the building. He is the leader of the technical team, working in much the same manner as the superintendent in the educational team.

His role has changed in recent years. Formerly an architect operated with solely technical information: the number of rooms required, the size and nature of the site, and the established budgetary limits. The best architects today plan schools suited to their individual educational needs. Today's schools are first and foremost for students. The contemporary architect *designs* schools; he does not simply assemble a plant.

In coordinated planning with members of the educational team, the architect develops a general, preliminary plan. After the community's approval of his initial efforts he works with the technical team to produce detailed plans—functional, safe, and economical. Compromises are often necessary for the design to be acceptable to all concerned. In the final planning, the architect must be alert to new materials, improved construction practices, and fluctuations in building costs to minimize the difficulties of the actual construction.

The architect makes frequent reports to the superintendent and governing board during the planning process and throughout the actual construction. During construction the school district's inspector works under the supervision of the architect. The final inspection of and the recommendation for acceptance of the finished school is also the architect's responsibility.

The scope of the architect's function is suggested by the following list of activities in which he usually is involved. He should:

1. Study and appraise the implications of the educational specifications furnished by the educational team.
2. Prepare preliminary sketches of the proposed site, considering its soil and subsurface structure, its topography, the interrelationships of the building's space requirements, its orientation, the location of its utilities and services, its access to transportation facilities, its drainage, and its surrounding property.
3. Prepare preliminary drawings of floor plans, their suggested elevations, the location of the school buildings on the site, and of the facilities to be included in any subsequent development.
4. Outline the specifications upon which preliminary costs might be estimated.
5. Secure written approval from the governing board of his final revisions on the preliminary drawings; he should then prepare blueprints.
6. Anticipate statutory and building code restrictions relating to the school being planned.
7. Secure written legal approval of his blueprints.
8. Prepare advertisements for construction bids, conferring with the governing board and its legal counsel as to their procedures.
9. Assist the board in opening and reviewing bids, and advise the board as to the responsibilities of the contractors if requested to do so.
10. Furnish all forms of agreement necessary for the completion of the building by the contractor.
11. Approve the selection of a supervisor and inspector of construction, each representing the best interests of the school district.
12. Act as a moderator between the governing board and the contractor on points of dispute. The architect may thus avoid unnecessary delays in construction; but he should not hesitate to recommend legal processes if they are needed.
13. Approve and certify the contractors' and subcontractors' payments.
14. Inspect the buildings with the contractors and the inspector, and upon satisfactory completion of all work, certify to the school board that all bills, liens, and other obligations have been met, and the school is ready for students.

Essentially, the architect's function is to design a total environment which will realize the district's educational objectives.

Choosing an architect is probably the most important decision that a school board must make, after it has selected its executive administrator. No successful formula has been found to select the necessary architect. The past accomplishments of an architect are the usual criteria. Sometimes younger, unknown architects are selected to design smaller and less complicated school plants; then results are appraised in terms of future demands.

In most instances architects are invited to appear before the school board and present evidence of their competency. They are able to present sketches, models, colored slides, and other data to indicate their past accomplishments. Investigating procedures verify his selection:

1. Visit school plants that he has designed.
2. Contact school district personnel who have previously worked with his firm.
3. Talk with contractors who have worked from his plans and specifications.
4. Invite his firm's representatives to qualify him before the board.
5. And finally, question him as to his objectives as a school designer. A joint committee of the National Council on Schoolhouse Construction and the American Institute of Architects has devised such a questionnaire.

The board of education examines these questionnaires by acceptable criteria. These criteria include items assuring the competency of the architect and his firm:

1. Is he a registered or licensed architect?
2. Does he have the staff and facilities to handle a project of such dimension?
3. Does he know school building requirements?
4. Has he designed specialized institutional buildings?
5. What is his knowledge of educational theory?
6. What are his professional affiliations?
7. In what school districts has he worked?

Further information can be obtained by reports from people who have knowledge about the firm and the architect.

INTER-DISTRICT QUESTIONNAIRE:
ARCHITECTURAL SERVICE

It has been brought to the attention of the _____ Board of Education that the architect and firm of architects _____ _____ was employed by your school district as a school designer. Our Board of Education would like your estimate of the competency of this architect and his firm.

In addition to any general statements you may make about them, will you kindly answer the following questions? All information will be kept strictly confidential.

1. Has _____ cooperated in every possible way during the project?

2. Were his final plans and specifications complete and detailed?

3. Was his planning creative and functional?

4. Did he promptly complete his work?

5. Did he follow all building, health, and safety codes, and were his plans economical?

6. Was his supervision to the best interests of the school district?

7. Did he cooperate with the builder and his subcontractors?

8. Were his plans and specifications clear enough to be followed to the letter?

9. Did he include in his services consultant services on structural and mechanical engineering, heating, ventilating, decoration, landscaping, and so forth?

10. Did he work with the educational consultants on the selection of the site, and the preparation and use of the educational specifications?

11. Does he have adequate knowledge of school design and construction?

12. Is he familiar with present day educational needs and practices?

13. Is he familiar with the newest building materials and methods of construction?

After such questionnaires have been returned, a composite rating of the architect can be prepared. The following architect rating form is an example of such comparative forms:

RATINGS OF ARCHITECTS

Scale for indicated characteristics	3—Unqualified approval
	2—Qualified approval
	1—Disapproval
Miscellaneous comment scale	5—Outstanding
	3—Good
	1—Questionable

Name of Architect	Cooperation	Complete plans and specs	Progressive & creative	Promptness	Compliance with codes	Supervision	Contractor cooperation	Meeting specifications	Inclusive fees	Knowledge of school architecture	Familiar education needs and practice	Familiar with new materials and methods	Miscellaneous evaluation	Total points
Rating 1														
Rating 2														
Rating 3														
Rating 4														
Rating 5														
Composite Rating														

Total points on composite ratings (possible 41)_____.

After screening the architect the board should visit the school plants and facilities he has designed. These tours should be preceded by an orientation to and a discussion of the educational and site problems that were to be solved, and an evaluation should be made of the specific solution. Not having designed a school building should not disqualify an architect for consideration: school structures are challenging to any competent architect.

The City Planner

The City Planner is a professional employed in planning for the general physical development of urban areas. He may be a private consultant or a planner on the staff of city and county planning agencies.

The role of the city planner in school planning varies according to the state and local legislation limiting planning and according to the laws governing the school organization and administration. The planner's work depends on the structure of the local government and the tradition of working relationships within and among government agencies.

The city planner may participate in school planning in two distinct ways. As an independent professional he may work in a staff as a direct consultant to a school board. This is a more specialized service the city planner can provide. Again, the city planner could work for a local planning agency, such as a city or county planning commission. To describe the role of such a planning agency it is necessary to set forth the nature of the planning function itself. The United States Chamber of Commerce, in a recent publication entitled *City Planning and Urban Development* defines this function as follows:[1]

> "City or urban planning, in its simplest terms, can be defined as intelligent forethought applied to the development of community. A plan for a town, city or metropolitan area is an outline which attempts to set down in words, maps and charts a guide for public officials and private citizens in developing and using land. This plan is commonly known as the comprehensive general or master plan for the community."

The planning agency in local government is a commissioned organization largely of lay citizens. The planning commission either relies on its own staff or calls on consultants for professional and technical advice.

The primary responsibility of the planning commission is to advise the legislative body of physical development. It also often serves in an advisory capacity to the executive officer, and less immediately to the more independent boards and commissions. The functions of the planning agency are:

1. To prepare and adopt a comprehensive and general long term plan for the physical development of the area concerned.
2. To recommend measures for carrying out the plan, including:
   a. Regulatory legislation under the police jurisdiction: zoning, subdivision control, and other official or precise plans.
   b. Programming of major public improvements.
3. To review specific proposals for development, testing their conformity to the master plan.

[1] *City Planning and Urban Development*, Chamber of Commerce of the United States, Washington, D.C., (October, 1952) p. 7.

The planning agency can furnish specific assistance to school planning in the following ways:

1. Cooperate with school authorities in the preparation of the master plan.
2. Furnish information to school boards and departments regarding:
   a. School population growth and changes in population characteristics.
   b. The programs and projects of other agencies: park, recreational, street and highway.
   c. The subdivision of activities; and other major private development projects.
3. Through subdivision control assist school boards to reserve school sites if they are considering new subdivisions.

After the development and adoption of the master plan certain efficient procedures should be followed by the planning agency and the school board. At the staff level there should be a continual liaison and interchange of information between the planning agency and school board. There should be an exchange of information between the planning agency and the school authorities on such matters as population trends and proposals for the development of public facilities and private developments, such as shopping centers and industrial developments. The school authority should also be furnishing the planning agency with data on enrollment, school policy and its standards, the general condition of the school plant, and the needed changes to meet new conditions, particularly those requiring capital expenditures. There should be a procedure referring such matters as new subdivisions, highway projects, and major public projects to the school authority for review. The school authority, on the other hand, should refer such matters as the changes of school sites and new school construction to the planning commission for review in the master plan.

The Structural Engineer

The structural engineer is generally a professional practitioner with his own business, designers, and draftsmen. He prepares complete structural drawings for buildings, approximately half of which are prepared by the architect. His is the responsibility of seeing that the designed building, when completed, will be able to withstand all conditions to which it might be subjected.

The architect and the engineer often operate in a single firm. Generally, however, the structural engineer is the architect's subcontractor.

The structural engineer must know building procedures, materials, costs, and methods of preparing estimates. He frequently is the architect's guide in effecting compromises between design, strength, and economy.

The structural engineer's work begins with an examination of the site. He will attempt to plan a firm foundation.

The architect will show the structural engineer the preliminary plans for the school plant, as conceived by the designer and school personnel, and the structural engineer will attempt to build upon them a satisfactory and economical building. The structural engineer may recommend to the architect certain modifications in the plans which are structurally sound and more economical. The architect and the governing board of the school district must then decide whether to accept or reject these recommendations. Sometimes the structural engineer does not have the opportunity to communicate directly with school personnel. His special competencies in structural matters are interpreted by the architect and incorporated into the plans.

The Mechanical Engineer

The mechanical engineer often has broader responsibilities than any other member of the technical team except the architect. His special concern is to determine the required heating and plumbing. On occasion he will assume the functions of the electrical, illuminating, and ventilating engineers.

The mechanical engineer is concerned with (1) water supply for all purposes, (2) drainage, (3) fuel supply and its distribution, (4) sanitary waste and sewage disposal, (5) heating systems and their controls, (6) provisions for ventilation, (7) plumbing fixtures and systems, (8) kitchen equipment, (9) fire protection systems, and (10) special laboratory, homemaking, and shop facilities.

The mechanical engineer is able to give valuable advice on site selection, utilities and their availability, building orientation, and the type of construction necessary in so far as it affects his special fields. Thus he works closely with the educational team, the architect, and other members of the technical team.

The Civil Engineer

The civil engineer advises the governing board and architect on the engineering requirements of potential school sites and on the development of the site which has been selected. He will be concerned with the development of the area surrounding the site and the effects that such development may have upon the school. He may do much of the work that might ordinarily be done by a foundation engineer if one is not employed.

The civil engineer is concerned with such factors as property description, land titles, the interpretation of title reports, the availability of utilities, storm drainage, the accessibility of the school to its neighborhood, and the limitations imposed on the site development by topographic conditions. He can be of assistance at every step: from the initial consideration for a site to its final selection and development; he can aid the architect in planning the most economical locations for building, playground, access roads, storm drains, and sanitary sewers.

The Foundation Engineer

The foundation engineer is a civil engineer specializing in the analysis of the physical properties of soils in relation to the construction of buildings. The foundation engineer provides valuable assistance at every stage of school planning—from the selection of the site through actual construction upon it. He is able to advise planners on the soil of the site, its best building locations, the most economical and adequate type of foundation, and on the grading, filling, and installation of the foundation. Although the foundation engineer does not design the foundations of a building, he recommends types of foundations and provides the basic information for the use of the structural engineer and architect.

Schools are relatively lightweight structures, but the cost of grading, filling, and providing a suitable foundation are a part of the cost of the site. Consulted prior to site selection, the foundation engineer uses topographic and geologic maps to determine the site's suitability, and may investigate subsurface conditions by test borings. In some areas, the best layout of structures on the site may depend upon subsurface conditions.

A foundation engineer will minimize the possibility of expensive errors. The necessity of employing this specialist will be determined, generally, by the type of structure planned, the site to be utilized, and the self-sufficiency of the other engineers. The architect, structural engineer, and civil engineer may be capable of doing the foundation engineer's work—but this work is unavoidable and if they lack competency a foundation engineer must be employed.

The Illuminating and Electrical Engineers

The illuminating and electrical engineers are considered together because their responsibilities are often handled by one engineer. Problems of illumination are architectural; they include such factors as lighting fixtures, reflective characteristics of surfaces, fenestration, light control, and the quality of illumination.

The proper distribution and adequacy of the light is a more important problem than the quantity of illumination. Using both natural and artificial light sources, the illuminating engineer's recommendations are basic to the design itself—to the healthful learning environment of the pupils.

The electrical engineer is concerned with the power needs of the school building, with problems of electrical service, load distribution, and communication. He should carefully plan outlets, telephone locations, and interclassroom communication systems. He will consider plans for distribution systems, motors, special power requirements, clock systems, program bells, intercommunication facilities, radio and television reception needs, and stage installations.

The Acoustical Engineer

The control of sound in the school is an important part of construction planning. There are two kinds of sound to be controlled: (1) noise from the outside of the school—from airfields, highways, railroads; and (2) sound within the classroom—echo and reverberation (sound decay).

The control of exterior noises begins with the selection of a school site; there are, however, instances where noise cannot be avoided. In such cases the acoustical engineer attempts to reduce the effects of the noise to a minimum—to ease the strain of oral communication. The effects of exterior noise in the classroom was measured by Dixon[2] in an articulation test.

The second instance of sound control in school buildings involves the measurement of reverberation (the time required for a given sound to dissipate, measured to one-thousandth of the sound's initial pressure). An acoustical engineer can determine the amount needed and the placement of sound absorbing materials to provide conditions approximate to the optimum reverberation time, assuring oral communication [0.72 seconds]. A study by Jentges[3] on acoustical efficiency in classrooms suggests that optimum reverberation times for classrooms may be much lower than previously reported.[4] Furthermore, there are indications that the effective acoustical treatment in classrooms eases oral learning—a basic means of teaching and organizing the curriculum; and decreases the hearing differences between pupils in the front of the room and those in the rear.

In larger areas such as corridors and auditoria, sound control of

[2] M. Ted Dixon, "Classroom Acoustical Control and the Efficiency of Verbal Communication" (unpublished doctoral dissertation, Stanford University, 1953).

[3] James E. Jentges, "An Experimental Study of Acoustical Efficiency in Classroom Environments" (unpublished doctoral dissertation, Stanford University, 1956).

[4] Vern O. Knudsen and Cyril M. Harris, *Acoustical Designing in Architecture* (New York: John Wiley & Sons, Inc., 1950).

flutter and echoes is effected by limiting the use of parallel surfaces. However, reverberation times can be controlled only by sound-absorbing materials.

Close cooperation between the acoustical engineer and the architect should result in an improved design as well as in sound conditioning throughout the school.

The increasing employment of acoustical engineers in the planning for schools should enhance the quality of future education.

The Color Consultant

The color consultant is becoming a key member of the technical planning team. Increased knowledge of the interdependence of light and color has focused attention on the importance of color in the learning environment.

The color consultant also creates an aesthetic setting in the school plant, and thus he should be employed in the planning stages of the building.

Color, properly used, serves practical ends—reflects light, curtails glare, minimizes fatiguing eye adjustments and eye strain. The use of color is a matter of science. For example, great differences in brightness tax the eye by demanding constant, tiresome adjustments. Thus the general view—of ceilings, walls, floors, furniture, table and desk tops—should be of uniform brightness—seeing at its most comfortable and efficient best.

The Landscape Architect

The landscape architect's function is planning the playground area, the building, and the landscape into a pleasant, functional, and integrated educational environment. He arranges hedges, fences, trees, shrubs, flower beds, and lawns. The landscape architect will work with the architect: his assignment is complex, unperformable by a layman, and, for his cost, his contribution is a valuable one, required in the initial planning stages.

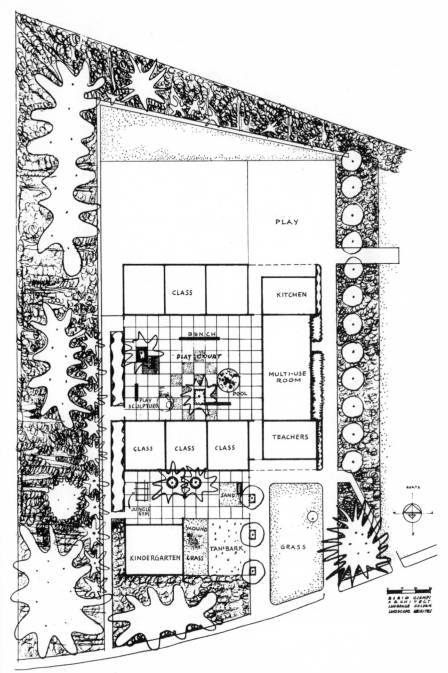

FIGURE 6. Landscape plan presented by landscape artist (*Courtesy Mario Ciampi and Lawrence Halprin*).

FIGURE 7. Landscape artist's concept of proposed court area in use (*Courtesy Lawrence Halprin*).

Government Agencies

The assistance offered by government agencies to schools differs between states. The state and its local school districts are responsible for public education. Some school systems are, however, independent of local government, while others are legally responsible to government agencies at the county and community level, at least in some facets.

The role of the state in school planning is usually as an advisor to the local governing board and to architectural firms. State personnel advise on procedures, state regulations, and technical matters. Typically, the state gives the formal supervision and approval to building programs required by law. Such relationships vary greatly from state to state. As a state gives financial support to building programs at the local level, its involvement can be anticipated. In any case, a superintendent or governing board should become familiar with state requirements before initiating a building program.

BIBLIOGRAPHY

American Institute of Planners, Advisory Planning Service, "Planning for School Capacities and Locations," Information Report No. 36 (March, 1952).

American Public Health Association, Committee on the Hygiene of Housing, Public Administration Service, *Planning the Neighborhood.* Chicago: R. R. Donnelly & Sons, 1948.

Beranek, Leo L., *Acoustics.* New York: McGraw-Hill Book Co., Inc., 1954, pp. 427-429.

Birren, Faber, *New Horizons in Color.* New York: Reinhold Publishing Corporation, 1955.

——, "Put Color to Work," *American School and University,* Vol. 24 (1952-53).

Blundell, W. J., "The Clerk of the Works in a Schoolhouse Construction Program," *American School Board Journal* (April, 1952).

Caudill, William W., *Toward Better School Design.* New York: F. W. Dodge Corp., 1954.

Edwards, John D., "The Evolving Role of the Educational Consultant in School Planning" (Doctoral thesis). Stanford, California: School of Education, Stanford University. Abstract: Dissertation Abstract 13:705, No. 5 (1953).

Engelhardt, N. L., *Planning School Building Programs.* New York: Teachers College, Columbia University, 1940.

Hereford, Karl, and Kenneth Gibbons, "A Look at New Schools," *School Executive* (April, 1954), pp. 63-93.

"Hints on Choosing an Architect," *American School Board Journal,* Vol. 126, No. 1 (January, 1953), p. 31.

Holy, Russell A., *The Relationship of City Planning to School Plant Planning.* New York: Teachers College, Columbia University, 1935.

Knudsen, Vern O., and Cyril M. Harris, *Acoustical Designing in Architecture.* New York: John Wiley & Sons, Inc., 1950.

Levin, Robert E., *The Visual Environment in Today's Schools,* Educational Administration Monograph No. 6. Stanford: Stanford University Press, 1955.

National Council on Schoolhouse Construction, *Guide for Planning School Plants.* Nashville, Tenn.: The Association, Peabody College, 1953.

Newman, Robert B., "Acoustics," *Architectural Forum,* 91: 52-53 (October, 1949).

"Selecting an Architect," *American School Board Journal*, Vol. 122, No. 1 (January, 1951), p. 21.

Smith, Lester W., and Evan E. Jones, "Working with the Architect," *American School and University*, Vol. I, 28th Edition, American School Publishing Corporation, New York, 1956-57, pp. 63-64.

Trends in School Planning, 1955 Report on School Planning Conference. Stanford, California: School of Education, Stanford University.

Wilson, Robert F., *Color and Light at Work*. London: Seven Oaks Press, 1953.

CHAPTER 3

FINANCING
THE SCHOOL PLANT

THE OVER-ALL CONSIDERATION

Financial planning is an important part of school planning. Few communities, if any, have sufficient financial resources to do all the building they would like to do or should do to house their children properly, and at the same time provide other desired community services. Values must be considered, immediate needs weighed against long-term goals and service priorities. The school building program and the total role of education cannot be considered independent of the needs of youth: their health, recreation, and welfare. The issue is not one of merely passing a bond issue; it is one of the

101

entire commitments of the community. Three steps are entailed in these financial considerations:

1. To determine the sources of finance.
2. To raise the finances.
3. To budget the finances between engineers, consultants, architects, and so forth.

A discussion of procedures to accomplish these steps follows.

SOURCES OF FINANCE

Federal Funds

There are three sources of funds for school building: federal, state, and local. For building purposes federal funds are usually a minor source; however, an investigation should be made of their availability. Federal funds are often paid to the state rather than to the local district and thus as federal funds, lose their identity. Furthermore, most federal funds are granted in support of some special program, for example, vocational education. Such funds are largely for service operations, and as such are not available for building costs. However, it is usually the rule that the more fully all such revenue is utilized the more local funds are available for capital purposes. An important exception to the general rule that federal funds are for service operations applies to those localities in which the federal government employs and/or houses large numbers of people. In such cases, the federal government recognizes that this places an extra burden on local school systems and sometimes grants funds in support of local schools. Thus a certain amount of income may be expected from the government, either through the state or in support of its own employees.

State Funds

Most states delegate the responsibility for educating children to the local community; but the state is responsible for the minimal schooling of all children.

The general pattern of state aid for building purposes varies greatly between these states. In some cases revolving loan funds, based upon the credit of the entire state, have been established. In other states outright grants-in-aid are made to needy districts. In several states the plan effects a combination of these two systems of aid.

Local Funds

The major responsibility for raising money to finance school buildings, equipment, and facilities is with the local district. To determine the funds available for purposes of school plant construction, an enumeration of local taxes available to the local district is necessary. The planner must become thoroughly acquainted with the legal framework and the financial structure of his district so as to be able to compute the present and future income available from these sources. Most school districts operate within a legal maximum bonding limit.

Typically, debt ceilings are set by state statute or constitutional provision. For example, the school laws of Montana provide that "the maximum amount for which any school district shall be allowed to become indebted by the issuance of bonds . . . is hereby fixed [at] . . . 5 per cent of the value of the taxable property therein. . . ."[1] This provision or an approximate variation of it is typical of states in which local bonding capacity is limited to a percentage of the total assessed valuation of the real estate and personal property lying within the boundaries of the school district. In some states there are special provisions for raising the limit. Some states provide for a majority vote of the electorate of the school district, while others provide for an appeal to the state tax commission by the governing board of the school district. Familiarity with these legal requirements is essential to the planner. In the preliminary stages of planning it is often advisable to obtain competent guidance on these matters and to ascertain the accuracy of these estimates of funds.

Possible assistance from other units of the local government should be explored. Some cities have charter provisions which permit the city—as distinct from the school district—to levy a tax for school support. Legal advice on such sources is essential. Following is a list of some of these sources:

[1] Montana School Laws, 1950 State School Supplement, page 2, "Limit of Indebtedness," Constitutional Amendment, Chap. 193, Sec. 1.

TABLE 5

ESTIMATED CAPITAL OUTLAY AND DEBT SERVICE, PUBLIC ELEMENTARY AND SECONDARY SCHOOLS (IN THOUSANDS OF DOLLARS)

State	Total capital outlay expenditures from all sources (Local, State, and Federal)			State Aid for Capital Outlay and Debt Service											
				State GRANTS for capital outlay and debt service									State LOANS for capital outlay and debt service		
				1953-54			1954-55			1955-56					
	1953-4	1954-55	1955-56	Capital outlay	Debt service	Total CO & DS	Capital outlay	Debt service	Total CO & DS	Capital outlay	Debt service	Total CO & DS	1953-4	1954-5	1955-6
(1)	(2)	(3)	(4)	(5)	(6)	(7)	(8)	(9)	(10)	(11)	(12)	(13)	(14)	(15)	(16)
Alabama	9,965	9,011	10,000			1,955			1,955			1,955			
Arizona	18,800	13,269	20,000												
Arkansas	13,584	13,600	13,600										1,313	1,109	1,300
California	282,635	318,966	350,000										46,417	52,297	60,000
Colorado	24,746	25,000	25,000	15		15									
Connecticut	28,775	33,527	36,000	1,659		1,659	2,099		2,099	3,002		3,002			
Delaware	8,593	9,665	6,743				7,638		7,638	150		150			
Florida	38,424	52,723	82,374			9,396			10,120			11,093			
Georgia*	71,587	183,691	71,122			14,322			14,312			14,327	51,355	158,650	48,122
Idaho	7,453	8,772	9,227												
Illinois	125,636	140,371	158,866												
Indiana*	39,776	46,572	52,000										10,000	11,000	12,000
Iowa	33,497	42,000	45,000												
Kansas	8,877	36,782	37,500												
Kentucky	5,474	16,285	18,000												
Louisiana	34,971	36,238	38,000												
Maine	5,045	4,000	5,000										570	577	20,999
Maryland	9,105	44,070	54,000	1,486	865	2,351	2,591	972	3,563		100	2,219	9,452	5,196	11,380
Massachusetts	39,314	54,000	60,000	3,750		3,750	5,300		5,300	6,000		6,000			
Michigan	113,336	115,000	125,000												
Minnesota	54,917	60,767	70,000												250
Mississippi	5,558	9,500	10,000												
Missouri	41,467	53,517	44,000	1,857		1,857	1,749		1,749	1,819		1,819			†
Montana	6,649	6,134	6,500												

Nebraska	7,227	7,500	10,000							
Nevada	5,553	8,456	6,000				500	500		
New Hampshire		4,602	6,500							
New Jersey	56,386	79,687	85,000							
New Mexico		59,962	85,301							
New York	357,906	332,368	358,800	5,394	5,394	6,971	9,447	766	933	2,700
North Carolina	41,118	31,580	40,000	25,000	25,000	25,000	25,000	179	35	70
North Dakota	2,652	6,300	6,300				2,500	251	1,555	2,000
Ohio	123,447			3,000	3,000	3,000				
Oklahoma	21,594	20,710	25,000							
Oregon	33,884	38,000	40,000							
Pennsylvania*	185,778	202,003	224,400	4,686	4,686	13,501	12,200	137,070	162,070	162,070
Rhode Island	2,699	4,418	7,000	7	7	7	7			
South Carolina	52,184	42,957	36,000	48,712	36,778	36,778	35,000			
South Dakota	4,660	5,628	6,000							
Tennessee	21,375	25,000	25,000	6,300	6,300	6,300	7,480			
Texas	78,418	72,534	75,000							
Utah	13,908	19,700	17,500	1,063	1,064	1,064	1,065			
Vermont	2,279	3,502	5,180	1,747	976	976	1,305			
Virginia	62,001	50,189	40,000	16,874	7,516	7,516	9,906	4,027	3,376	3,000
Washington	44,934	43,375	44,000	12,294	11,655	11,655	15,000			
West Virginia	19,872	14,420	20,136		33	33				
Wisconsin	28,437	53,284	68,284					1,808	3,494	2,500
Wyoming	2,714	6,305								

* Including cost of facilities constructed for a school administrative unit by a State building authority on a lease-purchase agreement, also holding corporations in Indiana.

† $60 million State bond issue bond available to counties as they reorganize.

Source: Courtesy Ray L. Hamon, Chief, School Housing Section, Office of Education, Washington, D.C. This table indicates the best up to date information on state and federal monies received by these states.

1. Special levies by the city, as distinct from the school district.
2. Special levies by the county or township.
3. Common use of recreational facilities by school and city (playgrounds, stadia, parks, and so forth).
4. Common use of other facilities such as the school and community auditorium, observatories, and so forth.

RAISING FINANCES

The planner has a definite list of the funds and revenues available for building purposes. He enumerates specific amounts of money. Now he must determine the money to be expected from each source. Each source supplies information of the availability of its funds.

Sources of Information About Federal Funds

1. U.S. Office of Education, Federal Security Agency, Washington 25, D.C. Complete information on legislation concerning federal funds is available from this agency. In addition, it provides school plant consultative services to state and local educational administrators.

2. National Education Association, 1201 Sixteenth Street, N.W., Washington 6, D.C. Several departments of the NEA publish materials and studies relative to school plant problems. The NEA Research Division provides bibliographies and current research information on request.

3. American Council on Education, Committee on Educational Buildings and Equipment, Washington 6, D.C.

4. Members of Congress. In most cases U.S. Senators and local Congressmen will supply information on technical matters which have federal implications.

5. State Departments of Education. More than half of the state departments employ school building specialists who devote all or most of their time to school plant problems. In other states the departments of education are prepared to answer inquiries and supply printed information.

6. Other school districts. Where neighboring districts are known to face similar problems they are often among the best sources of information.

Sources of Information About State and Local Funds

1. State Departments of Education. This is probably the most important single source of information. Several of the states have on their staffs field representatives able to assist the district directly, not only in financial planning, but in other phases of the building program.

2. Education codes, administrative codes, state constitutions, county charters, city charters, and other bodies of law are important primary reference sources necessary at all stages of planning.

3. Members of the state legislature.

4. Local officials: County superintendents of schools, city managers, school attorneys, tax collectors, treasurers, assessors, auditors, and so forth. These sources of information are of fundamental importance.

5. Special educational consultants: state colleges and universities, private universities, schools and departments of education, officials of other school districts, and other private consultants.

THE COMMUNITY'S SUPPORT

The determination of funds legally available for school facilities is necessary. But of essential importance is the community's willingness to participate in this expenditure.

The best way a school system can gain the community's support is by operating a good school system. Employing the most competent teachers, keeping the community informed of its accomplishments, as well as its expenses, will result in sympathy with the school.

This procedure has broken down in many communities due to the rapid increase in school population as well as to the influx of great numbers of new people. Thus schools must re-evaluate the communication techniques that once served their needs. School districts today are forced to use every available media to inform the public about their programs and financial needs.

Information about the needs of the school district for personnel and capital outlay purposes can usually be financed from school district funds.

Most school laws or codes prohibit local districts from financing radio or television programs or from publishing printed materials that request a "yes" vote from the taxpayer. A school district that organizes and successfully terminates a campaign for sufficient building funds to house its student body adequately is becoming a rarity. Much thought and organization is required to encourage continuing support for school plant needs. The following suggestions include some that every school district should use if its patrons are going to be adequately informed about its needs.

A SUGGESTED SCHOOL BOND CAMPAIGN

General Principles

1. *Purposes.* School bond campaigns are conducted to acquaint the voters with the school plant needs and to gain their approval of the plans for meeting these needs. The first part of such a campaign consists in stating the nature and extent of the problem to be met. The second part consists in securing acceptance of the proposed solutions by a majority of those who will vote at the election. The campaign moves from agreement upon the problem to agreement upon the solution.

2. *Board of Education.* The campaign must be justified to and unanimously accepted by the members of the board of education. A division of opinion within or uncertainty as to a course of action by the board will often defeat the proposed issue.

3. *Legal Details.* Legal details must be given close attention: the time and place of the elections, the amount of the bond issue, the schedule of retirements. A qualified bond attorney should be contacted early in the planning stages. Many bond elections have been declared void because of nonadherence to a legal requirement.

4. *Honesty.* The full details of the bond issue must be made available to the public, so that it can make the final decisions. The public is very quick to sense maneuvering or insincerity or lack of directness on the part of the governing board. *We hope*

5. *Coverage.* The support of all eligible voters must be solicited. A large number of citizens do not have children in school, yet are voters. Their interest must be solicited for the bonds. Sometimes the

heaviest property holders and some of the community's most influential citizens do not have children in the schools. Their interest can be kindled by appealing to their community pride, by stressing the effect of good schools on property values, and by emphasizing the effect of good schools on the development of the community and the district.

6. *Participation.* The community should be drawn into participating in the active work of promoting the bond issue. As many school patrons as possible should be included on the various committees, and the publicity committee should see that their names go to local newspapers.

7. *Time Schedule.* The campaign should be programmed in advance by preparing a time schedule and adhering to it. This schedule should cover at least the first and subsequent meetings of the executive and steering committee, the appointment of other committees, the speaking schedules, the publicity and advertising schedule, the contest date, the brochure dates, and the intensive activities just prior to the election.

BOND CAMPAIGN ORGANIZATION

There are two common patterns by which a bond campaign may be organized.

1. *The Administration Dominated Approach.* In this pattern the school administrator and his staff plan the campaign and do most of their own work. This approach is disadvantageous because the election may become an issue of the approval or disapproval of the administration and its policies.

2. *The Citizens' Committee Approach.* This approach involves the lay community. The committee is made up of interested citizens with a lay member as their leader. The school is represented on this committee by the local school administrator or his representative. Committee members may be the PTA president, the editor of the local paper, various merchants, service club members, union representatives, and so forth. This approach focuses the voters' attention directly upon the campaign issues, and minimizes the chance of school personalities becoming involved.

There follow some questions that should be thought about before the campaign starts. The answers to these questions will vary with the community, but they will help determine the guiding principles of the campaign.

1. How active should the Board of Education be in the campaign? Should board members actively participate in favor of the proposal?
2. How active should teachers be in the program?
3. How are funds to be raised to finance publicity? How much advertising is to be done, and what is to be the tone of this advertising?
4. Is it advisable to have a special election or to have the bond election held at a general election?
5. To what extent should students be used in influencing votes; how could their services best be utilized?
6. Which group or groups of people are likely to vote against the bond issue; what can be done to inform this group of the school's needs?

A suggested organization of a bond campaign using the Citizens' Committee approach follows:

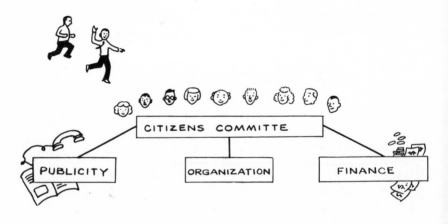

FIGURE 8. A Citizens' Committee should be responsible for publicity, organization, and finance.

The responsibilities of a *publicity committee* are to:

1. Take charge of newspaper releases.
2. Manufacture materials for distribution by block workers.

3. Prepare posters, bumper signs, lapel ribbons, door knob signs, and so forth.
4. Mimeograph printed material.
5. Conduct a slogan and/or poster contest.
6. Work with the editor of the student newspaper for a special edition.
7. Provide book marks for distribution at the library.

The responsibilities of an *organization committee* are to:

1. Conduct a "registration of new voters" drive.
2. Secure endorsements from organizations, business firms, and prominent citizens.
3. Organize a "house-to-house canvass" of all voters.
4. Organize separate "phone committees" and "poll watching committees" for election day.
5. Secure speakers and arrange the speaking engagements. Supply the speakers with all available factual materials pertaining to school needs.
6. Secure a sound truck for use on election day and on the preceding days. Prepare the recording on the script to be used.

The responsibility of the *finance committee* is to devise the means of securing sufficient funds for the bond drive.

BUDGETING

The purpose behind budgeting the finances is to anticipate as accurately as possible the needed income. The investigation should include all special funds available and the conditions to be met to qualify for them. Such conditions must be considered, the amounts available computed, and the totals indicated in the summary. In most cases income from state and federal sources are contingent upon such intangibles as the future school enrollment and the likely average daily attendance. Predictions of these factors should thus be indicated.

Local tax rates and assessed properties valuation should be recorded, and an attempt to predict their future levels should be made. In as much as the restrictions upon bonded indebtedness are tied to the amount of the district's assessed valuation, the amount of money legally raisable from future bonding must be predicted.

Prediction of future tax rates involves largely political considerations. Past experience must be considered, but no specific guide lines can be laid down: political sagacity is an elusive quality, to say the least. The school planner will ordinarily find it safer to base predictions of future tax rates upon existing laws and tax limitations, rather than upon the vagaries of future legislation. This is perfectly justifiable, since tax specifications are usually stable. However, many of the considerations which may affect the future amount of the district's assessed valuations are political in character. In so far as such factors can accurately be analyzed they should be considered. It would seem advisable to consult assessor; but in most communities little information is available from him: assessors are reluctant to make even tentative statements as to the future. Having established a tentative table of future tax rates and future assessed valuations, an exact computation of future income, fund by fund, year by year, should be made.

With this information it should be possible to evolve an approximate budget and financial program. A question likely to arise is as to the relative merits of bond financing as contrasted to a pay-as-you-go program. The technical aspects of this question are considered fully in the literature of public finance. A few broad generalizations can be safely made: (1) In actual practice the question is often academic; communities that have the problem of extending their building facilities are usually unable to finance a building program apart from bonding. (2) The disadvantage of bond financing is its high cost. During the twenty-year period which is required to amortize a typical school bond issue, at interest rates of from $2\frac{1}{2}$ to 3 per cent, a school will repay a total sum approximately 25 per cent greater than it originally received (see Table 6). In former years, when interest rates on school bonds often exceeded 6 per cent, schools not infrequently repaid a sum more than double that of the original bond proceeds. (3) In a period of rising building costs capital improvements can be purchased more cheaply today than at a future date. This saving, occurring during an inflationary period when interest rates on bonds are usually low, may offset the interest costs of bond financing. During a period of falling costs the reverse is true, and the only possible justification for bonding then becomes the immediate provision of funds otherwise unobtainable. (4) Bond financing does not preclude the use of available income, in so far as this income is available for capital expenditure.

TABLE 6

SALE OF HILLSBOROUGH SCHOOL DISTRICT BONDS

On June 7th the County Supervisors received bids on the sale of $275,000 in Hillsborough School District bonds.
Arranged in increasing bids, the following bids were received:

Firm	Interest Cost to District Net Amount	Net Rate (Per Cent)
American Trust Co.	$54,175.00	1.95225
Bank of America	54,223.50	1.95400
Blythe and Co.	54,739.00	1.97258
Kidder Peabody and Co.	56,248.00	2.02695
Schwabacher and Co.	58,327.50	2.10550

Based upon the bid of the American Trust Company, a schedule of amortization for the $275,000 issue follows:

TABLE 7

HILLSBOROUGH SCHOOL DISTRICT AMORTIZATION SCHEDULE

Bond Issue of June 6, 1955

Year	Amount Bonds Outstanding	Interest January 1	Payments July 1	Bond Retirements July 1	Balance
1955	$275,000	—	—	—	$275,000
1956	275,000	—	$6212,50	$10,000	265,000
1957	265,000	$2856.25	2856.25	15,000	250,000
1958	250,000	2481.25	2481.25	15,000	235,000
1959	235,000	2106.25	2106.25	15,000	220,000
1960	220,000	1993.75	1993.75	15,000	205,000
1961	205,000	1881.25	1881.25	15,000	190,000
1962	190,000	1768.75	1768.75	15,000	175,000
1963	175,000	1656.25	1656.25	15,000	160,000
1964	160,000	1525.00	1525.00	15,000	145,000
1965	145,000	1393.75	1393.75	15,000	130,000
1966	130,000	1262.50	1262.50	15,000	115,000
1967	115,000	1131.25	1131.25	15,000	100,000
1968	100,000	1000.00	1000.00	15,000	85,000
1969	85,000	850.00	850.00	15,000	70,000
1970	70,000	700.00	700.00	15,000	55,000
1971	55,000	550.00	550.00	15,000	40,000
1972	40,000	400.00	400.00	10,000	30,000
1973	30,000	300.00	300.00	10,000	20,000
1974	20,000	200.00	200.00	10,000	10,000
1975	10,000	100.00	100.00	10,000	—

Amount of gross interest.............................$54,525
Amount of premium................................... 350
Amount of net interest.............................. 54,175
Rate of net interest...................................1.95225%
Bonds sold to American Trust Co. June 6, 1955

Secure Competent Counsel

Bond financing is a highly technical field. Exacting procedural requirements have been imposed by statute particularly in the case of public bodies. A school district considering the borrowing of money through the sale of bonds should proceed only upon the advice of a qualified bond attorney. It is most important that consultation be had from the outset. The first formal step which the governing board should take is to consult a qualified bonding attorney. Thereafter, at every stage, through the final sale of the bonds, every move should be made with his counsel.

Financial Details on Policy Matters

The undertaking of an indebtment requires careful policy. Specific decisions have to be made. How large will the bond issue be? Over how many years is the issue to be amortized? Is repayment to be heaviest in the first few years, or is repayment to be deferred as long as possible? These and similar questions can be answered only in consideration of the over-all financial position of the district.

Secure the Lowest Possible Interest Rate

School bonds are securities purchased by investors, and as securities all school bonds are not equally valuable. To attract potential investors in school bonds they should be given detailed information on the school district's finances. Such information should be on such matters as the district's tax delinquency, total indebtedness, its assessment policy and its trends, the bonds' tax exemption status, and so forth. Many districts prepare a prospectus describing in some detail the district, its financial status, and the bond issue being offered. In most states school bond issues are sold in a block to investment banks or syndicates, who in turn sell individual bonds to private investors. Where this is the case the school district usually calls for bids on its bond offerings, in accordance with federal and state regulations and statutes. The most effective means of publicizing the district's proposal for bids should be drawn up by the district's bond attorneys. The process usually involves advertising in financial journals. Such advertisements should indicate that a district prospectus is available upon request. In addition, the district might send at its own discretion, a prospectus to each investment concern which is known to bid on school bond offerings in the area.

Adhere to All Commitments

In every state the purposes for which the proceeds of the school bond issue may be spent are specifically limited by statute. In most states, additional limitation is imposed by the local voters at the time of their approving of the district's proposal to issue bonds. In addition the school must justify its bond campaign in terms of specified needs.

It is essential that the school recognize and meet all these commitments. Some are required by statute, and their violation may lead to serious legal complications. But the school should always keep faith with its patrons. All promises, all commitments should be meticulously kept. It may be found that changes in building costs or other unforeseen contingencies require modification of the building plans. In such cases the school's obligation is to fully inform the public of its problem.

The central obligation of the school board is to consider the building program in relation to the entire educational process. The further wisdom, drawing upon special sources of revenue, must be given thorough consideration. It is this phase of the program, which is a challenge to the competent leaders of education.

All these bonds having been sold, this circular is provided as a matter of record only.

New Issue

$500,000
Chaffey Union High School District
San Bernardino County, California
2¾% and 2½% Bonds, Election 1953, Series I

Dated August 15, 1953   Due August 15, 1954-73, incl.

Payment and Registration	Principal and semi-annual interest (February 15 and August 15) payable at the office of the Treasurer of San Bernardino County in San Bernardino, California. First coupon (annual) payable August 15, 1954. Coupon bonds in denomination of $1,000 registerable only as to both principal and interest.
Tax Exemption	*In the opinion of counsel, interest payable by the District upon its bonds is exempt from all present Federal and State of California personal income taxes under existing statutes, regulations and court decisions.*
Legality for Investment	*We believe that these bonds are legal investments in California for savings banks, subject to the legal limitations upon the amount of a bank's investment, and are likewise legal investments in California for trust funds and for other funds which may be invested in bonds which are legal investments for savings banks, and are eligible as security for deposits of public moneys in California.*
Financial Statement	Assessed Valuation, 1952-53 (32%† of actual value) .... $88,298,120 Estimated Population 79,000

Total as of August 31, 1953	Direct Debt Only	Direct and Overlapping Debt
Gross Bonded Debt*...	$2,000,000	$9,034,370
Net Bonded Debt...	2,000,000	8,767,651
Net Debt, Percent Assessed Valuation.................	2.27%	9.93%
Net Debt, Percent Estimated Full Value...............	0.68%	2.96%
Net Debt, Per Capita..	$25	$111

*(row label: **Direct and Overlapping Debt**)*

†Reported by State Board of Equalization for common property only; utility roll of $9,994,980 is assessed at 50% of actual value.
*Reported by California Municipal Statistics, Inc. including new issue but excluding loans from State of California.
The Chaffey Union High School District will have $2,500,000 authorized but unsold bonds. Unsold overlapping debt totals $1,308,614. The City of Ontario may vote again on $1,250,000 sewer bonds and $1,300,000 water bonds. Annexation of an additional area to the Metropolitan Water District is under consideration.

Fiscal Year	Assessed Valuation	Secured Tax Levy	Delinquency as of June 30th Amount	Percent
1947–48................................	$65,243,060	$3,314,332.61	$ 69,003.62	2.08
1948–49................................	68,043,080	3,532,965.14	100,923.01	2.86
1949–50................................	70,814,470	3,761,868.01	77,786.58	2.07
1950–51................................	75,073,140	4,255,203.45	73,768.29	1.73
1951–52................................	80,706,620	4,543,681.81	67,508.53	1.49
1952–53................................	88,298,120			

*(row label: **Assessed Valuation and Tax Collection Record†**)*

†Reported by California Municipal Statistics, Inc.

Description of Area	The Chaffey Union High School District is located on the eastern edge of the Southern California metropolitan area, adjoining Pomona. 25% of assessed valuation is in the City of Ontario and 11% in the City of Upland. 39% is in the Fontana School District including the newly organized City of Fontana. The unincorporated towns of Cucamonga, Alta Loma, Guasti and Etiwanda also are in the District. A well established agricultural section, the District is noted for grapes, oranges, lemons, dairy products, poultry, deciduous fruits, nuts and garden truck. The Kaiser Steel plant is a large taxpayer and has been expanded substantially in recent years. Other industries include General Electric, Pacific Airmotive, Koppers Co., various wineries, citrus packers, and steel products makers. Southern California Edison has a new 250,000 kw. steam plant at Etiwanda. Residents also commute to Los Angeles County.

Amount	Coupon Rate	Due	Price to Yield	Amount	Coupon Rate	Due	Yield or Price	Amount	Coupon Rate	Due	Yield or Price
$25,000	2¾%	1954	1.70%	$25,000	2½%	1961	2.25%	$25,000	2½%	1967	2.55%
25,000	2¾	1955	1.80	25,000	2½	1962	2.30%	25,000	2¾	1968	2.60%
25,000	2¾	1956	1.90	25,000	2½	1963	2.35%	25,000	2¾	1969	2.65%
25,000	2¾	1957	2.00	25,000	2½	1964	2.40%	25,000	2¾	1970	2.70%
25,000	2¾	1958	2.10	25,000	2½	1965	2.45%	25,000	2¾	1971	100
25,000	2½	1959	2.15	25,000	2½	1966	100	25,000	2¾	1972	2.80%
25,000	2½	1960	2.20					25,000	2¾	1973	2.80%

*(row label: **Amounts, Rates, Maturities and Yields or Prices**)*

(Accrued interest to be added)

Purpose, Security	These bonds, to be issued for various school purposes, in the opinion of counsel will constitute the legal and binding obligations of the Chaffey Union High School District and will be payable, both principal and interest, from ad valorem taxes which, under laws now in force, may be levied without limitation of rate or amount upon all of the taxable property, except certain personal property, within said District.
Tax Gain, Amortization of Premium	*These bonds will be initially issued by the above named political subdivision at not less than their par value, and a taxable gain may accrue on bonds purchased at a discount. Investors are required under existing regulations to amortize any premium paid thereon.*
Legal Opinion	*The above bonds are offered when, as and if issued and received by us and subject to approval of legality by Messrs. O'Melveny & Myers, Attorneys, Los Angeles, California.*

September 1, 1953.

No person has authority to make any statement or representation respecting this issue other than as set forth herein. The information contained herein, while not guaranteed, has been obtained from sources which we consider to be accurate and reliable.

FIGURE 9. Chaffey Union High School District bond election (*Courtesy Bond Investment Department, Bank of America*).

116

BIBLIOGRAPHY

Bailey, C. M., "Problem of School Finance," *Vital Speeches*, 21:1523-27 (October, 1955).

Barr, William M., "The Capital Need and Taxpaying Ability of Indiana Public Schools" (Doctor's thesis). Bloomington: Indiana University, 1953. Abstract: Dissertation Abstracts 13:1058-59.

Burke, Arvid J., "Some Proposals for Better Financing of Schoolhouse Construction," *Nation's Schools*, 53:48-51 (February, 1954).

——, *Financing Public Schools in the United States*, pp. 507-12. New York: Harper & Bros., 1951.

Close, Wendell C., "The Effective Marketing of School Bonds," *California Journal of Educational Research*, 5:51-56 (March, 1954).

Ellinwood, D. M., "Better Break for Your Taxpayers," *American School Board Journal*, 130:69-70 (January); 43-45 (February, 1955).

Engelhardt, W. L., Sr., "What Size School Sites?" *American School and University*, Vol. I, 28th Edition, American School Publishing Corporation, New York, 1956-57, pp. 65-70.

Engleman, F. E., "White House Conference and School Finance," *National Education Association Journal*, 44:397-98 (October, 1955).

Federal Security Agency, *State Provisions for Financing Public-School Capital Outlay Programs*, Cooperative Study. University of California, Berkeley, 1951.

Graham, David R., "Some Economic Factors to Consider Before Building," *American School Board Journal* (January, 1951), pp. 48-51.

Hutchins, Clayton D., and Albert R. Munse, *Public School Finance Programs of the United States*, Misc. Document No. 22. Office of Education, Department of Health, Education and Welfare, Washington, D.C.: Superintendent of Documents, (1955) p. 251.

Ireland, Dwight B., "A Plan of Presentation for a School Bond Issue," *American School Board Journal* (August, 1950), p. 31.

"Is There a Better Way to Pay for Schools?" *Architectural Forum*, 101:108-11 (October, 1954).

James, H. T., "How Can Public Schools Be Supported?" *School Executive*, 74:48-51 (August, 1955).

Johns, R. L., "Money for Schools," *School Executive*, 74:88-9 (January, 1955).

Linn, Henry H., "Reducing Costs for School Construction Without Jeopardizing the Curriculum," *American School Board Journal*, Vol. 129, No. 4 (October, 1954), pp. 41-42, 74.

Misner, P. J., "New School," *Phi Delta Kappan*, 37:179-83 (January, 1956).

Morphet, E. L., "Financing Our Schools," *The Saturday Review*, 38:22 (September, 1955).

National Education Association, Committee on Tax Education and School Finance, *Tax Losses from Property Tax Exemptions*. Washington, D.C.: The Association, March, 1954.

Page, L. C., "More Indigenous Design Will Result from New Emphasis on Economy," *Nation's Schools*, 51:88 (January, 1953).

Reller, Theodore L., "School Building Authorities," *American School Board Journal*, 127:61-62 (September, October, 1953).

Rovegno, Joseph P., "The Public Authority as an Agency for School Building Construction" (Doctor's thesis). Pittsburgh: University of Pittsburgh, 1953.

Swalls, F., "Basic Principles in Financing Education," *Teachers College Journal*, 26:50-51 (January, 1955).

CHAPTER 4

SITE
SELECTION

Since the site should be selected far in advance of immediate building needs, it is impossible to determine exactly the nature of the future building and the needs it will serve. Education and planning consultants can usually provide basic population information to guide the board in selecting the best probable general location for the proposed site, but the opinion of an architect and/or an engineer is necessary when the purchase of specific land areas is being considered.

In rapidly growing areas where prescience in site selection is not possible, it is sound procedure to employ the architect on a specific project before the site is selected. The efforts of planning consultants should also be coordinated at this time.

The preliminary statement of the use to which the buildings will be put is followed by an analysis of all the factors affecting the school site, in terms of the space needs of the school and the community's educational program. The architect can then proceed to prepare the preliminary site plans.

IMPORTANCE OF SITE SELECTION

The importance of sites and their needs was rendered in a report by the U.S. Office of Education's School Housing Section in their School Facilities Survey Reports (1951-52). The report of the Status Phase, published in 1953, was based on returns from forty-three states enrolling 20,156,045 pupils. For all schools reporting, 82,362 acres of land were needed for new sites and improvements and 42,075 acres were needed for the enlargement of existing sites and for the improvement of additional land. A total of 124,437 acres of land was needed for elementary, secondary, and combination types of school plants. The estimated expenditures required to enlarge and improve existing sites and to purchase and improve new sites were also reported. The cost of land was determined by its fair market value. For all schools reporting, $53,139,903 was estimated as the cost for improvement of existing sites, $137,340,268 was needed for the enlargement of existing sites and improvement of additional land, and $169,541,893 was the reported estimated cost for new sites and their improvements. The estimate represented a total expenditure of more than three hundred sixty million dollars.

More than one-half of the funds needed in the forty-three states —$190,480,171—was designated to improve and/or enlarge existing school sites. "From these data it may be assumed," the report stated, ". . . that many existing sites are either too small or are in need of major improvements."[1]

TRENDS IN SITE SELECTION

De Shaw[2] and Gray[3] have stressed the need for changes in school

[1] *Report of the Status Phase of the School Facilities Survey*. U.S. Department of Health, Education and Welfare (Washington, D.C.: Office of Education, School Housing Section, 1953), p. 73.

[2] Elton R. de Shaw, "Planning the School Grounds," *The American School and University* (1951-52), pp. 217-20.

[3] Archie L. Gray, "Needed Research in the School Plant Fields," *Review of Educational Research* (February, 1951), pp. 63-68.

planning and in site selection. Strayer and Engelhardt[4, 5, 6] conducted surveys throughout the United States, most of their recommendations determining present standards of school building. As schools were being increasingly used for centers of recreation and adult education, school plants were, in turn, doing double service. Thus it became doubly important that these plants be properly located and adequately developed.

The National Council on Schoolhouse Construction states:

> With the expanding concept of the compass of school activities and of the relation of the school to the community, there is an increasing need for greatly enlarged acreage of school sites. This need is enhanced by many factors such as outdoor instructions supplementing regular classroom instruction, provision of facilities for games and recreation for groups of various ages including adults, preservation of natural sites such as a grove for community picnics, and the relationship of the school site to overall community planning and to other available public use areas.[7]

While the Council and other organizations and agencies have contributed significant research and study to general school planning problems, there remains much to be accomplished in certain of the specific areas, particularly site selection. Site standards, established by drawing from the experience of leaders in the fields of education, architecture, and engineering have been extensively cited in school literature, with respect for the conclusions drawn. This was done by Schneider[8] in his study of the site selection practices of various state departments of education.

However, Gray and Blake have made important observations based on their study of trends in school sites:

> Noteworthy developments in functional design are the tendency toward larger school sites with ample space for recreational and education areas; and the tendency toward L-shaped, finger type, or even campus plan, one story buildings. There has been a prevailing

[4] George D. Strayer and N. L. Engelhardt, *School Building Problems* (New York: Bureau of Publications, Teachers College, Columbia University, 1927).
[5] George D. Strayer and N. L. Engelhardt, *Standards for Elementary School Buildings* (New York: Teachers College, Columbia University, 1923).
[6] George D. Strayer and N. L. Engelhardt, *Standards for High School Buildings* (New York: Teachers College, Columbia University, 1924).
[7] National Council on Schoolhouse Construction, *Guide for Planning School Plants* (Nashville, Tennessee: The Council, 1953 Edition) p. 21.
[8] Raymond C. Schneider, "Factors Affecting School Sites" (Unpublished doctoral dissertation) School of Education, Stanford University, Stanford, California: (May, 1955), Chapter III.

idea that there is still plenty of land on which to erect modern one story schools. . . .[9]

Gray and Blake cited various studies to indicate that it is erroneous to assume that land is available—that most cities and many suburban areas have none. The high cost of land in seriously congested areas reduces sites, and multi-storied structures become the only answer to the problem.

FACTORS AFFECTING SCHOOL SITE SELECTION

It is important to understand that all legalities can be followed, and yet a school district will find itself in serious difficulties when engaged in a school site selection project. Older people who have had a satisfactory education on a three-acre high school site near the center of town often do not understand the need for the school district to purchase a fifty-acre site in an area where there are few, if any, residences. The changing curricular demands, as well as the growth trends of the present generation have not been entirely interpreted to the public by school officials. The increased cost of land is also a factor encouraging taxpayers to seek a justification for departures from an earlier accepted pattern.

Thus many boards of education ask for outside assistance, for consultants to re-evaluate the factors under consideration, before the final site decision is made. A wrong move by the board may result in obtaining the site but in losing the bond issue.

Property values become inflated when school districts indicate an interest in purchasing land for school site purposes. The lack of master planning, as well as the inability of school districts to anticipate community growth trends, has resulted in excessive expenditures for school sites.

Anticipating long-range school plant needs, promoting legislation to provide for the employment of impartial appraisers, and devising means of informing the public about school plant needs are among the many necessary steps that school officials can take to acquire adequate school sites without conflict.

[9] Archie L. Gray and Jerald Blake, "Trends in Materials and Design," *Review of Educational Research* (February, 1951), p. 29.

DEVISING A SITE EVALUATION RATING SHEET

The future, fortunately, is not as bleak as Gray and Blake's findings indicate. In most areas of rapid growth school sites are plentiful from the start. Foresight and active planning in advance of the immediate need will insure the choice of an adequate site.

Strayer and Engelhardt[10] cite an intensive study of four thousand titles on school building problems, and discuss what they considered to be important. Little attention, however, was given to the school site as one of the more pressing problems. This became apparent upon any review of previous standards, techniques, and even current practices regarding some school site selections.

The changed concepts (since 1920) of educational, recreational, and community activities to be sponsored in a modern school make the older rationale of school site selection grossly inadequate. The increased demand on school sites for an expanded physical education curriculum for the schools as well as for total, community uses has led to the increased emphasis in school site selection procedures.

The problem is to examine all the factors pertinent in any way to the assumptions that the current and impending needs of the school district are real and that there is an immediate need for steps to be taken to acquire new sites upon which to locate new facilities. The community will grow; it will enlarge by annexing outlying areas; its zoning ordinances will change because of real estate development; its attendance areas will shift; its existing schools will prove inadequate; its transportation routes will shift; its population and school enrollments will increase; its business, commercial, and industrial potential will change.

Constant effort is made to improve forms for scoring sites, and one recently developed is presented in this chapter. Such a scoring device affords the investigator the opportunity to evaluate the factors affecting a particular site, and to compile a series of numerical ratings as an aid to the final choice. Such ratings will be corroborated against facts, will lead to further investigations and appraisals, and will initiate the method of acquisition deemed most expeditious and fair.

One of the following methods of site acquisition is usually employed by a school district:

[10] George D. Strayer and N. L. Engelhardt, *School Building Problems* (New York: Bureau of Publications, Teachers College, Columbia University, 1927).

Method	Procedure	Advantages	Disadvantages
Purchase from owner	District purchases land from owner or owners	A business transaction where all parties are usually satisfied when the transaction has been completed	Owner has opport nity to ask more th market price and request special favo such as harvestii crops, privileges, eas ments, and so forth.
A negotiated purchase	An uninterested party acquainted with land values names a figure that is agreeable to the school district as well as to the owner.	Usually takes less time to consummate transaction. When price is agreed upon both parties tend to be satisfied.	Allows too much cr dence to the know edge and honesty the negotiator.
Condemnation	Authorized land appraisers, usually not less than three, submit a suggested market value price to a school district.	Fair price is more likely to be arrived at.	Often results in leg implications that a time consuming Can result in po community relatio between owner a school district.

Some State laws provide for the setting aside of land for school purposes.[11] Outright gifts have been made of tracts of land for

[11] Section 1342. Nevada Compiled Laws, 1929.
[The owner may plat lands and]
MUST CAUSE ACCURATE MAP TO BE MADE.—WHAT TO SET FORTH AND DESCRIBE. APPRAISEMENT OF LANDS.—ADDITIONAL DESCRIPTION. S. 2.

Whenever any lands are hereafter laid out and platted as mentioned in section 1, the owner or owners of the same or any trustee or trustees selected by such owner or owners, shall cause to be made out an accurate map or plat, particularly setting forth and describing:

1. All parcels of ground so laid out and platted by their boundaries, course and extent, and their position with reference to monuments erected or constructed, not less than one to each four blocks, with definite and exact relation to the center lines of the streets of such plat or subdivision, and whether they are intended for avenues, streets, lanes, alleys, commons, or other public uses, together with such as may be reserved for public purposes, and every map or plat of ground so laid out shall, if it covers forty or more acres of land, show one block for every quarter-section of land in the parcel of ground so mapped or platted, and the block so designated upon the map shall be forever devoted and dedicated to the uses of the public school system of the district in which it is located; provided, that whenever any such dedicated lands shall become unsuitable, undesirable or impractical for any school uses or purposes, the school board of the particular district shall proceed to appraise such lands and offer the same for sale. Said lands shall be appraised in the following manner: The governing body, in the county in which any such lands may be, shall appoint one appraiser, the assessor of the county shall appoint one appraiser, and the two so appointed shall select a third appraiser, and these three persons shall constitute a board of appraisers, who shall proceed to make a just and fair appraisal of such lands and report the same to the governing body of the county in which lands are situated. The said governing body shall thereupon proceed to sell said lands by giving notice, by posting in three public places in the district in which said lands are situated, for a period of ten days, inviting bids therefor. At the expiration of notice as provided herein

SCHNEIDER   SITE   EVALUATION   RATING   SHEET

	WEIGHTINGS	Accessibility	Acquisition	Community Use	Drainage	Environment	Expansion	Population	Preparation	Topography	Traffic	Utilities	Zoning	Acreage	Option No. 1	Option No. 2	TOTAL SCORE
		1	2	3	4	5	6	7	8	9	10	11	12	13	14	15	
	10																
	9																
	8																
	7																
	6																
	5																
	4																
	3																
	2																
	.1																
	0																

Site Desig. Final Rating
Location _____
District _____
Local Option #1 _____
Local Option #2 _____

Date _____ , 19 ____
Evaluated by _____

CALCULATION: A/B x 1000 = Final Rating

A. TOTAL SCORE
B. ITEMS SCORED

FIGURE 10. Schneider Site Evaluation Rating Sheet (*Courtesy R. C. Schneider*).

school site purposes by the owner or owners, especially by subdividers who recognize the value of adequate school sites in the proper location in areas that are being developed. This is more often the case when the land has been purchased at a reasonable price by the developer.

The criteria of scoring on school sites used in the Schneider Site Evaluation Rating Sheet, Figure 10, were the comparative merits of a given site to all other sites rated in the same area and the optimum conditions surrounding and affecting the location of the new plant in that area.

The factors used in this rating sheet are accessibility, acquisition, community use, drainage, environment, expansion, the proximity to a population center, site preparation, topography, the proximity to traffic hazards, the location of its utilities, area zoning, the acreage

said governing body shall sell said lands to the highest and best bidder; provided, that no bid shall be accepted for less than ninety per cent of the value thereof as set by said board of appraisers.

2. All blocks and lots, whether intended for sale or otherwise, by numbers or letters and their precise length and width.

3. By course and distance, the position of one or more of the monuments with reference to a known and established corner of the public-land survey.

4. Each monument or mark by which the location of the blocks, lots, streets, alleys, and public places have been fixed by survey upon the ground. As amended, Stats. 1919, 111; 1921, 34; 1929, 339.

available (size), and the space for two local options. The implications of each of these factors are briefly presented.

1. *Accessibility*. Each of the potential sites should be accessible from most places in the attendance area. One of the most acute problems facing school administrators today is that of pupil transportation. Considerations affecting the ease with which pupils may be transported to and from school; their safety in walking, cycling, or driving; and the ease with which public and school people may come to and leave the school grounds are of importance in evaluating the accessibility of a school site to its surrounding area.

2. *Acquisition*. Title to the land of a potential school site is held by some individual, group of individuals, or corporate group. The school's position is simpler when there is but one person with whom to negotiate and against whom to file a land condemnation suit. Hence the availability of land for acquisition is rated by the number of its owners. This knowledge is available in local records and official maps. An appraisal of the true value of the property should be made by a competent appraiser prior to its final acquisition.

3. *Community Use*. This factor is introduced because of the school's importance to the people in its immediate area. Driving or walking distances to school-community functions, parking facilities available on or near the site, and the site's general accessibility are factors to be considered. A basic question to answer in considering this factor is: "Is the site in proximity to a present or future community center and in such a position as will promote better school-community relations?"

4. *Drainage*. Drainage is a problem of the general topography of a site. The land should not be situated in a flood plain or in an area subject to serious crosswashing due to seasonal deluges. Subsurface conditions should be ascertained by competent engineers, and an adequate drainage system planned for the site.

5. *Environment*. General considerations for a good school environment are rated in this category. These might include such factors as landscaping for protection from noise, wind, and unsightly local conditions; proximity to public parks and recreational areas and the general desirability of the total surrounding area. Today's schools, with few exceptions, enhance property values in their residential areas.

6. *Expansion*. Many communities lack foresight in selecting adequate sites. It is necessary for additional land, adjacent to a potential

choice, to be available for future use. Delay in acquiring this land usually results in excessive expenditures.

7. *Population.* In some areas it is not necessary for a site to be close to a certain population or community center. In most instances, however, a new school will so enhance surrounding properties that it will create a new population center. In instances in which entire new neighborhoods are developed, a site of sufficient size to meet the educational and recreational needs of its residents should be set aside by the developer. The existing population and its potential growth should be continually appraised as a part of the district's long-range planning program.

8. *Preparation.* The degree of difficulty involved in preparing the site for the construction of the physical plant should be noted. A check of the surrounding structures, if any exist, will generally reveal any adverse effects on those structures due to settling caused by poor subsurface conditions. A final check should be made by competent foundation and structural engineers. They should familiarize themselves with the conditions in the area and advise the district concerning the initial grading and the preparation for the school's foundations. Estimates of the cost of the site preparation should not be made until test borings have been evaluated with respect to the size of the anticipated structure. Tests can usually be made prior to the acquisition of the site on consent of the owner of the land.

9. *Topography.* Natural topographical features should be appraised with respect to the plant and educational program anticipated for the site. Such features as shape, contour, drainage, land faults, subsurface conditions, existing structures, roads, railways, rivers, swamps, wooded areas and other geological and topographic hazards must be considered in this rating.

10. *Traffic.* Potential sites should be rated with respect to their proximity to through streets, arterial highways, and principal freeways. Their positions may be found on city maps. A check with county and state planning offices will reveal future plans regarding new construction in any particular area. It is important to have knowledge of the location of all railways, bridges, viaducts, underpasses, canals, rivers and creeks that have to be crossed by children going to and from schools. Public and school transportation routes must also be charted and evaluated.

11. *Utilities.* Prior to the selection of a site in a particular area

the location and sizes of the following utilities should be ascertained with respect to the anticipated new plant needs: water, gas, sanitary and storm sewers, and electric power lines. These should be rated with respect to their potential service connections, easements, and nuisance to play and building areas.

12. *Zoning.* Zoning factors may be appraised by an examination of the city and county or regional zoning ordinances and maps. From school documents the effects of industry and commerce on the school environment, with respect to smoke, noise, odors, and other hazards, can be made. The growing number of local and commercial airports is another important factor to consider in studying zoning provisions. Information can be obtained by contacting airport officials as to their future plans for expansion.

13. *Acreage.* All open and relatively undeveloped area suitable as a potential school site should be appraised on the basis of local school needs. The educational program determines the size of a school site. Most of the nationally recognized standards are *minimum* standards only. Most school districts try to exceed these minimum standards by twenty to thirty per cent—overcrowding occurs rapidly where minimums are used as adequate.

14. and 15. *Local Conditions Options.* Each community has particularities not anticipated on a general rating scale. These may be special items a community rates specially—items not to be found in any other district. These may be such factors as proximity to the existing attendance areas of similarly organized school districts, proximity to the existing attendance areas or site of another school in the same area, or proximity to an airport or its take-off and/or landing patterns and the noise and safety hazards created.

METHOD OF SCORING

Each site is scored on a ten-point scale. Important sites may be scored on the basis of only fourteen items—thirteen plus local option No. 1. Others may be rated on only thirteen or, if needed, on all fifteen items. In any event the options should be shown on the rating sheet.

As each item is comparatively scored (though not necessarily on all items), a dot is placed on the shaded spot opposite the weight assigned to it and below its corresponding item. When all items are scored, a line is drawn connecting each of the dots so scored, forming a graph.

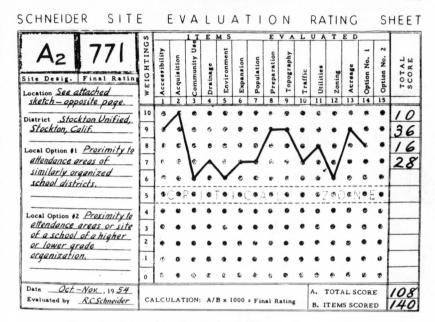

FIGURE 11. Example of Schneider Site Evaluation Rating Sheet completed (*Courtesy R. C. Schneider*).

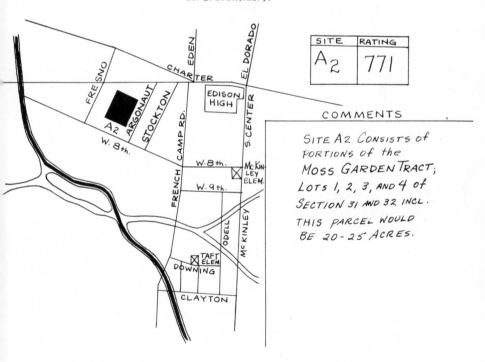

FIGURE 12. Map of the site rated.

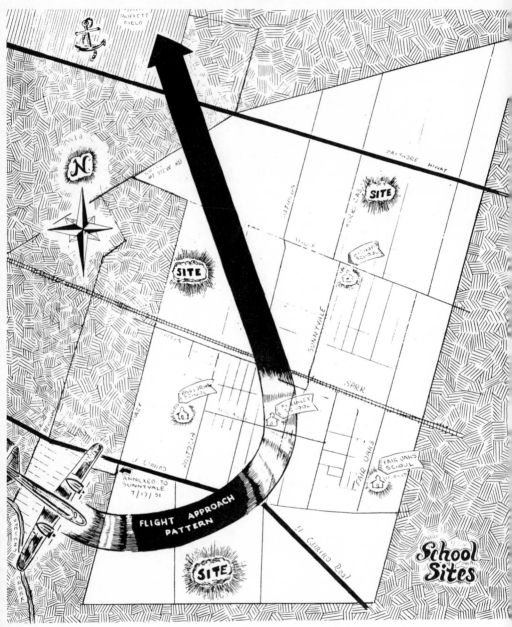

FIGURE 13. Flight approach pattern.

The scores opposite each of the weightings are tallied and multiplied by their value and totaled in the Total Score Column at the extreme right edge of the rating sheet. These Total Scores are then added in the A. *Total Score* box. The number of items rated is entered in the B. box *Items Scored*. This fraction is converted into a decimal carried out to three places, and then multiplied by 1000 to remove the decimal. This calculation yields the *Final Rating* based on a 1000 point scale. This figure is then entered for comparison with the scores of all sites rated.

The graph is drawn to reveal the strong and weak points of the site. Sites having several points in or below the critical zone should not be considered, or re-examined if their use is deemed necessary. Sites having an approximate straight line (one or two point deviation) above the critical zone should be acceptable. A district is fortunate when there are alternate sites with favorable ratings.

OTHER TECHNIQUES USED IN SITE EVALUATION

In addition to the Site Evaluation Rating Sheet discussed above, other criteria are available in making a complete site study of an area.

AERIAL PHOTOGRAPHS

A district should avail itself of aerial photographs for the latest pertinent information regarding a particular area in its district. There are three usual types of aerial photographs. They are defined with respect to the angle the axis of the camera lens makes

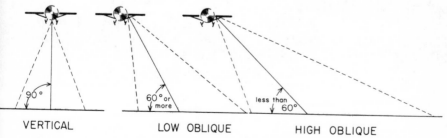

FIGURE 14. Three types of aerial photographs.

with the earth and the horizon. An example of these three types of photographs is shown in Figure 14; vertical, low-oblique and high-oblique. The vertical photographs are frequently taken during a controlled flight at a given altitude, depending upon the scale of photograph desired.

There are three practical uses of aerial photographs to obtain: (1) a simple picture of the terrain; (2) matched groups of photographs called mosaics; and (3) a fund of information for the data of relief maps or maps showing the differences in elevation in land strata (topographic maps).

FIGURE 15. Aerial photograph (vertical) (*Courtesy R. L. Copeland, Piedmont, Calif.*).

FIGURE 16. Aerial photograph (low oblique) (*Courtesy R. L. Copeland, Piedmont, Calif.*).

FIGURE 17. Aerial photograph (high oblique) (*Courtesy R. L. Copeland, Piedmont, Calif.*).

TOPOGRAPHIC AND GEOLOGIC MAPS

Another aid for ascertaining conditions and school sites is the government map. There are two types of maps in general use, (1) geologic maps which show subsoil conditions and land faults; (2) topographic or contour maps which show roads and buildings in the area, as well as wooded areas, swamps, railroads, canals, and so forth. Geologic maps will indicate foundation difficulties; topographical maps will indicate accessibility, drainage lines, grading problems, and any unusual settlement in the area. An example of this latter type, which has been enlarged to study a particular site problem, is shown in Figure 18.

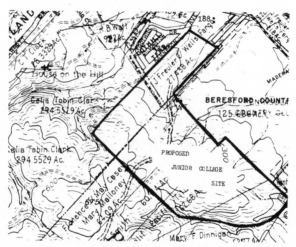

FIGURE 18. Topographic map showing proposed Junior College site.

TEST BORINGS

Maps usually show surface conditions only in a general way. Qualified engineers should be consulted to make test borings for more accurate reports of the subsurface conditions. A drawing of such a test plot, together with the graphic results, is shown in Figures 19, 20, and 21. These tests revealed the shearing strength, bearing capacity, and type of soil found in the area shown on the plot plan. From these diagrams (Figure 20) the engineers were able to design the foundation.

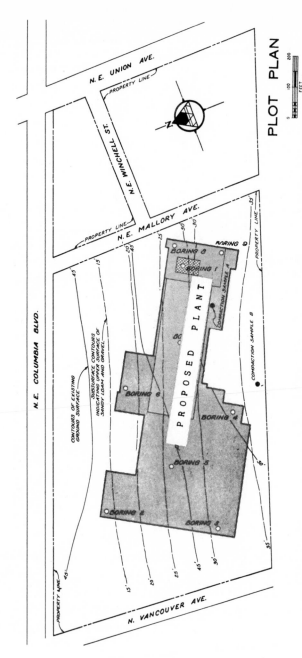

PLOT PLAN

FIGURE 19. Test boring plot plan (Courtesy Dames and Moore, Foundation Engineers, San Francisco, Calif.).

135

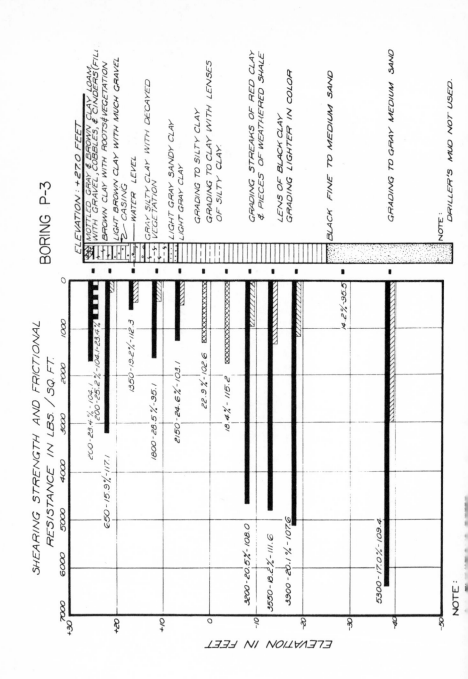

BORING P-3

SHEARING STRENGTH AND FRICTIONAL RESISTANCE IN LBS. / SQ. FT.

ELEVATION: +27.0 FEET

MOTTLED GRAY & BROWN CLAY LOAM WITH GRAVEL, COBBLES, & CINDERS (FILL)

BROWN CLAY WITH ROOTS & VEGETATION

LIGHT BROWN CLAY WITH MUCH GRAVEL

WATER LEVEL

2" CASING

GRAY SILTY CLAY WITH DECAYED VEGETATION

LIGHT GRAY SANDY CLAY

LIGHT GRAY CLAY

GRADING TO SILTY CLAY

GRADING TO CLAY WITH LENSES OF SILTY CLAY.

GRADING STREAKS OF RED CLAY & PIECES OF WEATHERED SHALE

LENS OF BLACK CLAY
GRADING LIGHTER IN COLOR

BLACK FINE TO MEDIUM SAND

GRADING TO GRAY MEDIUM SAND

NOTE:
DRILLER'S MUD NOT USED.

200 - 23.4 % - 104.1
200 - 25.2 % - 104.1 - 23.4%

1350 - 19.2 % - 112.3

650 - 15.9% - 117.1

1800 - 28.5 % - 95.1

2150 - 24.6% - 103.1

22.9 % - 102.6

18.4 % - 115.2

3200 - 20.5% - 108.0

3550 - 18.2% - 111.6

3900 - 20.1 % - 107.6

14.2 % - 95.5

5300 - 17.0% - 109.4

ELEVATION IN FEET

NOTE:

136

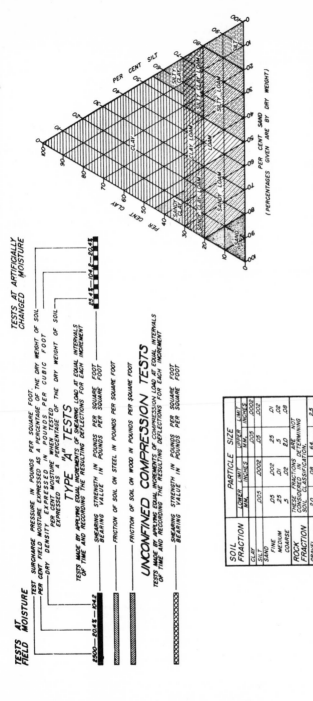

PER CENT SILT

PER CENT CLAY

PER CENT SAND

(PERCENTAGES GIVEN ARE BY DRY WEIGHT)

SILT
SILTY CLAY LOAM
SILTY LOAM
CLAY LOAM
CLAY
LOAM
SANDY CLAY LOAM
SANDY CLAY
SANDY LOAM
SAND

■ INDICATES DEPTH AT WHICH UNDISTURBED SAMPLE WAS EXTRACTED

TESTS AT ARTIFICIALLY CHANGED MOISTURE

TESTS AT FIELD MOISTURE

2500 — 2043 — 104.2   23.4 % — 104.6 — 20.4

TYPE "A" TESTS

—TEST SURCHARGE PRESSURE IN POUNDS PER SQUARE FOOT.
—PER CENT FIELD MOISTURE EXPRESSED AS A PERCENTAGE OF THE DRY WEIGHT OF SOIL
—DRY DENSITY EXPRESSED IN POUNDS PER CUBIC FOOT
—PER CENT FIELD MOISTURE WHEN TESTED EXPRESSED AS A PERCENTAGE OF THE DRY WEIGHT OF SOIL

TESTS MADE BY APPLYING EQUAL INCREMENTS OF SHEARING LOAD AT EQUAL INTERVALS OF TIME AND RECORDING THE RESULTING DEFLECTIONS FOR EACH INCREMENT

——— SHEARING STRENGTH IN POUNDS PER SQUARE FOOT
——— BEARING VALUE IN POUNDS PER SQUARE FOOT

——— FRICTION OF SOIL ON STEEL IN POUNDS PER SQUARE FOOT

——— FRICTION OF SOIL ON WOOD IN POUNDS PER SQUARE FOOT

UNCONFINED COMPRESSION TESTS

TESTS MADE BY APPLYING EQUAL INCREMENTS OF COMPRESSION LOAD AT EQUAL INTERVALS OF TIME AND RECORDING THE RESULTING DEFLECTIONS FOR EACH INCREMENT

——— SHEARING STRENGTH IN POUNDS PER SQUARE FOOT
——— BEARING VALUE IN POUNDS PER SQUARE FOOT

SOIL FRACTION	PARTICLE SIZE			
	LOWER LIMIT		UPPER LIMIT	
	MM.	INCHES	MM.	INCHES
CLAY			.005	.0002
SILT	.005	.0002	.05	.002
SAND FINE	.05	.002	.25	.01
MEDIUM	.25	.01	.5	.02
COARSE	.5	.02	2.0	.08
ROCK FRACTION	THESE FRACTIONS ARE NOT CONSIDERED IN DETERMINING SOIL CLASSIFICATION.			
GRAVEL	2.0	.08	64.	2.5
COBBLES	64.	2.5	256.	10.
BOULDERS	256.	10.		

SOIL CLASSIFICATION CHART
AND
KEY TO TEST DATA

DAMES & MOORE
FOUNDATION ENGINEERS

FIGURE 20. Log of borings (Courtesy Dames and Moore, Foundation Engineers, San Francisco, Calif.).

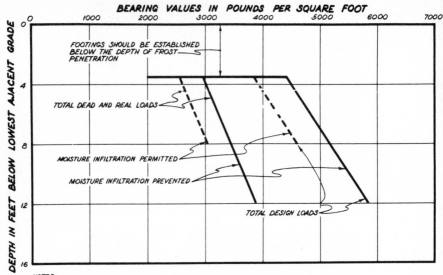

BEARING VALUES IN POUNDS PER SQUARE FOOT

DEPTH IN FEET BELOW LOWEST ADJACENT GRADE

FOOTINGS SHOULD BE ESTABLISHED
BELOW THE DEPTH OF FROST
PENETRATION

TOTAL DEAD AND REAL LOADS

MOISTURE INFILTRATION PERMITTED

MOISTURE INFILTRATION PREVENTED

TOTAL DESIGN LOADS

NOTES:
    THE INDICATED BEARING VALUE IS THE FOOTING PRESSURE WHICH
    MAY BE IMPOSED IN EXCESS OF THE PRESSURE DEVELOPED BY THE
    ADJACENT OVERBURDEN
    TOTAL DESIGN LOAD BEARING PRESSURES ARE DETERMINED BY
    YIELD POINT BEARING VALUES OF THE SOILS

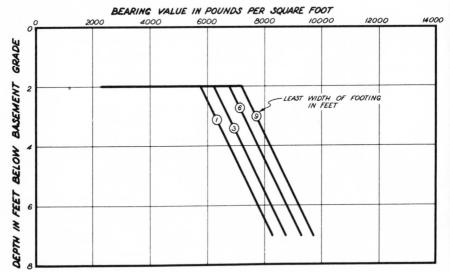

BEARING VALUE IN POUNDS PER SQUARE FOOT

DEPTH IN FEET BELOW BASEMENT GRADE

LEAST WIDTH OF FOOTING
IN FEET

NOTES:
    THE INDICATED VALUES APPLY TO FOOTINGS FOUNDED AT LEAST ONE
FOOT INTO THE SAND STRATUM.
    ALLOWANCE HAS BEEN MADE FOR THE CONFINEMENT DEVELOPED BY
A 4INCH-THICK REINFORCED CONCRETE SLAB.
    THE INDICATED VALUES APPLY TO THE TOTAL OF ALL LOADS, DEAD,
LIVE AND SEISMIC.

FIGURE 21. Bearing values (*Courtesy Dames and Moore, Foundation Engineers, San Francisco, Calif.*).

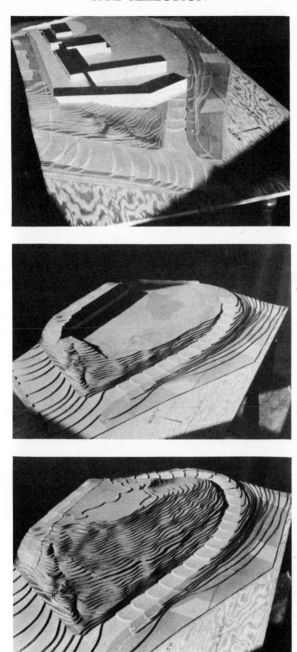

FIGURE 22. A-B-C. Contour models (*Courtesy San Francisco City Schools, San Francisco, Calif.*).

FIGURE 23. Topographic map of contour models area (*Courtesy San Francisco City Schools, San Francisco, Calif.*).

MODELS

Contour models of the site are frequently made for study by the architect, engineer, school administrators, and board members. Photographs of such a model are shown in Figure 22. Figure 23 which accompanies the photograph of the contour model is a topographic map of the area included in the model.

BIBLIOGRAPHY

American Association of School Administrators, *American School Buildings*, 27th Yearbook. Washington, D.C.: The National Education Association of the United States, 1949.

Broome, Edwin W., "Characteristics of a Good School Site," 19th Yearbook, 1947-48, *American School and University*. New York: The American School Publishing Corporation, 1947.

Burns, Arol, "Where Shall We Build?" *Nation's Schools*. Chicago: The Modern Hospital Publishing Company, April, 1955.

Committee on Educational Buildings and Equipment, "Things to Consider in Planning Educational Plants." American Council on Education Studies, Series VII—School Plant Research, No. 4, Vol. XII. Washington, D.C., August, 1948.

Cowgill, C. H., and B. J. Small, *Architectural Practice*. New York: The Reinhold Corporation, 1952.

De Shaw, Elton R., "Planning the School Grounds," *American School and University* (1951-52), pp. 217-20.

Engelhardt, N. L., "Anticipatory School Site Selection and Purchase," *American School Board Journal*, 116, 33-34, 73-75 (January, 1948).

"Facilities for Physical Education," Bulletin 13A, State Department of Education, Tallahassee, Florida, 1954.

Gray, Archie L., "Needed Research in the School Plant Fields," *Review of Educational Research* (February, 1951), pp. 63-68.

Gray, Archie L., and Jerald Blake, "Trends in Materials and Design," *Review of Educational Research* (February, 1951), pp. 28-35.

McFadzean, John, "Examples of Site Planning with Emphasis on the Fifty Acre Community-High School Recreation Area in Reno," *Nation's Schools*, 44:34-39 (July, 1949).

National Council on Schoolhouse Construction, *Guide for Planning School Plants*. Nashville, Tennessee: The Council, 1953 Edition, p. 21.

New England School Development Council, *How to Choose a School Site*. Cambridge, Mass.: The Council, February, 1947.

Nichols, John E., and others, "Sites, Building, and Equipment," *46th Yearbook, Part II*, National Society for the Study of Education. Chicago, Illinois: University of Chicago Press, 1947.

Parker, Harry, and John W. MacGuire, *Simplified Site Engineering for Architects and Builders*. New York: John Wiley and Sons, 1954.

"Planning and Caring for Our Schools," *Report of the 1953 Conference*, Stanford University, School of Education. Stanford, California: Stanford University Press, 1953.

"The Planning and Construction of Louisiana School Buildings," State Department of Education of Louisiana, Bulletin No. 711, Revised, 1954.

"Planning Together for Better School Buildings," Bulletin No. 412, Superintendent of Public Instruction, Lansing, Michigan (1950).

Report of the Status Phase of the School Facilities Survey. U.S. Department of Health, Education and Welfare; Office of Education, School Housing Section, Washington, D.C. (December, 1953), p. 73.

"Rules and Regulations of the State Board of Education Relating to School Housing," reprinted from *California Administrative Code*, Title 5. Education, Chapter 1, Department of Education, California State Department of Education, Sacramento, California.

Schneider, Raymond C., "Factors Affecting School Sites," unpublished Doctoral dissertation, School of Education, Stanford University, Stanford, California (May, 1955).

School Planning Manual, Volume XXXVII, No. 7, School Building Service, State Department of Education, Richmond, Virginia (November, 1954).

Stoffer, Robert J., "Engineering Surveys for School Sites," *American School and University*, 22:97-102 (1950-51).

PART 2

PLANNING FOR THE PLANT

CHAPTER 5

EDUCATIONAL SPECIFICATIONS

Perhaps the weakest link between planning and building is interpreting the needs of those using the completed facilities. This problem of interpreting demands a fresh approach to school planning—a formulation of a systematic procedure for designing facilities for schools. To accomplish a functional and economical school design, facts are needed concerning the school program during the initial planning stage. The proposed procedure is, in essence, a fact-finding process—a cooperative task of educators, students, and lay people to analyze, describe, and interpret the program so that it can become the base for the architect's decisions. The program materials prepared for these purposes are the "educational specifications."

These educational specifications are tentative, and relative to particular situations. Paragons of planning and absolute standards

145

cannot be developed for schools because of many complex variables: the needs and interests of the community, the administrator's competency in group dynamics and human relations, the competency of teachers with techniques and processes, the specific class sizes, the available amounts and types of tools, materials, furniture, and equipment, the geographical location, and the community's finances.

The suggested procedure for developing educational specifications for facilities encompasses three steps:

(1) Analyzing the functions of the facility: a description of the program.

(2) Developing a theoretical formulation of the facility: the implications of the functions for a systematic analysis of the basic factors of school planning.

(3) Describing, suggesting, and illustrating the facilities that will encompass the functions and these basic factors in school planning.

The *first step* is operationally described as follows:

(1) Surveying the community to ascertain the needs and interests of students and adults. This survey should be part of the master planning for the proposed school. Its facts may be gathered by an educational consultant service team, by high school students, or by civic organizations. Questionnaires may be sent to each home or house-to-house surveys may be organized by the above groups. Some historical and factual information may also be obtained from municipal offices, community libraries, or various organizations, such as the Chamber of Commerce. Committees are then formed: responsibilities for particular sections of educational specifications delegated by the administrator.

(2) Utilizing a taxonomy to analyze two raison d'etre functions of educating students: the teaching process—the communicating of knowledge, skills, and attitudes; and the learning process—the acquiring of knowledge, skills, and attitudes. The rubrics include:

2.1 *Curriculum structure:* organizing the number of periods and probable sizes of classes, based on projected and current class enrollments. Each community must work out its own desirable pupil-teacher ratios.

2.2 *Purposes:* developing the aims and objectives of the program based on the survey, and by other methods such as conducting public forums, forming discussion groups in the local service organizations, and consulting leading educators.

2.3 *Personnel:* describing the necessary qualifications of the teachers for effective teaching of the proposed program.

2.4 *Clienteles:* designing the program in terms of the characteristics, developmental tasks, and imperative needs of the students.

2.5 *Culture:* planning the program with an understanding of the changing culture of the school, community, and American culture.

2.6 *Content:* selecting the number and kinds of activities for the program based on data of the survey and value judgments of the planning committees. This section is concerned with possible curriculum revision. The various committees in each area will evaluate the existing curriculum.

2.7 *Process:* suggesting that the teaching-learning procedures be based on democratic procedures and insight into psychological factors of learning, such as motivation and individual differences.

2.8 *Product:* recognizing that the outcomes of process are twofold: the student as product and the student's educational product.

The *second step* is the problem of relating the factors of school planning to the school program. This part of the procedure is concerned with such factors as (1) zoning, (2) supervision, (3) flexibility, (4) thermal environment, (5) color-conditioning, (6) acoustical treatment, (7) utilities, (8) luminous environment, (9) maintenance and safety, (10) audio-visual considerations, and (11) storage, furniture, and equipment. During this part of the procedure, the planning committee will work in close relationship with the administration, architect, custodian, and engineers. Additional research by the committee may include visiting nearby schools; reading related school planning literature; studying floor plans and the descriptions of facilities found in the current literature; looking at blueprints of schools under construction; and interviewing architects and representatives of furniture, tools, materials, and equipment companies.

The *third step* is concerned with the arduous task of describing, suggesting, and illustrating the proposed facilities. This thinking is based on the knowledge of the school program and related factors in school planning. Operationally, this step includes: (1) making a spatial relationship diagram for each activity in terms of location, processes, storage needs, display spaces, and special utility needs; (2) describing in detail each activity in terms of the proposed number of work stations; and the amounts, types, and sizes of tools, materials, furniture, and equipment needed for each station; and (3) making sketches or models for further communication with the architect. These sketches will be for clarification only. These are not dictated plans for the architect to follow. During this part of the procedure the committee would have conferences with the administrator, educational consultant, architect, engineer, and custodian.

Continuous two-way communication must be maintained at all times. The esprit de corps of the planning committees may be affected if any changes by administrator, architect, or engineer in the emerging educational specifications are not forwarded to the committees.

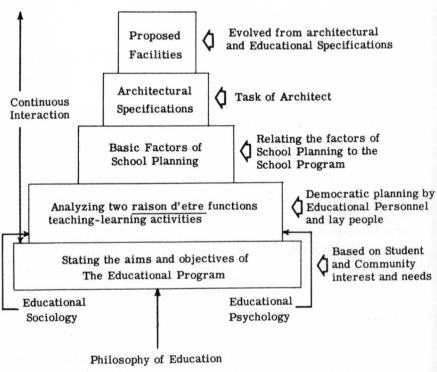

FIGURE 24. A procedure for planning facilities for schools.

The weakest link between the recognition of the need for a school plant and the completion of the structure is the fact that the planners must interpret the requirements of those who will use the facilities. The educational specifications usually include a detailed description of the number of pupils to be accommodated in the proposed building, their activities, and the stress these will put on the building and site. But further details as to specific activities in designated areas necessitates a detailed description of necessary equipment, furniture, storage areas, and so forth—a description often inadequate and vague.

Those responsible for the educational specifications are in a position to evaluate alternative costs. Educational specifications should build toward more space and more building per dollar spent. Adequate, well-conceived educational specifications are the basis for the best architectural specifications.

FIGURE 25. Educational Consultant and librarian plan educational specifications for a new library.

THE ROLE OF THE EDUCATOR

Throughout the planning process the responsibilities of the members of the planning team vary with the evolvement of the project. However, the major responsibility is carried by the school administrators, teachers, and consultants who survey the total situation and determine the procedure to achieve maximum results.

To stress the importance of a close working relationship between curricula and school planning groups, some school systems have selected building staff representatives to serve on curriculum committees. An example of this procedure is shown below in a school district's partial list of its current curriculum groups:

A. CURRICULUM GROUPS

   1. ART:
     Chairman
     Consultant
     Building Representative
     Delegates (4)

   2. BUSINESS:
     Chairman
     Consultant
     Building Representative
     Delegates (6)

   3. FOREIGN LANGUAGE:
     Chairman
     Consultant
     Building Representative
     Delegates (4)

PROCEDURES FOR DETERMINING EDUCATIONAL SPECIFICATIONS

Each level of school planning has its peculiar problems, but those of grade schools pose certain problems which can be solved only by a recognized program. The following aids are illustrative of those that are of assistance to planning groups:

Media	*Advantages*
1. 2″ x 2″ Slides (Colored preferred)	Present examples of existing situations that have possible adaptations to the local situation.

2. Film Strips

Frames on a film strip can be confined to a concentrated area.

3. 16 MM Films

Films on school buildings and community activities have been well planned, and show many different situations in a short period of time.

4. Opaque Projections

Make possible the showing of maps, charts, pictures, and so forth.

5. Photographs

Demonstrate proposed or existing school plants for observation.

6. Maps, Graphs, Charts

Show comparisons between different situations.

7. Flannel Board

Shows relationships between items.

8. Magnetic Planning Board

Provides for a variety of combinations of classroom or building units in specific spaces.

9. Scaled models

Present the proposed structure or room arrangements in three dimension.

10. Isometric Drawings

Give the illusion of three dimension.

11. Field Trips

Provide first-hand experiences and make possible an evaluation of existing facilities.

THE COMPLEXITY OF PREPARING THE EDUCATIONAL SPECIFICATIONS

The preparing of educational specifications increases in complexity from the elementary school through the college and university. Moreover, certain administrative policies must be understood before progress can be made in the planning. These will vary among school districts but in general they are concerned with: the maximum size of proposed school plant; the desired teacher-pupil ratio; the contemplated educational program; the transportation plans; the community use of school facilities. This list could be expanded indefinitely.

Although all of those working on the planning of the plant will not be concerned with each phase, their work should deal with the same details of each item. Furthermore, each worker should have a work outline covering all phases of the planning.

The guide (page 156) for planning educational specifications for a senior high school provides a framework adaptable to the planning of most secondary and higher education schools.

FIGURE 26. A typical classroom (*Courtesy Schmidts, Hardman and Wong, Architects, Berkeley, Calif.*).

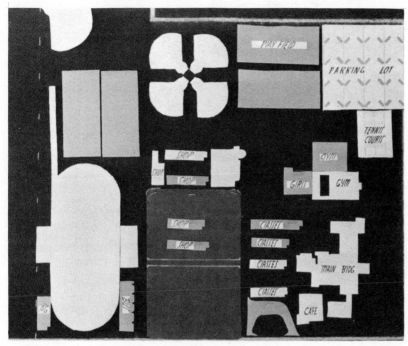

FIGURE 27. Flannel board presentation for a secondary school plant addition.

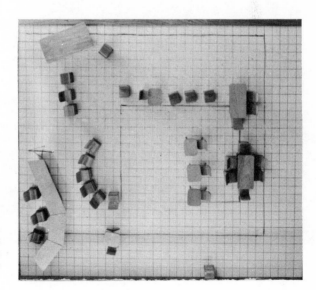

FIGURE 28. Magnetic planning board showing possible classroom arrangement.

FIGURE 29. Model of a possible machine shop arrangement.

FIGURE 30. A scaled model for a proposed elementary school on a hillside (*Courtesy Hertka and Knowles, Architects, San Francisco, Calif.*).

FIGURE 31. Isometric drawing of a proposed secondary school concourse (*Courtesy of Mario Ciampi*).

FIGURE 32. Rendering of a central court for a proposed high school (*Courtesy of John Lyon Reid and Partners, San Francisco, Calif.*).

A SUGGESTED GUIDE FOR PLANNING
EDUCATIONAL SPECIFICATIONS FOR A
SENIOR HIGH SCHOOL

1. AREA
   1.1* Number of areas; Names of areas; Shape desired. (A detailed description of activities to be performed will usually dictate the shape of area, in terms of square feet.)

2. RELATIONSHIP TO OTHER AREAS AND ORIENTATION

3. ACTIVITIES WITHIN THIS AREA
   3.1 School curriculum
   3.2 Adult training
   3.3 Community use

4. TRAFFIC CIRCULATION
   4.1 Within area
   4.2 In relationship to other areas
   4.3 In relationship to other outdoor activities
       4.3-1 Auto traffic
       4.3-2 Auto parking
       4.3-3 Receiving and distribution of supplies

5. GENERAL CONSIDERATIONS AND FUTURE TRENDS
   5.1 Flexibility
   5.2 Safety
   5.3 Maintenance

6. FURNITURE AND EQUIPMENT
   6.1 Fixed
   6.2 Portable
   6.3 Special kinds or sizes
   6.4 Special work surface or surface treatment

7. STORAGE
   7.1 Equipment
       7.1-1 Size (will be determined by an inventory of equipment)
       7.1-2 Location in relation to other storage
       7.1-3 Location in relation to class activity
   7.2 Supplies
       7.2-1 Size and amount
       7.2-2 Location in relation to class activity
   7.3 Projects storage
       7.3-1 Size and number
       7.3-2 Location

* This code numbering system is suggested as a convenience for architects and all planning committee members.

7.4 Personal storage
　　7.4-1 Size; location; purpose
7.5 Special storage for specific uses
　　7.5-1 Size
　　7.5-2 Special material or treatment if needed

8. OTHER SPECIAL NEEDS WITHIN THIS AREA
8.1 Electrical system
8.2 Ventilation system
8.3 Exhaust system
8.4 Air outlets
8.5 Gas outlets
8.6 Other utilities
8.7 Door sizes or location
8.8 Receiving and dispensing area or platform
8.9 Displays
　　8.9-1 Show cases desired and their location
　　8.9-2 Teaching surfaces

9. COLOR, DECORATING, AND ACOUSTICS
9.1 Special considerations

10. UTILITIES
10.1 Heating
10.2 Ventilating
10.3 Electrical
10.4 Water
10.5 Toilets
10.6 Others

11. AUDIO-VISUAL FACILITIES
11.1 Special considerations

Once the various team members have been properly oriented, they will become engaged in preparing educational specifications for their particular area. Occasional meetings with the total committee will be necessary in order to insure proper coordination.

No pattern of procedure can be recommended for any particular area. The following technique was used by an art instructor to insure an adequate sample of planning ideas from his fellow art teachers and supervisors in the school system.

Planning for Art Rooms in a Proposed Senior High School

1. AREA

Code No. 1.1

Number of art rooms necessary in high school of approximately 2,000 enrollment.

Check one:

_____	1
_____	2
_____	3
_____	4
_____	5
_____	Others

_____

Comments:

_____

Code No. 1.1

Room size that would be desirable.

Check one:

30' x 40'
30' x 50'
35' x 50'
30' x 45'
_____
_____
_____

Comments and _drawings_ on back if necessary.

2. RELATIONSHIP TO OTHER AREAS AND ORIENTATION

Code No. 2

Is it desirable to have the arts and crafts rooms near:

Please check
one or more:

_____ Little theater

_____ Industrial arts

_____ Auditorium

_____ English

_____ Science

_____ Others

_____

Please make _comments_ to justify selections.

Considering adult education and landscape drawing should the art rooms have any of the following:

Check one
or more:

     _____ Outside entrance

     _____ Secluded outside area

     _____ Rest rooms easily accessible

     _____ Others

     _____

Comments:

3. ACTIVITIES WITHIN THE ART AREA
    Code No. 3.—Curriculum

    It is anticipated that all art rooms could be flexible enough to engage in all of the following activities:

1. advertising art	8. ceramics
2. color and design	9. jewelry—metals
3. art service	10. plastic work
4. drawing	11. textiles—printing
5. illustration	12. weaving
6. lettering	13. carving
7. painting	14. making displays
	15. silk screen

Can you add others and *comments?*

4. TRAFFIC CIRCULATION
    Code No. 4.3-3

    In receiving supplies should there be any special considerations such as:

Check one or
more if
necessary:

     _____ Central receiving room

     _____ Special door in the art room for receiving

     _____ Others

     _____

Comments:

5. GENERAL CONSIDERATION AND FUTURE TRENDS

Code No. 5.1

Make any *comments* you have in the line of making the art rooms flexible.

6. FURNITURE AND EQUIPMENT

Code No. 6.1

What kind of fixed furniture or equipment should the art rooms have:

Check:

——— Blackout curtains
——— Island sinks
——— Sinks
——— Power tools
——— Kiln
——— Others
———

——— Grinder
——— Buffer
——— Jigsaw
——— Drill press
———
———

Comments:

Code No. 6.3

What special furniture or equipment should the art rooms have:

Check here:

——— Easels
——— Looms—size?
——— Lighting effects on booms
——— Stands for models
———
———

Please add others and *comments.*

Code No. 6.4

What kind of work surface should there be for:

1. Jewelry benches

_____

_____ Asbestos

_____ Stainless steel

_____ Wood

_____ Tile

_____ Others

2. Silk screen

_____

_____ Stainless steel

_____ Masonite

_____ Others

_____

3. Clay

_____

_____ Masonite

_____ Wood

_____ Others

_____

Others and please *comment* on back.

7. STORAGE

Code No. 7.1   Equipment

How should large equipment be stored, such as easels, looms, etc.:

_____ In store room

_____ In special cabinet

_____ In art room

Comments and *drawings* if necessary.

Code No. 7.1

How should small equipment be stored, such as jewelry, tools, etc.:

_____ In special cabinet

_____ In store room

_____ Others; e.g., toolcart

_____

Comments and *drawings.*

Code No. 7.1-3

Where should the cabinets of the above items be located in relation to class activities:

_____ In storeroom

_____ One end of room

_____ Special cabinets

Comments and *drawings.*

Code No. 7.2   Supplies

Indicate the *size* and *number* of the following items (plus any of your additions) the art room should store and *where*, i.e., storeroom, cabinets, etc.

Specific Size	Number or Quantity	Where Stored	
			Water colors
			Oil paints
			Poster paint
			Brushes
			Pencils
			Chalk
			Tape
			Wire
			Metal
			Ink
			Paper

Specific Size	Number or Quantity	Where Stored	
			Paper
			Paper
			Paper
			Paper
			Paper
			Cardboard
			Cardboard
			Cardboard
			Cardboard
			Charcoal
			Paste
			Glue
			Plastic
			Leather
			Leather fastenings & tools
			Linoleum
			Silk screen paint
			Solvents
			Clay
			Glazes
			Clay tools
			Pens
			Rulers
			Erasers
			Yarn
			Thread
			Photo chemicals

On the back of this page make any drawings necessary and suggestions for supply storage, such as: adjustable shelves, drawers on rollers, etc.

Code No. 7.3   Project Storage

Indicate the size and number of the following items that would likely be stored in the art rooms.

Size	Number or Quantity	Where Stored	
24 x 30"			Drawing boards
			Tote trays
			Paintings
			Drawings
			Clay projects—green
			Clay projects—bisque & glazed
			Sculpture

Comments or *drawings*.

Code No. 7.4   Personal Storage

If you think there should be storage in the art area for the following, please indicate the size and location.

Size	Location	
		Student coat lockers
		Teacher lockers
		Office space for teachers

Code No. 7.5   Special Storage

If the art rooms should have any special storage facilities please indicate the size and amount needed.

8. OTHER SPECIAL NEEDS WITHIN THE ART AREA

Number or Quantity Needed	Kind or Type	Where Located	
			Electrical
			Ventilation system
			Exhaust system
			Compressed air outlets
			Gas outlets
			Other utilities
			Tacking space
			Show cases
			Bulletin boards
			Peg board

Comments:

9. AUDIO-VISUAL FACILITIES

How Much	Where Is It to Be Stored?

Comments:

BIBLIOGRAPHY

"A Framework for Public Education in California," California Framework Committee, *California Elementary School Journal*, Vol. XVIII (1949), pp. 208-251.

Beard, Cora, and others, "Elementary School Classroom Design and Equipment—Specifications of Teachers," *American School and University*, Eighteenth Annual Edition, pp. 203-208. New York: American School Publishing Corporation, 1946.

Beatty, W. W., "What's Needed in Administrative Spaces?" *Nation's Schools*, 56:62-7 (July, 1955).

Bennion, Lynn M., "School Personnel Planned Educational Specifications for this Utah Elementary School," *Nation's Schools* (February, 1952), p. 56.

Burk, Carl J., "Teachers Participation in a School Building Program," *American School Board Journal* (March, 1952), p. 52.

Bursch, Charles, Charles Gibson, and Henry L. Wright, "Classroom Size," *School Executive*, 68:26-27 (January, 1949).

Cochran, Lee, "Multiple Use of Space," *School Executive*, 68:56-57 (January, 1949).

"Creating a Good Environment for Learning," Association for Supervision and Curriculum Development, Department of the National Education Association, 1954 Yearbook.

Easton, J. A. G., "Specifications for School Shops," *American School and University*, 22:335 (1950-51).

Edwards, H. Griffith, *Specifications*, Stat. p. 294. New York: D. Van Nostrand, 1953. 311 p.

Ingraham, Joseph C., *Modern Traffic Control*, New York: Funk & Wagnalls Company, 1954.

"Movable Schoolroom Equipment," *American School Board Journal*, Vol. 121, No. 6 (December, 1950), p. 36.

"Planning Tomorrow's Secondary Schools," School Planning Laboratory, School of Education, Stanford University (1954).

Seagers, Paul W., "Developing Educational Specifications," *Bulletin of School of Education, Indiana University*, Vol. 24:6 (November, 1953).

Sellew, R. W., "What Information Should Educators Furnish the Architects?" *American School Board Journal*, 130:49-50 (May, 1955).

Shaw, Archibald B., "Educational Planning of Schools," *School Executive*, 73:84-85 (January, 1954).

"Trends in School Planning," School Planning Laboratory, School of Education, Stanford University (1955).

MINUTES OF A SCHOOL PLANNING ADVISORY COMMITTEE

The School Planning Advisory Committee met Tuesday, May 3, at 3:45 p.m., in the Board Room of the Administration Building, Chairman Brown presiding.

The Advisory Committee Chairman reported that members of the committee are being invited to participate in the preschool conference to be held in August so as to give the committee the opportunity to work with the Curriculum Council. He explained that attendance at this conference is voluntary, and arrangements have been made to pay the expenses of any member of the committee who attends. A confirming letter and reservation form will be sent out from the Superintendent's office. The reservation form should be returned as soon as possible to the office of the Director of the Curriculum.

The Superintendent of Schools reported that the architect selected for the new senior high school has had considerable experience in planning school buildings and is widely known for his work in this field. The need for cooperative planning was stressed as an essential function of this committee. We would like an arrangement whereby the particular insights, abilities, and skills of instructors will predominate the program of educational specifications to guide the architect in his development of plans for the new senior high school. The superintendent explained that such a design would be a new pattern and experience for us because in the past we have had a different grade organization. He reassured the group that the program could be handled successfully, with the benefit of everyone's thought.

Throughout this planning budgetary limitations will have to be kept in mind. The people on this committee have been brought into this planning because of their ability to cope with this problem and because of their professional experience.

The Superintendent briefly explained the process used in selecting an architect for the senior high school. Various representatives from the architects' offices were presented.

At this point the Educational Consultant gave a brief report of what

168

had been done to date. A good start has been made by the committee. Several groups have had two or three meetings with the consultants and have visited a number of senior high schools in the area. They saw a school in the area which was the result of poor planning. As this program progresses, the committee will attempt to avail itself of the ideas of other teachers. When the school is finished it should be one of the leading educational buildings and school plants.

In order to have material ready for the staff to write up prior to the preschool conference, it will be necessary for them to have the data before the summer vacation. The architect will begin to make preliminary drawings from the material. These will be reviewed to see if the architect's interpretation has been sufficient. After the conference the committee will review the plans, and the architect will then begin the final drawings.

The architect emphasized the importance of function and space. He stressed the importance of justifying the disposition of all space. Storage space will be checked room by room.

The Educational Consultant reported that Miss Jones and Mr. White will make the first reports on the progress of their work to date, since they have had previous experience in planning school facilities.

Miss Jones, high school gym teacher, explained the work of teachers in the girls' physical education department. The chairman of each department was asked to make an evaluation of present facilities for handling such activity, and to make suggestions for a future building. These evaluations became part of a ten-page report given to the Educational Consultant. After the report was returned for further information, each teacher was given a particular problem, and an additional report was compiled giving complete details regarding shelving, storage for equipment, and so forth. The thinking of all teachers in the girls' physical education department is represented in this report.

Mr. White gave a brief report on the development of the material for the boys' physical education department. The first attempt to compile the report was found to be too general. Keeping in mind the functional use of the building, his group went over the existing high school gym to determine the changes to be made for the new senior high school gymnasium. Mr. White and Mr. Johnson compiled the over-all report, which was submitted to each teacher for further comment. Sketches and drawings for the outside area were also completed. When the suggestion to include a swimming pool was made, a new addition had to be included in the report. The pool, its outside area, and the exercise room will be used by both boys and girls. In planning the whole gym area, his group kept in mind that the facilities would also be used by community groups.

After the above reports were completed a question-and-answer period followed. The following questions were asked:

1. Will equipment be dealt with in the building contract? *Answer:* usually only fixed equipment will be included in the contract. All other furniture and equipment will be bought separately.

2. What type of structure will the building be? *Answer:* the entire building was not as yet designed, but it is envisaged, at least initially, as a one-story structure. The commercial and academic sections will be in separate structures. The building is intended to conform to the educational program.

3. Will it be possible to use general plans? *Answer:* plan for your own needs. It is unlikely that other plans would fit your program.

4. What will be included in the library? Will the library be used as a study hall? *Answer:* the attempt will be made to design a library rather than a visual arts and book storage room. Stack areas, however, should be convenient to the audio-visual staff.

The chairman reported that another trip will soon be planned to enable the remainder of the committee to visit additional schools in the area. The committee was again requested to order its data in preparation for its conference with the Educational Consultant.

The meeting adjourned at 5:00 p.m. The next meeting will be held Wednesday, May 25, in the Board Room of the Administration Building.

Respectfully submitted,

Secretary

CHAPTER 6

PLANNING
THE ELEMENTARY SCHOOL

To a certain extent school plants and facilities are a reflection of the educational philosophy and stated educational needs of the community. Formerly, the teacher was conceived of as a strong regimentarian in charge of rows of children at fixed desks. The materials provided each child included only textbooks and some writing materials. The teaching method consisted largely of drill and the recitation of bits of factual material, and all youngsters were expected to learn the same things in the same way. The classroom and the facilities were planned with these methods and purposes in mind. Despite the claims of the proponents of the "tough" pedagogy, many students failed to learn even the simplest reading, and eagerly sought to leave school at the first opportunity. Many of the others, although mastering certain techniques and facts, were not particularly well-adjusted and did not understand how their competencies could best be used. It is a truism that children do not learn by words alone, but learn through experience and activity. Yet this idea was slow to be accepted and it has only recently been the case that planned experiences and activities have become an integral part of the elementary school.

Our concept of the purposes of education has broadened from a notion of the simple mastery of certain facts and techniques to include such concepts as: the mastery of the tools of learning and communication—the competency, within the individual's level of achievement, to use the basic tools of language and mathematics; the development of the capacity for independent thinking; the development of moral and spiritual values; development of socialization and personality; the development of an awareness of the modern world and its influence on everyday life; the development of an appreciation of and a responsibility for citizenship; the development of economic and consumer skills and techniques; the development of appreciations and skills for leisure time activities; the development of an understanding for and an appreciation of the various arts; the protection of the child's health during the school years and his development of the knowledge and habits that will enable him to live a healthful life.

Educational method is largely concerned with activity and experience, and a visit to an elementary school indicates simultaneity of many activities. Typically, in a first grade one group of youngsters is working with the teacher in the development of their reading skills; another is working individually at tables sharpening their reading skills; some children are enjoying books at the library table —a few may be engaged with manipulative puzzles or toys or interested in dramatic play; and others may be at tables or easels with crayons, paints, or clay. Such a room can be orderly despite the multiplicity of activities. Developmental activity is the keynote of the contemporary elementary school, but this activity is carefully and completely planned. The confused child-directed school envisaged by the critics of "progressive" education is largely a figment of the critics' imaginations. A modern activity program involves, to be sure, much bustle and noise, but these are the sounds of work rather than of confusion.

Needless to say, the old classroom, with its fixed seats and outmoded facilities, does not suffice for elementary education today. The elementary school plant and facilities will have to be planned on the basis of the individual's education.

Although there has been increasing elementary school construction in the last few years, there is still insufficient construction to provide for the increased enrollments and the constantly evolving educational programs. It is more important than ever that adequate planning precede construction so that the actual plants meet the needs of the community—not only providing sufficient space to accommodate the school population but also providing the right kind of space. The school plant is more than a shelter from the weather; the adequate plant implements and facilitates the instructional program. A new elementary school, aesthetic, flexible, functional, is the result of careful and conscientious planning, involving the resources of many people over a long period. The focus, during all of the planning, is the child and his activity; the planned building is a reflection of the manner in which children are taught and of the community's philosophy of education.

In order to plan effectively for the elementary school's needs it is essential to develop a total approach, based on expected school populations, educational and community philosophies, teaching methods, and desired outcomes. This total approach must correlate with the total community planning. It should be in harmony with the financial structure of the community and must be subject to constant and careful evaluation, to enable changing conditions and concepts to be incorporated. A rigid and inflexible total plan is no longer considered to be educationally or financially proper.

Perhaps the most important single factor in determining school plant needs is that of school population. How many children are in school now? How many children will be in school next year? In five years? In ten years? School districts are constantly embarrassed by new plants totally inadequate to take care of the future school population. It is not unusual to find newly opened plants operating on double sessions. This often occurs because future school population was not considered in the initial planning. In planning the elementary school, then, future need should be determined through careful population studies, as discussed in Chapter II. However, the determination of the need is only the first of many steps in good planning.

Knowing the space required to house a certain number of students each year is a partial basis for determining the total space requirements, to be supplemented by an evaluation of the kinds of spaces required. These requirements depend on the activities planned, the teaching methods used, and the furniture and facilities desired. It must be borne in mind that these activities are not ends in themselves but a series of carefully planned and structured experiences aimed at helping children become more effective in all of their relationships.

The nature of the activities has to be established for each phase, each level, of the elementary school. What goes on in the kindergarten? What facilities are required? What furniture is to be used? What spaces are needed for special activities? What lighting levels are desired? How much and what kind of storage is needed? What kinds and amounts of chalkboard, tackboard, easels, and other teaching spaces are needed? What audio-visual provisions should be made? What kind of access to the outdoor play areas should be provided? What type of door is desired?

Function, then, has to be defined in terms of physical requirements translatable into meaningful descriptions for the use of the architect and the engineer. This translation is not made independently of the architect, nor is it regarded as the final set of educational specifications. It develops through an evolving process, in which the various planning groups, the architect, the teachers, the administrative staff, the board, and the consultants work together. Moreover it should be understood that the planning groups do not develop architectural specifications—but develop guides to aid the architect in his design. Architects plan schools while educators plan *for* schools.

The presentation of educational specifications to the architect in the form of sketches and suggestions, along with exact specification, is the most effective means of handling the planning during the developmental stage. A suggested and effective order of the specifications is as follows:

A general statement followed by a statement of:

(a) The school's relationship to other areas and its orientation.
(b) Activities.
(c) General considerations and trends.
(d) Traffic circulation within the school area.
(e) Utilities.
(f) Color, decorating, and acoustics.
(g) Furniture and equipment.
(h) Storage.
(i) Special needs.

FIGURE 33. A new model school built in the south (Frances Lacy Elementary School, Raleigh, N.C.) (*Courtesy Edward Waugh, A.I.A. Architect, Loewenstein-Waugh Associates*).

It is essential that the planning be inclusive, structured, efficient—unguided and formless planning sessions are unproductive. While adequate for kindergarten planning, planning for other elementary school grades, junior high schools, senior high schools, and college areas could be developed by following the same general format.

Committee membership, time allocation for meetings, methods of communication with the architect, and revision procedures will vary with different situations. However, a planning committee consisting of administrators, teachers, community groups, and classified personnel works effectively. Members of the consultant staff should coordinate and guide the planning sessions, and communication with the architect should be maintained so that time losses do not occur between the initial planning and final revision. Sketches and comments from the architect can be accepted and incorporated into the educational specifications, or rejected and discussed with the architect prior to the development of the school's final specifications.

THE SELF-CONTAINED CLASSROOM

Typically, the kindergarten is self-contained in all schools. All its activities take place within the total unit, which includes the patio-indoor-outdoor-playground area. The unit contains all the spaces and facilities necessary for kindergarten activities. Included are toilets, lavatories, dining spaces, library facilities, music facilities, play space, rest space, art space, construction space, table space, and storage space for all the materials necessary for the efficient performance of these activities.

The child in the kindergarten is made to feel at home while away from home. He is adjusting to a new environment in many ways not different from the only other environment he has known.

The notion of a self-contained classroom is to an extent applicable to other components of the elementary school, although practice differs between schools. Professionals have expressed the desirability of using the self-contained classroom for the tenth grade and above, and it is not at all uncommon in present usage to find it in the eighth grade. The significance of the self-contained classroom is that it provides for *all* activities. Such a classroom does not necessarily imply that a class must spend all its time in one classroom, but that the group participates in the broad experiences and activities of the modern elementary school.

PLANNING THE KINDERGARTEN UNIT

It is desirable that the kindergarten be completely self-contained, and of a size sufficient to care for the children enrolled—usually 1,200-1,500 square feet. Lighting should be uniform and glare-free. Daylighting should provide pleasant and cheerful areas for work and play. The kindergarten, as the transition place between home and school, should retain as much of the home atmosphere as is practical; an institutional appearance should be avoided. The kindergarten is conceived as an area for children just entering school life.

Kindergarten planning will vary with the situation. The following is an illustration of a typical set of educational specifications for the kindergarten.

1.1 *Relationship of the kindergarten to other areas of the elementary school, and the orientation of the kindergarten.* The kindergarten should be located on the school's first floor, easily accessible to the play area and to the outside entrance. The desirability for adequate daylighting suggests a southern exposure and fenestration. The kindergarten should be isolated from the rest of the plant, both as to its building and play area, but should be readily accessible to other parts of the plant, including administrative offices and the multi-use areas.

1.2 *Activities.* Daily kindergarten activities include:

Removal and securing of wraps
Health inspection
Toilet usage
Play and work periods
Midmorning and noon lunch
Rest and/or nap periods
Storing supplies and equipment

The kindergarten must have space for:

Group play
A housekeeping corner
Workbench (construction)
Clay area
Black area
Art area (easels)
Fingerpainting area
Plants
Pets (Terrarium)
Aquarium
Sink for play and cleanup
Music area

Book area
Story area

'Areas' in which the various construction projects can take place. These could include such units as:

The home
The farm
The store
The circus
Trains

Outdoor areas will vary with climatic conditions, but can generally include:

Lawn
Sandbox
Wading pool
Swings
Jungle gym
Garden

1.3 *General considerations and trends.* The kindergarten is characterized by space for physical movement in the various work and play activities. The youngster is given a wide range of different experiences, many occurring simultaneously. One of the basic objectives of the whole kindergarten program is the development of a sense of belonging to a group, which aim is furthered by this wide and varied participation.

Creative work and play are encouraged, particularly in terms of the simple construction of such things as a car, a truck, or a train, and in the various arts, such as finger-painting, clay modeling, and crayon work. Expression is also possible through simple rhythm instruments, and varied dramatic endeavors (playing store, house, or trucks).

Frequent rest periods and nap periods necessitate space and facilities. Floor mats or cots will require about 35 square feet of floor space per unit.

Optimums rather than minimums should be attempted in the school planning stages—whether considering space requirements or educational objectives. It is usually necessary, because of financial limits, to use the play room as a restroom and for a dining area; however, separate restrooms and dining areas have many advantages.

In the entire process of planning and designing the kindergarten, care must be taken that space is provided for all the activities. The structure should not, however, resemble a fieldhouse or a gymnasium, either as to size or appearance. Flexibility and adaptability should characterize the structure.

1.4 *Traffic circulation within the kindergarten.* Divers activities involving all of the children will occur simultaneously. It must be possible for youngsters to go from any activity to another with a minimum of effort and with little disturbance.

Among the areas provided in the kindergarten are: the teacher's area, the music center, the food preparation and serving area, the toilet and lavatory areas, the wraps' storage area, the reading corner, the science center, the art center, the construction area, the main play areas, the rest area, and the outdoor area.

1.5 *Utilities.* A washup and play sink must be provided, with both hot and cold water, conveniently available to the art and clay centers. The drinking fountain should not be incorporated in this play and cleanup sink, but should be a separate unit.

Since the kindergarten children do not work and play at one spot and on one level, lighting of good brightness and high quality should be available throughout the area. Brightness, balance, and the reduction of glare, maintained with a sufficient quantity of light, must be attained.

Because much of the activity in the kindergarten takes place on the floor, it is essential that the floor be kept warm and dry. Mechanical ventilation is desirable to aid in maintaining normal temperatures as well as to provide fresh air.

Toilet and lavatory facilities, within the kindergarten unit, are essential.

Food preparation and serving facilities are essential.

1.6 *Color, decorating, and acoustics.* There is evidence to show that children respond favorably to gay and varied colors, especially the younger children of the kindergarten group.

Ceilings should be light, with high reflectance for lighting considerations (85 per cent). Walls should be relatively light, in the 60 per cent area, and the lower wall must be readily washable. Flat paints should be used throughout, with no use of high gloss paints because of their glare. Floors should be light, and of a material readily cleanable and which does not block the passage of the heat from the radiant floor panels.

There is considerable noise in the kindergarten; its control is possible through acoustic treatment of the ceiling, but without overcontrol and its consequent "dead" room.

1.7 *Furniture and Equipment.* All furniture and equipment for use by the children should be of a convenient size and height.

Teacher's corner. A desk, chairs for adult visitors, filing cabinets for records.

Music. A small piano (low enough for the teacher to be able to see over), a record player, records.

Food. A stove or a large hotplate, a refrigerator, a sink, and cupboards.

Reading. A library table and chairs, bookshelves to accommodate the large picture books used in the kindergarten.

Science. Terrarium, aquarium, pet cages, display space.

Art. Waterproof clay and painting tables, easels, sink facilities.

Construction. Work benches, tools, near a sink.

Play. Blocks, indoor play equipment.

Toilet and lavatory. Small size units, low mirrors, and towels.

Rest. Folding cots or mats.

General. Blackboard, tackboard, bulletin space low enough for the children to use.

Outdoor. Swings, slides, jungle gym, sandbox, wheel toys, and other outdoor play equipment.

There should be drinking fountains both indoors and outdoors.

1.8 *Storage.* It is essential that storage areas be planned to accommodate the specific materials to be used. Art paper storage facilities must be of such a size that the art paper and finger painting paper can be easily stored. Shelving should be provided for storing the 18″ x 22″ finger painting sheets, the 24″ x 26″ art paper, the 24″ x 36″ tagboard, the 26″ x 38″ cardboard.

Roll papers in 36″, 24″, and 18″ rolls are also used, and must be stored within the kindergarten unit. Newsprint, of the type generally used in the kindergarten, comes in 9" x 12" x 24" bales, although other bale sizes might be used.

Clay, paints, crayons, and other art materials should be stored close to the art area, as should the various art papers.

Teacher's corner. A closet for the storage of wraps and various teaching supplies.

Music. Provision must be made for storage of the record player, records, and the rhythm instruments.

Food. Cupboards should be provided for utensil and canned food storage.

Reading. If window seats are provided, storage can be provided beneath the seats.

Science. Storage space for the equipment necessary to make simple scientific demonstrations is needed.

Construction. Storage space for tools, wood, and other construction materials should be provided.

Play. Storage space is needed for the large blocks, and the interior toys.

Toilet and lavatory. Storage is needed for extra soap, towels, toilet paper.

Rest. If separate rest areas are provided, provision should be made to use the areas for play and consequently, storage space must be provided for mats and cots. If the main room is used for rest, mats and cots will have to be stored in a place and manner that makes them readily accessible—at floor level or on movable carts.

General. Storage is needed for student projects, usually as bins, and so forth.

Outdoor. Some storage facility is needed for storing the wheel toys, the sandbox toys, garden tools, and other outdoor toys.

1.9 *Special needs.* Kindergarten handles the difficult transition period between home and school, and as such should minimize the institutional look.

Although the self-contained classroom is not exclusively kindergarten, it is an essential part of the kindergarten.

Flexibility and functionality are essential in the kindergarten. Provision must be made for the many different activities which take place. Its construction must be such that the teacher can see and supervise many simultaneous activities.

Because the kindergarten child is so young and inexperienced, it is essential that the building be safe, without dangerous protrusions and booby traps. Although there may be some aesthetic value in an irregular wall, roof, and floor line, it is desirable to use straightened designs.

During clement weather indoor-outdoor living is a part of the kindergarten program. Ready access to the outdoor areas is essential; large window areas on the playground side of the building are desirable.

PLANNING OTHER COMPONENTS OF THE ELEMENTARY SCHOOL

Since all schools are different in their teaching space requirements no attempt will be made to structure a planning procedure applicable to all situations. Planning principles must be applied to specific situations to ensure the adequacy of the planning.

PLANNING THE PRIMARY CLASSROOM

Primary classrooms should be self-contained, though not to the extent of kindergartens. Primary grade children have their lunches in the cafeteria and use the auditorium and gymnasium. However, it is desirable that all facilities required in the primary program be within the confines of the primary area. This would include toilet and lavatory facilities, sink facilities, all work centers, and the patio-outdoor-play area.

Individual abilities are greater in the primary grades than in the kindergarten. Some youngsters in the first grade are proficient in handling numbers and words, while other youngsters are still engaged exclusively in kindergarten activities.

Educational planning for primary classrooms will follow a program similar to kindergarten planning. Specific planning should be done for each classroom and for each grade level, since requirements will differ. Even for a school of two or more first grades, each should be separately planned.

PLANNING THE INTERMEDIATE CLASSROOM

The self-contained classroom is also used by intermediate grades. Many educators hold that all classrooms should be self-contained during the entire elementary school career; others propose specialized courses in separate spaces, that is, art is taught in an art room, music in a music room, science in a science room, and so forth. The cost of an elementary school plant of self-contained classrooms is slightly higher than the total cost of a plant with special spaces, since self-contained classrooms must be larger and replete. The problem, however, is essentially not of cost, but of philosophy and method. In either choice planning should be adequate planning.

PLANNING SPECIAL FACILITIES

The Multipurpose Room

Similar plans are followed for the multipurpose room as for any other space. The activities of the room, the participating individuals, its space facilities must be determined. The following specifications are illustrative of a workable method for developing these educational specifications.

The multipurpose room is planned to house specific activities; activity shifts determine its dimensions. The functional use of storage space and movable furniture is essential. Daily changes in room use add to custodial labor. This area is likely to be used by various adult groups. Its uses are likely to be extended in the future; hence, the room should be adaptable and flexible.

1.1 *Orientation and relation to other components.* The multipurpose room should be convenient to classrooms. The entrances and exits, as well as the service facilities, should be accessible. The multipurpose room should be so located that disturbing noises from adjacent activities do not interfere in its activities. The multipurpose room should be self-contained to the extent that its utilities—heat and light—can be controlled apart from the whole of the plant.

1.2 *Activities.* In planning the multipurpose room it is necessary to know its activities, as in the case of all careful planning; but con-

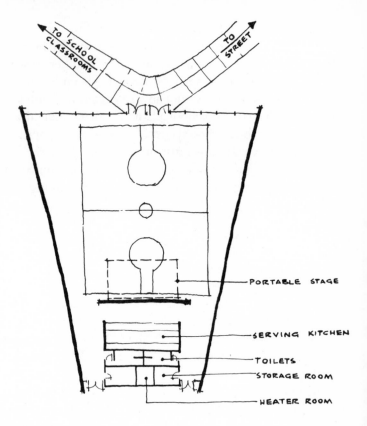

MULTI - USE UNIT

sideration of its particular activities is more extensive in so far as various activities have priority. In certain areas climatic conditions force physical education activities into the multipurpose room. These activities require open floor space; the room should be able to be stripped. Lunches may be eaten in the room; hot lunches necessitate table facilities and cooking facilities; the room must be planned to hold folding tables. The room may be used for all-school assemblies, or for large groups. Seating must accommodate the groups anticipated; storage must be provided so that the room can be cleared for other activities. Activities will be presented to groups of children, both on the floor and on the stage areas, and for groups of varying sizes. Choral and instrumental music practice and presentation—both for children and for the community—may take place in the room and on the stage. The room may be used by various adult groups, for meetings, dramatics, social purposes, banquets, luncheons, dancing, and parties. It may also be used by other community organizations, such as the scouts, and for meetings and demonstrations.

1.3 *General factors and trends.* Multipurpose rooms are used to enrich the educational program and for various community functions. Present tendencies are to schedule full use of the area every period of the day, and to have numerous evening activities. As teachers become aware of the program enrichment available through the facilities of the multipurpose room, its full utilization can be planned.

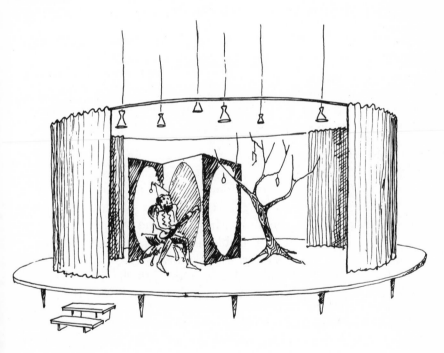

PORTABLE STAGE
MULTI-USE UNIT

1.4 *Utilities.* The room should be able to be darkened, so that audio-visual materials may be used. Television facilities may be introduced. The room should have sufficient electrical outlets and a bell and clock system tied to the school's system. Speakers and jacks should be provided for a public-address system. The stage should have separate lighting controls. The kitchen, a basic unit in various community activities, should be sufficient and adaptable for future needs.

1.5 *Traffic circulation within the area.* It is desirable that student traffic between this area and the rest of the school be direct. Direct entrance and exit into the room, from both the outside and the classroom side is desirable. Doors must be planned so that emerging groups and entering groups can be accommodated at the same time. Participants in programs should be able to enter upon the stage without going through the general seating area.

1.6 *Color, decoration, and acoustics.* Color treatment of the multipurpose room should be similar to color treatment in the classrooms. The total decorative scheme, including furniture and built-in equipment, should be harmonious and attractive. The floor should be light colored, of a material and finish permitting easy maintenance. The room should be acoustically treated.

1.7 *Equipment and furniture.* For student use at assemblies and passive group participation, suitably sized chairs must be available; these should be stackable or folding chairs so that the floor can be readily cleared for physical education activities. Other chairs should be available for adult group use. Mats, balls, and other physical education materials should be available to the area. The kitchen should contain a stove, a refrigerator, utensil storage space, a dishwashing facility, and nonperishable food storage space. It should be arranged and constructed to permit expansion for a hot lunch program.

1.8 *Storage.* Storage must be provided for the different kinds and sizes of chairs that will be used in the room. If the stage is above 30″, and is permanent, storage under the stage is advised. If the stage is lower, or portable, then the chairs will have to be in storage rooms on storage carts. The success of the activities in the multipurpose area depends upon the speed and ease in which the area can be changed for different activities. If music activities are to take place in the area, music and instrument storage places should be provided; contemplated future expansion of the music program requires that storage needs be anticipated at this time. A piano, for use in certain music and physical education activities, should be provided, and provision should be made to remove it from the area during other periods. Portable storage units will provide flexible perimeter storage spaces for further materials and equipment.

1.9 *Special needs.* The area should be flexible and functional to encompass the different activities. Safety is of extreme importance; it is essential that wall protrusions, and other building hazards, be held to a minimum. The floor should be of a material that can be cleaned easily and upon which people will not skid. The physical education program necessitates the protection of lights, windows, and glass doors. Walls should be of a material and finish that can be easily cleaned.

Administrative Facilities

These would contain space for the principal, vice-principal, guidance personnel, attendance and school records, public and student receptions, conference work, and storage. The areas provided, and their mutual relationships, depend upon administrative policy and the function of the school.

The Health Suite

This would contain facilities for dental and medical examinations, first aid, resting, dressing, receptions, and conferences. Its completeness and its location is determined by school policy.

Library Facilities

These would contain reading areas, book storage space, an office, checking facilities, card catalogs, audio-visual facilities, and workrooms. Again, the size, location, and extent of the facility would be determined by the use to be made of it and the school policy.

Maintenance and Operation Facilities

These should consist of areas for keeping records and making assignments (the office), shop facilities for making school repairs, storerooms for such supplies and equipment as are needed for the district's purchasing and storing, custodial workrooms with sinks and equipment storage space convenient to the school sections, and lavatory-shower facilities for the custodians.

Teachers Facilities

These would usually consist of a kitchenette, a restroom, a workroom, and a lavatory.

Lavatory Facilities

These should be conveniently located in the areas of children's activities.

Playground Facilities

As in the case of planning the school building and its interior facilities, playground facilities can be planned only by determining the spaces required for recreational activities. Usually, outdoor spaces of three types are required—surfaced areas, turf areas, and apparatus areas. Surfaced areas should be economical to install and to maintain, all-weather resilient and paintable. Blacktop, prepared according to climate, is useful. Areas surrounding apparatus should be protected by some soft, resilient material, such as tanbark, cork, sand, or sawdust. Additional playground information is available in specific publications.[1]

The following are suggested minimum area requirements for carrying out a successful playground program.

[1] Harold J. Cornacchia and John E. Nixon, *Playground Facilities for Rural and Small Elementary Schools*, Educational Administration Monograph No. 4 (Stanford: Stanford University Press, 1955).

Kindergarten Requirements.

Activities	Performed in	Nature of Area
Rhythm	Squares, circles, lines	Surfaced and turf
Games	Squares, circles, lines;	Surfaced and turf
Relays	or unmarked areas	Surfaced and turf
Stunts and	Squares, circles, lines;	Surfaced, turf,
Self-check	or unmarked areas	and apparatus
	Unmarked areas	

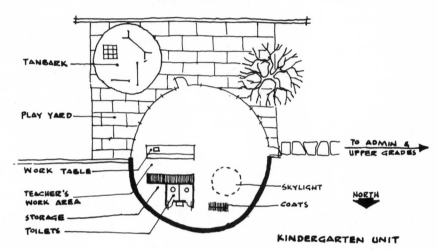

Thirty foot circles, 30' x 30' squares, lines 20' apart, are adequate unmarked area limits, totaling approximately 900 square feet. Areas for wheeled toys, outdoor classrooms, and garden areas bring the minimum recommended surfaced area to 2,000 square feet, and the minimum recommended turf area to 2,000 square feet.

Apparatus requirements for the kindergarten area:

	(sq. ft.)
Swing	400
Slide	375
Climbing Apparatus	225
Balance Beam	220
Turning Bar	200
Traveling Rings	200
Sand Box	375

A total of 1,975 square feet for apparatus and a grand total of 6,000 square feet is sufficient for the kindergarten outdoor area.[2]

[2] Allan Ray Elliott, *Space and Facilities for Physical Education and Community Use in Public Schools*, unpublished Ed. D. dissertation (Stanford University, 1953), pp. 261-264.

FIGURE 34. Kindergarten area. Sand box in left background wa
providing play space for 19 kindergarten children when this pictur
was taken.

FIGURE 35. Kindergarten sand box.

FIGURE 36. New type
of cement sand box.

Requirements for Grades 1, 2, and 3. The outdoor activities are similar to those of kindergarten children and are performed in similar spaces. Primary activities include: rhythm, hunting, relays, stunts, and low organizational athletic games. These would require 2,000 square feet of surfaced area for the first grade, 2,000 square feet of surfaced area for the second grade, and 3,000 square feet of surfaced area for the third grade, or a total of 7,000 square feet of surfaced area for the primary grades. Turf requirements would be the same as surfaced requirements, making a total turf and surfaced requirement of 14,000 square feet.

The following apparatus for the primary rooms could be combined and used on a rotating basis or simultaneously:

	(sq. ft.)
Sandbox	900
Climber	400
Turning Bar	200
Swings	600
Balance Beam	200
Slide	450
Traveling Rings	250

A total of 3,000 square feet for the primary apparatus area and a grand total of 17,000 square feet is sufficient outdoor play area for Grades 1, 2 and 3.

Requirements for Grades 4, 5, and 6. The outdoor activities are similar but more complicated and more demanding of space requirements. Typical activities of children in grades 4, 5, and 6 include the following low organizational games:

Basketball	Volley ball	Individual check
Playground ball	Rhythm	Relays
Soccer ball	Hunting	Tumbling

The fourth grade would require about 8,000 square feet of surfaced area and about 10,400 square feet of turf, the 5th grade would require about 8,000 square feet of surfaced area and 10,400 square feet of turf, and the sixth grade would require about 12,000 square feet of surfaced area and about 22,500 square feet of turf.

Apparatus requirements are lower, with the following being desirable:

FIGURE 37. First grade: 30-foot circle.

FIGURE 38. Second grade: 20-foot circle.

FIGURE 39. Third grade: two 20-foot circles.

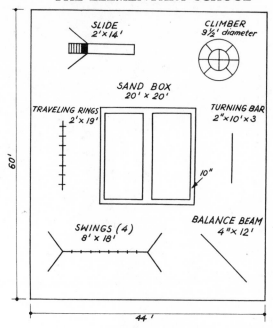

SLIDE
2' x 14'

CLIMBER
9½' diameter

SAND BOX
20' x 20'

TRAVELING RINGS
2' x 19'

TURNING BAR
2"x10'x3

10"

SWINGS (4)
8' x 18'

BALANCE BEAM
4"x 12'

60'

44'

FIGURE 40. Primary grades apparatus area.

FIGURE 41. Primary apparatus layout.

FIGURE 42. Primary grades apparatus. Horizontal ladder. Giant strid‹

FIGURE 43. Primary grades apparatus. Outdoor gym.

FIGURE 44. Primary grades apparatus. Eighteen children on one outdoor

(*sq. ft.*)

Horizontal Bars	250
Traveling Rings	450
Balance Beam	200
Swings	700
Rope Climbs	375

A total of 1,975 (2,000) square feet for the apparatus area and a grand total of 73,300 square feet is sufficient outdoor play area for Grades 4, 5 and 6.

Total requirements for the minimum physical education program kindergarten through grade six would be 96,300 square feet. The community use of the school site will determine how much additional land beyond these necessary requirements will be needed.

BIBLIOGRAPHY

American Association of School Administrators, *American School Building*, Twenty-seventh Yearbook. Washington, D.C.: The Association, a department of the National Education Association, 1949.

Bennion, Lynn M., "School Personnel Planned Educational Specifications for this Utah Elementary School," *Nation's Schools* (February, 1952), p. 56.

Brown, Paul R., "A Complete Elementary School," *American School Board Journal* (April, 1951), p. 41.

Bursch, Charles, Charles Gibson, and Henry L. Wright, "Classroom Size," *School Executive*, 68:26-27 (January, 1949).

Cochran, Lee, "Multiple Use of Space," *School Executive*, 68:56-57 (January, 1949).

Cocking, Walter D., James H. Bailey, and Archibald B. Shaw, "Project Planning on the Elementary School," *American School and University*, Twenty-first annual Edition. New York: American Publishing Corporation, 1949, pp. 92-100.

Cornacchia, Harold J., and John E. Nixon, *Playground Facilities for Rural and Small Elementary Schools*, Educational Administration Monograph No. 4. Stanford: Stanford University Press, 1955.

Elliott, Allan Ray, "Space and Facilities for Physical Education and Community Use in Public Schools," unpublished Doctoral dissertation, School of Education, Stanford University, Stanford, California (1953).

Hiatt, H. W., "Toilet Provisions in Elementary Schools," *American School and University* (1954), pp. 409-14.

Perkins, Lawrence B., and Walter D. Cocking, *Schools*. New York: Reinhold Publishing Corporation, 1949.

Rice, Arthur H., "What Research Knows About Color in the Classroom," *Nation's Schools*, 52:I-VIII (November, 1953).

Shaw, Archibald B., and Lawrence B. Perkins, "Planning the Elementary School," *American School Board Journal* (July, 1954), pp. 58-64.

Waechter, Heinrich H., and Elizabeth Waechter, *Schools for the Very Young*. New York: F. W. Dodge Corporation, 1951.

Whitehead, Willis A., and others, "A Guide for Planning Elementary School Buildings," Columbus Bureau of Educational Research, Ohio State University (1947), Chap. I, pp. 1-33.

CHAPTER 7

PLANNING
THE JUNIOR HIGH SCHOOL

Since the turn of the century the conception of the junior high school has been accepted by many state boards of education. The original purposes of the junior high school have been modified somewhat. There is general acceptance of the idea that in junior high school the adolescent youngsters can make a fruitful and pleasant transition from the general experiences of the elementary school to the more specific and intensive experiences of the high school. The junior high school in most school systems is comprised of the seventh, eighth, and ninth grades in systems organized on a 6-3-3 grade distribution basis. The discussion of junior high schools in this chapter is based on this grade distribution.

The junior high school was originally made up of grades 7 and 8 and was part of a 6-2-4 grade organization.

Many opportunities are provided for exploratory learnings in a wide range of fields. The guidance program, while taking cognizance of later vocational needs, is primarily concerned with personal adjustment and socialization. There is recognition of and provision for individual differences. Various aspects of socialization are emphasized, while previous learnings are consolidated and integrated.

SCHOOL PLANT SIZE

The availability of students in the community dictates the size of the plant; however, with the increased school enrollments the decision of providing one, two, or three school plants has led to a policy on the size of junior high schools. Junior high school educators indicate a minimum of 600 and a maximum of 900 students per plant as the most desirable limits.

The first junior high schools were established in many school districts as a solution to critical housing shortages. School districts developing a philosophy and a specific curriculum for the junior high school have been satisfied with it; others have regarded it as a low-level high school, and have found it less successful.

There are different patterns of curricular offerings in the junior high schools, but a certain number of courses are more or less consistently taught. These courses include those discussed below.

COURSES IN THE JUNIOR HIGH SCHOOL

English and Languages

At the seventh grade level all junior high schools require English and/or the study of a foreign language. On the eighth and ninth grade levels language instruction is also required, though the actual course matter varies.

Mathematics

Junior high schools have a specific mathematics requirement at the seventh and eighth grade levels, in arithmetic and general mathematics. Most junior high schools have a mathematics requirement at the ninth grade level as well; the course varies with the individual: college preparatory students take algebra, other students continue in general mathematics.

Science

All junior high schools require a course in science, though there is considerable variation as to the form of the program and the level of its presentation. Modern technological advances and our culture's increasingly scientific orientation, necessitate the anticipation by planners of an increased emphasis on science and its instruments.

Social Studies

Almost all junior high schools have a social studies requirement at the seventh and eighth grade levels, and the majority have a social science requirement on the ninth grade level. Course designations and titles vary considerably, and actual requirements are dependent on local regulations.

Physical Education

Almost all junior high schools have physical education requirements at all three grades, although actual activities vary widely. Shortsighted planning of facilities will result in inadequate physical education programs. Both indoor and outdoor facilities have to be provided to accommodate the expanded physical education activities program needed by junior high school students.

Art and Music

Art and music are usually required on the seventh grade level, though the actual participation within schools having the requirement takes different patterns. Often, music and art are taught to all the seventh graders as a home room activity and require movable

FIGURE 45. Music room (*Courtesy Schmidts, Hardman and Wong, Architects, Berkeley, Calif.*).

furniture and ample space. Few eighth and ninth grades have a music-art requirement, but nearly all junior high schools offer either one or both as electives.

Industrial Arts and Homemaking

Some junior high schools require an industrial arts or homemaking course in the seventh and eighth grades—seldom on the ninth grade level.

FIGURE 46. Homemaking room (*Courtesy Schmidts, Hardman and Wong, Architects, Berkeley, Calif.*).

Home Room

Many junior high schools have home room classes, during which administrative details, orientation, library activities, student government, and certain guidance functions are discussed.

Electives

In addition to the foregoing requirements junior high schools offer a wide range of electives. These electives introduce the student to new studies. The following list, by no means exhaustive, indicates some of the electives that may be offered:

Mathematics
　algebra
　geometry
　business arithmetic
　shop mathematics
Communicative arts
　journalism
　public speaking
　dramatics
Foreign language
　Spanish
　French
　Latin
　German
Industrial arts
　general shop
　wood shop
　metal shop
　arts and crafts
Homemaking
　cooking
　sewing
　interior decoration

Social studies
　American history
　ancient history
　geography
Science
　general science
　biology
　life science
Physical education
　basketball
　baseball
　swimming
　golf
Music
　chorus
　band
　orchestra
　appreciation
Art
　water color
　line drawing
　ceramics
　appreciation

PLANNING CORE-CURRICULUM ROOMS

The heart of the junior high school program is the learning and mastery of the skills and techniques necessary for efficient living in a modern world. The ability to communicate skills with numbers, concepts of human interrelations, and the understanding of science are essential to the development of civilized men. Core-curriculum rooms or academic classrooms represent the center of the junior high school scholastic program. The following approach to the planning of academic classrooms can serve as a general guide for individual school planning.

1.1 *Relationship of the academic classrooms to other areas of the school plant and orientation of the classrooms.* These classrooms must be readily accessible to the administrative offices, the library, the cafeteria, the health area, lavatory facilities, playgrounds and physical education facilities, and to any other special facilities areas for students. Adequate day or artificial lighting should be provided. It is desirable to limit junior high schools to single-story structures.

1.2 *Activities.* The common-learnings program in the junior high school will include such activities as:

(a) Total group learning situations in which all youngsters will be reading, writing, listening, and discussing as an entire class. Space must be provided for sufficient chairs and tables to accommodate all the students.

(b) Small group activities in which the class is subdivided into ability groupings to facilitate the learning process. Actual makeup of these subgroups will vary with the task; consequently, the classroom must be large enough and furniture and equipment movable so that different subgroupings are possible at any time.

(c) Committee activities in which the class is divided into various committees which are working toward the solution of a common problem. For these small group activities sufficient space is essential so that work can continue without undue disturbances and yet with the supervision of all groups by the teacher.

(d) Dramatics, student government, music, and art.

1.3 *General considerations and trends.* Class organization, student government, committee work, planning and working together toward the solution of common problems all contribute toward the development of citizenship.

1.4 *Traffic circulation in the classroom.* Junior high school students are generally awkward and muscularly uncoordinated. It is essential that there be sufficient room for movement within the classroom.

1.5 *Utilities.* A sink and work counter should be provided in each room. It is desirable for each room to have its own drinking fountain, separate from the sink.

Intensive sight activities such as reading require lighting with good brightness ratios and high quality illumination. The heating and ventilating systems should be adjustable. Adequate outlets, for use of audio-visual and other electrical equipment, are necessary.

1.6 *Color, decorating, and acoustics.* The wide use of color in the classroom minimizes the institutional aspects of the school environment. Classrooms are no longer decorated exclusively with "institutional" browns and grays, but in a wide variety of pleasing colors.

Glossy paints should not be used; lower walls should be washable. Floors should be light in color and of a material that can be readily cleaned and maintained. (See 1.6 in "Planning the Elementary School.")

Floor coverings should be relatively noiseless; acoustically treated walls and ceilings minimize noise.

1.7 *Furniture and equipment.* Separate chairs and desks should be provided for the youngsters. Student furniture should be light colored, dull finished, and of such construction and design as to be comfortable and durable. Teachers' furniture should harmonize in design and finish with the student furniture. All rooms will require a book and reading area, blackboard, tackboard, work surface, and specific materials.

Coat storage should be provided in or adjacent to classrooms; the teacher's coat should be hung near her desk.

1.8 *Storage.* It is necessary to provide storage spaces such as the following:

Teacher storage of coat and personal effects

Bookcases (actual sizes and amounts dependent on the program, proximity to the library, and kinds of books kept in the classrooms)

Records

Paper

Instructional supplies

Project materials

Art materials

Project storage

Use of flexible storage facilities make it possible to vary the educational program. For example, if additional blackboard or tackboard and less cabinet storage is needed, it would be possible to move out certain cabinet units and move in additional blackboard and tackboard sections. With the exception of the sink-worktable space, it is probably desirable to minimize built-in cabinet space.

1.9 Special needs. Aside from the fundamental learning, many exploratory experiences are offered necessitating the close integration of activities.

OTHER COMPONENTS

Any specific planning has to be done on the basis of specific considerations and requirements. The following components are taken from the summary recommendations for "Chief Moses Junior High School," Moses Lake, Washington (planned to accommodate approximately nine hundred students).

Area	Storage Provisions	Area* Sq. Ft.	Number of Rooms	Unit* Sq. Ft.
Administrative				
Principal		144	1	144
Vice-Principal		120	1	120
Mimeograph	Current duplicating jobs	60	1	60
Reception	Records of pupils	600	1	600
Storeroom	Instructional supplies—for one term	120	1	120
Lavatory		60	1	60
Vault	All permanent records	60	1	60
Arts and Crafts	Materials used in jewelry, leather craft, woodcarving, plastics, textiles, photography, painting and pottery	1,200	2	2,400
Cafetorium (combination cafeteria and auditorium)				
Dining Room	1,400 cu. ft. for storing tables	3,750	1	3,750
Kitchen	Cabinets for cooking utensils and condiments	900	1	900
Storeroom	Nonperishable materials used in kitchen	225	1	225
Office	Files and cabinets for business operations	80	1	80
Handwashing Alcoves	200 cubicles for books of pupils	20	2	40
Refuse	Garbage cans	75	1	75
Employee Locker and Toilets	Street clothes of employees	70	1	70

Stage and Anterooms	350 folding chairs and steel dollies, musical instruments	750	1+2	750
Public Toilet	Men	300	1	300
Public Toilet	Women	300	1	300
Multiuse Room				
Main Activity		8,364	1	8,364
Boys' Wing—				
Instructor's Office	Files, books, magazines, records, supplies	224	1	224
Instructor's Locker, and so forth		130	1	130
Towel and Equipment	Towels & daily issue athletic equipment	182	1	182
Equipment Storage	Athletic equipment	156	1	156
Custodian	Soap, wax, mops, brooms, pails, and so forth	104	1	104
Locker Shower Toilet		1,971 ⎫ 730 ⎬ 204 ⎭	1	1,971 730 204
Entrance and Corridor		240	1	240
Corrective and Gymnastics		896	1	896
Girls' Wing—				
Instructor's Office	Files, books, magazines, records, supplies	224	1	224
Instructor's Locker, and so forth		130	1	130
Towel and Equipment	Towels & daily issue athletic equipment	182	1	182
Equipment Storage	Athletic equipment	156	1	156
Custodian	Soap, wax, mops, brooms, pails, and so forth	104	1	104
Locker Shower Toilet		1,917 ⎫ 730 ⎬ 234 ⎭	1	1,971 730 234
Entrance and Corridor		240	1	240
Correctives		896	1	896
Business Education				

Commercial	Paper and other materials needed	900	1	900
Business Practice	Current materials in processing	260	1	260
Curriculum				
Languages	Materials used: special provisions for school publications	1,170 1,170 900	1 1 3	1,170 1,170 2,700
Mathematics	20 cu. ft. for exhibitions of models 10′ x 26′ storage room to serve both rooms	900 900 900 900	4 4 1 1	3,600 3,600 900 900
Social Science	40 cu. ft. for instructional and display material	1,040 1,040	4 4	4,160 4,160
Corridors	Lockers for pupils			14,400
Counseling		130	4	520
Custodian				
Office		120	1	120
Storeroom	Janitorial supplies for one-half year	240	1	240
Lavatory		50	1	50
Faculty				
Workroom	2 cu. ft. for grocery items and dishes	40	1	40
Restroom		390	1	390
Reparation area		520	1	520
Lavatory		25	2	50
Health				
Reception		300	1	300
Rest Room		100	1	100
Dental and Medical		500	1	500
Storage	5 cu. ft. for supplies	36	1	36
Lavatory		24	1	24
Homemaking				
Cooking	50 cu. ft. material and dishes	1,170	1	1,170
Sewing	150 cu. ft. for individual projects, 50 cu. ft. for display	810	1	810
Fitting	(Included in Sewing Room)			
Dining	5 cu. ft. for tableware and dishes	225	1	225

Library

Reading	Open shelves for 7,500 books and 50 magazines	2,080	1	2,080
Book Room	900' of shelving	390	1	390
Office	20 cu. ft. for books	160	1	160
Audio-visual	40 cu. ft. for projectors, films, slides and screens	100	1	100
Workroom	50 cu. ft. for books	520	1	520
Music	Cafetorium			
Activities				
Student-Public		900	1	900
Shops				
Metal		1,040	1	1,040
Drawing Room	Drawing boards and instruments, paper	900	1	900
Wood	50 cu. ft. for projects	1,040	1	1,040
Finishing	10 cu. ft. for materials	200	1	200
Supply	Vertical and horizontal racks	108	1	108
Tool Room	Trays and racks for tools	120	1	120
Office	2 cu. ft. for exhibits	120	1	120
Bicycle Storage	Adjust to local need			
Lavatory				
Boys'	Provide entry of 50 sq. ft.	300	3	900
Girls'	Provide entry of 50 sq. ft.	300	3	900
				85,115

* All figures are approximate and listed here as a guide for the architect.

(*Note:* The decision of the Board to increase music facilities, plus the areas needed for utilities raised the square footage to approximately 100,000 square feet.)

OUTDOOR PLAY AREAS

Youngsters of junior high school age will participate in both co-educational and separate outdoor physical education activities. Dancing, mixed rhythm games, and mixed group games will require circles, squares, and lines.

Hard-surfaced areas for junior high schools are used for certain dancing and games activities, and for certain court and diamond activities. A surfaced area 90' x 110' accommodates three basketball courts, three volleyball and badminton courts, and one softball diamond, by making use of portable and movable nets and backboard facilities; such an area accommodates approximately thirty-five students simultaneously. A junior high school for six hundred youngsters would require approximately 35,000 square feet of blacktop, which would provide for tennis, handball, dancing, and so forth, in addition to court and diamond games.

Turf areas are desirable for such activities as track, archery, golf putting, pitching, fly casting, bait casting, and softball. Total recommended turf area, including room for eight softball diamonds and three track-archery-golf-gymnastics areas, is 280,000 square feet.

Outdoor apparatus requirements for junior high schools include horizontal bars, parallel bars, rope climbers, and balance beams, with a minimum recommendation of 2,500 square feet of tanbark, to be placed under apparatus.

A swimming pool is desirable at the junior high school level. A pool 75' x 165' with decking and other facilities could adequately accommodate a junior high school of six hundred students.

FIGURE 47. Chief Moses Junior High School, Moses Lake, Washington (*Courtesy Hovind, Harthorne & Smith*).

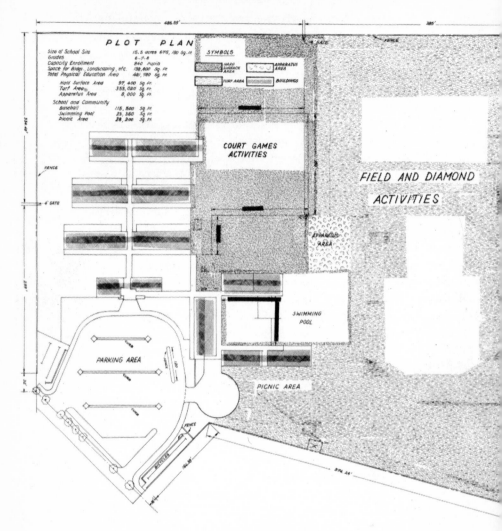

FIGURE 48. Plot plan of Covington School (*Courtesy Los Altos (Calif.) School District*).

BIBLIOGRAPHY

Engelhardt, N. L. and Doris McMillan, "Planning the Art Suite for a Junior High School," *American School Board Journal*, 124:33-5 (January, 1952).

Fowlkes, John Guy, "What Are the Trends in Planning and Constructing of Junior and Senior High School Buildings and Plants?," Bulletin of the National Association of Secondary School Principals, 33:214-17 (May, 1949).

Grover, E. C., "Fair Lawn Builds a Low Cost Junior High School," *American School Board Journal*, 128:39-42 (April, 1954), pp. 39-42.

"Guide for Housing and Layout of School Shops in California," *The Department*, California State Department of Education (1950), pp. 3-4.

Leggett, Stanton, "Trends in Educational Space in Junior High Schools," *American School and University*, Vol. XXVI (1954-55), pp. 219-28.

Mayfield, Tom J., "Artesia Completes a Junior High School," *American School Board Journal*, 123:27 (July, 1951).

"Modern Planning for Business Training in Georgia," Georgia Business Association, *Business Education World*, 33:220 (January, 1953).

National Facilities Conference, *A Guide for Planning Facilities for Athletics, Recreation, Physical and Health Education*, American Association for Health, Physical Education and Recreation (Washington, D.C.: National Education Association (1947).

Niemi, Allan L., "Housing School and Community Music Activities," *American School Board Journal*, 125:44-5 (August, 1952).

Orput, Allan L., "Designed for Social Living," *Nation's Schools*, 49:56-58 (March, 1952).

"Review of Educational Research School Plant and Equipment," *The Association*, National Education Association Bulletin (February, 1951), pp. 10-15.

Richardson, John S., and others, *School Facilities for Science Instruction*. The National Science Teachers Association (Washington, D.C., 1954).

Shaw, Archibald B., "Educational Planning of Schools," *School Executive*, 73:84-85 (January, 1954).

Shear, Bruce, "Physical Facilities for Pupil Personnel Services," *American School Board Journal*, 120:25-27 (January, 1950).

"Suggested Courses of Instruction in Industrial Arts for the Junior High School Level," California Industrial Arts Committee (California State Department of Education, 1953).

Thomas, Orpha Mae, "Planning the School Lunchroom," *School Executive*, 72:113-120 (February, 1953).

Van Duzee, Roy R. and others, "Shop Layouts of Various Kinds," *Industrial Arts and Vocational Education Magazine*, 137:90-7 (March, 1948).

CHAPTER 8

PLANNING
THE SENIOR HIGH SCHOOL

Schools organized on an 8-4 plan house grades 9-10-11-12 in their senior high school, while in the 6-3-3 plan the ninth grade is omitted. The educational specifications and space allocations examples provided in this chapter are for four year high school grade organizations.

There is probably no greater challenge to the school planner than in the development of specifications for a modern high school plant. It is not enough, in our changing society, to rely only on the classroom—much of its emphases are not oriented to specific circumstances. For example, a commercial department may be planned carefully and fully to develop competencies in a type of bookkeep-

213

ing no longer used by business and industry. Similarly, a biology room may be planned for pickling specimens, where biology students today study live creatures, or models of them.

Actual planning must start with some understanding of the aims and objectives of secondary education for the community. It is here proposed that secondary education should aid students to acquire saleable skills, acquire and maintain good health, develop contributive citizenship, contribute to a happy family life, master consumer techniques, understand and use science and the scientific method, appreciate the best in our culture and engage in creative activity, use leisure time wisely, select sound moral values, and master the skills of communication. These should be expanded and detailed in terms of the particular needs of the district, and they should be stated in terms of behavioral theory.

A senior high school plant will serve both the youth and the adults of a community for thirty to fifty years. Its plan should be modern and progressive. The curriculum in science is illustrative of the change. The following educational specifications apply to all-purpose science courses.

ALL-PURPOSE SCIENCE FACILITIES

Formerly, high school science facilities were patterned after college facilities—were used exclusively for a lecture-recitation-observation educational program aimed at developing students' research competencies. Such specialized presentations are still given to students planning to major in chemistry or physics in college. However, the main effort today is to relate the data to the extra curriculum.

1.1 *Relationship to other areas and orientation of the all-purpose science facilities.* All science rooms should be grouped together to communize storage spaces, water, gas, electricity, fume hoods, and special plumbing.

Natural science areas should have access to outdoor areas for planned plant propagation and animal husbandry.

The science rooms should be readily accessible to the library. They also have to be conveniently located in relation to the audio-visual center, which may be planned as a part of the library. The

INTERIOR OF
SCIENCE ROOM

science area should be accessible to school shops and arts and crafts facilities.

1.2 *Activities.* Typical science students will engage in the following activities:

Arranging equipment and conducting experiments.
Demonstrating experiments and projects.
Carrying on exploratory research.
Examining consumer projects.
Caring for, cleaning, and storing equipment.
Examining specimens.
Preparing exhibits.
Carrying on discussions in large or small groups.
Considering committee problems.
Reporting.
Participating in field trips.
Viewing demonstrations and audio-visual materials.
Listening to recorded materials.
Interviewing resource people.
Engaging in club work.
Constructing projects and displays.
Collecting exhibits.

Collecting written materials and pictures related to topics.

Making drawings, sketches, posters, models, replicas, and displays.

Reading textbooks and supplemental materials.

Writing reports, descriptions, and assignments.

1.3 *General considerations and trends.* Contemporary life is more complex largely because of technological developments. Common activities show the influence of science—from brushing one's teeth on a mass produced synthetic bristled toothbrush to setting the thermostat. Thus, it is advisable for a member of our society to have a knowledge and understanding of science.

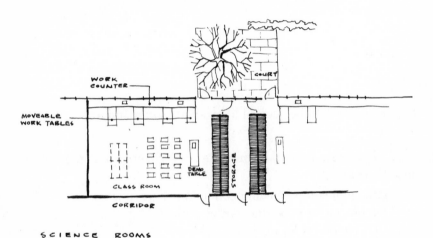

SCIENCE   ROOMS

Typically, high schools tend to offer more integrated, general courses and fewer of the rigid, traditional subjects. Physics, as such, is offered in approximately half of the high schools, where formerly it was taught in all but the smallest high schools.

High school science instruction is not concerned with training specialists, but with providing learning experiences for all students to help them secure the understanding, the problem-solving techniques, and the general competencies necessary for civilized living in the contemporary world.

This understanding must include the ability to use the fundamental concepts of science, and to interpret correctly conditions and happenings in both the natural and the artificial environment.

The science courses include extensive committee and group activity apart from emphases on the acquisition of facts, though this is by no means excluded. Class discussion and individual effort, both formal and informal, effectively encourage interest and provide for individual efforts. Course content is related more closely to the everyday environment, with projects and problems arising directly out of personal and community problems.

A need exists for science courses in such areas as aviation, electronics, horticulture, health, agriculture, and so forth. This need should not be met by specific courses, but by integrated science programs encompassing the major divisions of science, including astronomy, geology, geography, botany, biology, zoology, physiology, physics, and chemistry.

Spaces should be provided in the science rooms to provide for a wide range of activities. It should be possible for small groups and individuals to work on projects, displays, and problems; at the same time, it should be possible for the class to meet and work as a unit. Portable and multi-use furniture and equipment will make the classroom flexible and spacious.

1.4 *Internal traffic circulation.* It should be possible for a student or the teacher to go from group to group without interfering with other groups and individuals.

1.5 *Utilities.* Adequacy, economy, convenience, and safety are the primary factors to be considered in installing utilities. The use of perimeter experiment and project stations in place of island stations saves money without restricting the program.

Science rooms should have provisions for darkening; space should be planned for a projector and a screen. It is desirable to introduce gas, electricity, water, and distilled water in each science room.

Plumbing fixtures should be acid and corrosion resistant. Compressed air should be available in all science rooms.

1.6 *Color, decoration, and acoustics.* Science rooms should be attractively designed and decorated. The high level of illumination requires walls, the ceiling, floors, furniture, and equipment to have acceptable reflectance value (*See* Planning the Elementary School Kindergarten) and to be free from glare. Blacktopped work stations are to be avoided, but paints should be lead free and fume resistant. Floors should be of chemically resistant materials, and of light color.

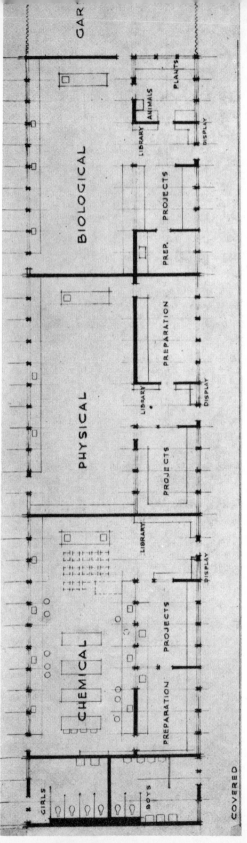

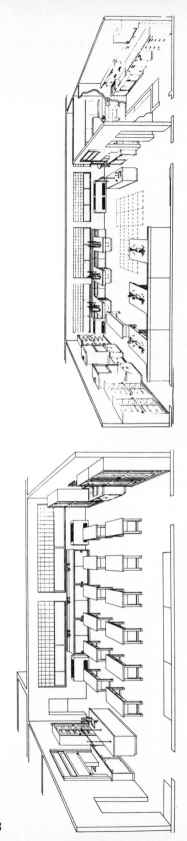

FIGURE 49 Gilroy Union High School, Science Wing Planned for Ultimate Capacity of 800 (*Courtesy Kewaunee Mfg. Co.,*
Adrian, Michigan, and J. F. Richards, Architect, Santa Clara, Calif.)

218

1.7 *Furniture and equipment.* There should be a demonstration desk so located that all of the students can see the demonstrations while seated. This desk should be equipped with gas, electricity, water, and compressed air, and it must have an acid resistant top. Conveniently arranged storage compartments and drawers should be provided at one end of it so that a movable demonstration table or laboratory truck can be moved into place to extend the length of the desk and to provide storage and transportation for prearranged apparatus. Special illumination for the demonstration area is desirable.

Close to the demonstration area, and readily visible to seated students, should be a blackboard. One of the boards can be permanently ruled with horizontal and vertical lines for use as a graph and for the illustration of certain experiments.

Tackboard should be in convenient locations. Map and chart racks should be available, though not necessarily built-in.

Movable student seats should be provided. Multiuse tables require only ordinary chairs. If work facilities from the experimental station areas are not multiuse, tablet arm chairs or chairs and tables should be provided. The room should be equipped with darkening devices, with the actual type dependent on fenestration and construction detail.

1.8 *Storage.* An effective science program requires the use of much apparatus, equipment, materials, and supplies. Convenient and accessible storage spaces should be provided. Actual storage requirements depend on the program, but for flexibility movable storage units should be used. Storage requirements within the room are dependent on the program.

It is desirable to provide storage rooms, accessible to the classroom, for the storage of apparatus and materials not immediately needed. A preparation room-dark room can be combined with this storage room.

1.9 *Special needs.* Floors and table tops must be resistant to oxidizing and reducing agents, organic solvents, and other chemicals. Drainage must be handled through sinks and lines which are not affected by these materials. Walls and floors should be free from vibrations since delicate measuring instruments will be used extensively. Temperature control is important to the area, since many sustained experiments require a specific temperature range. Dangerous fumes and other noxious odors must be removed, and it may be necessary to provide ventilated storerooms.

Science facilities should permit the students and teachers to carry on sustained experimental work and projects without moving or dismantling equipment. It may be that this sustained experimental work could best be accomplished in a room adjacent to the storeroom, separated from the classroom by glass panels; this area could also serve as a preparation room, work room, and conference room.

OTHER COMPONENTS

There is no shortcut to effective school planning. The development of complete and precise specifications is the only way to secure functional plants to serve the needs of the educational program and of the community.

Other areas to be planned and provided for in the senior high school include:

Administrative Area:
  Principal
  Vice-principal
  Reception and secretary
  Attendance
  Duplicating
  Dean of boys
  Dean of girls
  Reception for deans
  Test service office
  Counselors
  Conference
  File
  Men's lavatory
  Women's lavatory
  Utilities
  Teacher's room
  Custodian's closet

Health Suite:
  Dental and medical
  Reception
  Rest rooms
  Storage
  Lavatories

Toilet Rooms:
  Boys' lavatory
  Girls' lavatory

Arts and Crafts:
Arts and crafts classroom
Photography, art-metal classroom
Storage

Cafeteria:
Dining room
Kitchen
Storeroom
Office
Teachers' dining room
Employees' lavatory and locker
Store and snack bar
Dishwashing room
Refuse and garbage
Men's lavatory
Women's lavatory
Boys' lavatory
Girls' lavatory

Commercial:
Typing
Business machine
Classrooms
Distributive education room

Academic:
  Language arts
  Mathematics
  Social studies

Science:
  All-purpose science
  General science
  Biological science

Homemaking:
  Cooking laboratory
  Sewing laboratory
  Home management laboratory

Music:
  Office
  Instrumental
  Choral
  Practice rooms

Shop:
  Auto
  General
  Metal
  Wood
  Mechanical drawing

Library:
  Reading area
  Book room
  Office
  Audio-visual aids
  Work room
  Storage
  Conference
  Viewing room
  Listening room

Little Theater:
  Main room
  Stage
  Dressing
  Lavatory

Auditorium:
  Main
  Stage
  Dressing
  Lavatory

Gymnasia:
  Main gym
  Girls' gym
  Boys' gym
    Office
    Staff locker, lavatory, shower
    Issue
    Equipment storage
    Custodian
    Locker, lavatory, shower for students
    Exercise
    Drying
    First aid
    Varsity locker
    Corrective
    Conference

  Girl's area
    Office
    Staff locker, lavatory, shower
    Issue
    Equipment storage
    Custodian
    Student locker, lavatory, shower
    Exercise
    First aid
    Corrective
    Conference

Custodian:
  Office
  Storeroom
  Locker, lavatory, shower

Lockers:
  One per student, corridor area

Service:
  Maintenance shop
  Boiler room
  Control panels

Parking:
  Student
  Faculty
  Public

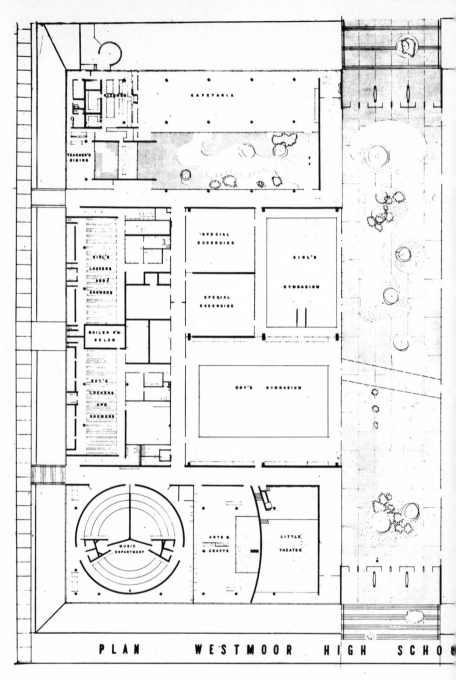

FIGURE 50. Westmoor High School plan (*Courtesy*

224

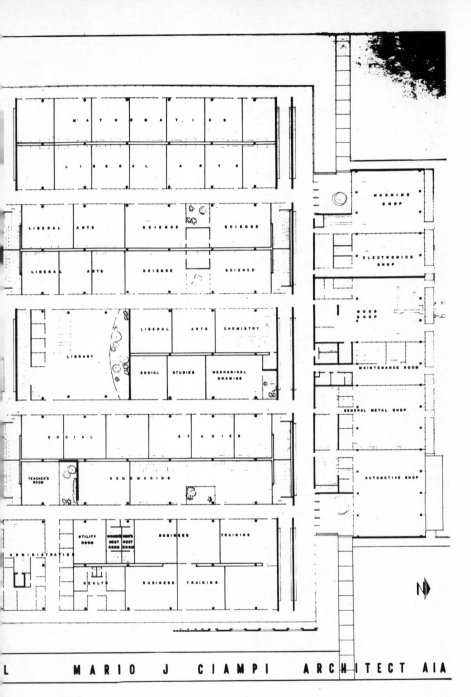

MARIO J CIAMPI ARCHITECT AIA

Mario Ciampi, Architect, San Francisco, Calif.).

FIGURE 52. Westmoor High School: main entrance court (*Courtesy Mario Ciampi, Architect, San Francisco, Calif.*).

FIGURE 53. Westmoor High School: library and court (*Courtesy Mario Ciampi, Architect, San Francisco, Calif.*).

FIGURE 54. Westmoor High School: cafeteria and court (*Courtesy Mario Ciampi, Architect, San Francisco, Calif.*).

227

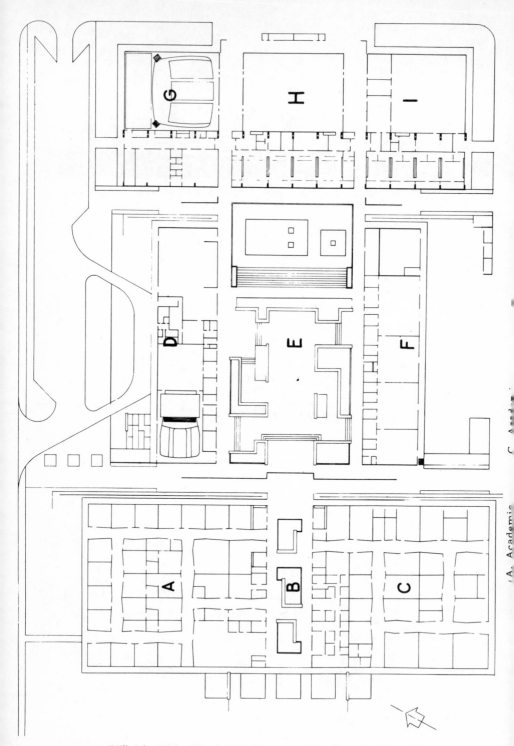

FIGURE 55. Hillsdale High School plan (*Courtesy John Lyon Reid and Partners, San Francisco, Calif.*).

228

Detailed educational specifications were prepared for the Hillsdale High School Plant. Figures 55 and 56 are the drawings of the plant resulting from the architect's interpretation of these specifications.

The following detailed educational specifications were developed for the Westmoor High School, Daly City, California.

Space Provisions Recommended for First Increment, Westmoor High School

Section 1 projects information and ideas that indicate the first increment of the Westmoor High School should be planned to take care of 1,000-1,250 students with a second increment to provide for between 500-750 additional students. Considering the community it will draw these students from, together with the past and present trends, the following space provisions are recommended. Full consideration of the type of curriculum the school and community would need has been considered in these recommendations.

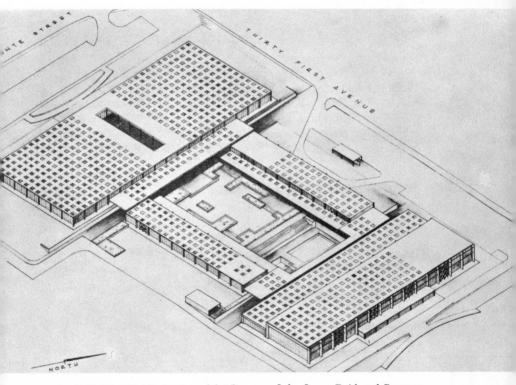

FIGURE 56. Hillsdale High School model (*Courtesy John Lyon Reid and Partners, San Francisco, Calif.*).

ADMINISTRATION AREA

No. of Units	Name of Unit	Size	Total Sq. Ft.*
1	Principal's office	12 x 14	168
1	Vice-principal's office	10 x 12	120
1	Reception room and		
	Secretary's office	10 x 18	180
1	Attendance office	28 x 32	896
1	Vault	6 x 10	60
1	Mimeograph and Duplicating		
	room	8 x 10	80
1	Dean of men's office	10 x 12	120
1	Dean of women's office	10 x 12	120
1	Reception room (Dean's		
	and Counselor's)	12 x 15	180
1	Test service director's room	10 x 12	120
2	Counselors' offices—each	10 x 12	240
1	Conference room	10 x 12	120
1	File room	10 x 12	120
1	Toilet & washroom for men	6 x 8	48
1	Toilet & washroom for women	6 x 8	48
16			2,620

* All figures in this and the following tables are approximate and listed here as a guide for the architect.

In the Administration area the units should be placed in relation to each other as follows:

(a) The Attendance Office should have a conspicuous location with the vault and mimeograph-duplicating room adjacent.

(b) The Principal's Office, Vice-principal's Office and reception room with secretary should be near (a) above but so located that these units do not have to sift out the general office traffic. The Principal's Office should have a clothes closet, storage closet and toilet-wash room facilities.

(c) The Dean's, Counselor's and Test Service Director's Offices should be located so the reception room is easily accessible to them. The file room should be centrally located but still protected from general unauthorized use.

(d) The toilets and wash rooms should be conveniently located in the administration area for use of all the workers in this area.

This whole unit should be located in the school building so ready access is possible for both school staff, students and visitors.

HEALTH SUITE

No. of Units	Name of Unit	Size	Total Sq. Ft.
1	Dental & Medical office	20 x 25	500
1	Reception room	15 x 20	300
1	Rest room	10 x 10	100
1	Storage room	6 x 6	36
1	Toilet & washroom	6 x 6	36
5			972

TOILET ROOMS

No. of Units	Name of Unit	Size	Total Sq. Ft.
3	Boys' toilet room	15 x 20	900
3	Girls' toilet room	15 x 20	900
6			1,800

ARTS AND CRAFTS AREA

No. of Units	Name of Unit	Size	Total Sq. Ft.
2	Classroom (for Art, Artmetal, Ceramics, Photography, etc.)	30 x 50	3,000

One room should be arranged for artmetal, ceramics, and photography. The other room should provide for the remainder of art courses.

CAFETERIA

No. of Units	Name of Unit	Size	Total Sq. Ft.
1	Dining room (Seating 400)		6,000
1	Kitchen	30 x 35	1,050
1	Storeroom	20 x 20	400
1	Office	10 x 12	120
1	Teachers' dining room	20 x 32	640
1	Locker & toilet room for employees	10 x 12	120
1	Store & snack bar	10 x 20	200
1	Dishwashing room	10 x 15	150
1	Refuse & garbage can storage room	10 x 15	150
1	Toilet facility (men)	15 x 20	300
1	Toilet facility (women)	15 x 25	375
2	Handwashing alcoves and 200 cubicles for book storage		100
13			9,605

(a) The faculty dining room should be adjacent to the student dining room to take advantage of close proximity to food preparation area.

(b) The handwashing alcoves and cubicles for book storage should be located at the entrances to the dining room.

COMMERCIAL AND BUSINESS PRACTICE ROOMS

No. of Units	Name of Unit	Size	Total Sq. Ft.
1	Typing room	30 x 35	1,050
1	Business machine and duplicating machine room	30 x 40	1,200
1	Utility room	30 x 35	1,050
1	Multiuse room	30 x 35	1,050
4			4,350

(a) The utility room should provide facilities for typing and transcription and, therefore, should be another typing room.

(b) The multiuse room should be constructed to provide facilities for bookkeeping, stenography, and so forth.

CORE-CURRICULUM ROOMS

No. of Units	Name of Unit	Size	Total Sq. Ft.
3	Language arts rooms	30 x 40	3,600
7	Language arts rooms	30 x 32	6,720
4	Mathematics rooms	30 x 32	3,840
5	Social studies rooms	30 x 32	4,800
2	Multiuse science rooms	30 x 50	3,000
1	General science room	30 x 48	1,440
1	Biology science room	30 x 48	1,440
23			24,840

(a) The large language arts rooms should be equipped with a movable stage.

(b) The two multiuse science rooms should provide for physics, chemistry and additional general science facilities. It's quite likely that the physics and chemistry taught the first year will be practically negligible but the second year it will be needed. Therefore, plans should be made to use these rooms for that purpose.

(c) It is desirable to arrange the rooms for the various core-curriculum in close proximity to each other.

HOME MAKING ROOMS

No. of Units	Name of Unit	Size	Total Sq. Ft.
1	Cooking laboratory	30 x 50	1,500
1	Practice dining room	15 x 20	300
1	Sewing laboratory	30 x 40	1,200
3			3,000

(a) The fitting area may be located in the sewing laboratory.

(b) The practice dining room shall be adjacent to the cooking laboratory and have an opening into it.

MUSIC BUILDING

No. of Units	Name of Unit	Size	Total Sq. Ft.
1	Instrumentation room	40 x 40	1,600
2	General music rooms	30 x 40	2,400
1	Office	10 x 12	120
2	Practice rooms	8 x 10	160
6			4,280

(a) Rooms should be sound proofed. Since the auditorium will come in the second increment it will be necessary to include this building in the first increment or make additional provisions in the main building planning.

LIBRARY

No. of Units	Name of Unit	Size	Total Sq. Ft.
1	Reading area (for 150 students) *		3,000
1	Book room (depository)	20 x 26	520
1	Librarian's office	10 x 12	120
1	Visual aids room	10 x 12	120
1	Work room	20 x 26	520
2	Conference rooms	15 x 18	540
7			4,820

* A partition could be used to separate this area into a library and study hall, to be removed later when second increment is built, if more seating capacity is needed in the library.

(a) The adjoining area should be so planned to allow enlargement of the library when the second increment is built.

(b) The conference rooms should be glass-partitioned and visible to the charging desk.

PUPIL AND COMMUNITY ACTIVITIES ROOM

No. of Units	Name of Unit	Size	Total Sq. Ft.
1	Room	26 x 35	910

(a) It is recommended that this room be easily accessible to the outside entrance since this room may be used by outside school people.

GYMNASIUM AREA

No. of Units	Name of Unit	Size	Total Sq. Ft.
1	Gym (Stage and Bleachers)		10,000
Boys' Wing			
1	Office for instructor	14 x 16	224
1	Lockers, showers and toilet for instructor	10 x 13	130
1	Towel and equipment daily-issue room	13 x 14	182
1	Equipment storage room (permanent)	12 x 13	156
1	Custodian room	8 x 13	104
1	Locker area	30 x 70	2,100
1	Shower area	25 x 30	750
1	Toilet area	12 x 18	216
1	Entrance and corridor area from main activity floor	12 x 20	240
1	Special exercise room	28 x 32	896
1	Drying room	20 x 30	600
1	Resting room	8 x 10	80
Girls' Wing			
1	Office for instructor	14 x 16	224
1	Lockers, showers and toilet room for instructor	10 x 13	130
1	Towel and equipment daily-issue room	13 x 14	182

1	Equipment storage room		
	(permanent)	12 x 13	156
1	Custodian room	8 x 13	104
1	Locker area	30 x 70	2,100
1	Shower area	25 x 30	750
1	Toilet area	12 x 18	216
1	Entrance and corridor area		
	from main activity room	12 x 20	240
1	Special exercise room	28 x 32	896
1	Resting room	8 x 10	80
24			20,756

(a) There should be a movable partition through the center of the gymnasium which will divide it into two small gymnasiums. The boys' wing and the girls' wing should be arranged adjacent to the portion of the gym each will be using.

(b) In arranging the relation of each of the units adjacent to the gym, consideration should be made for future increase when the second increment is built. This means that toilet, shower, locker space together with other small space must be increased to provide for an additional 500 or more students. The most logical solution would be to provide gym facilities for the girls in the second increment and convert present girls' wing into use for boys.

CUSTODIAN'S OFFICE, STOREROOM AND TOILET AREA

No. of Units	Name of Unit	Size	Total Sq. Ft.
1	Office	8 x 10	80
1	Storeroom	12 x 14	168
1	Toilet, washroom	5 x 6	30
1	Locker and dressing room	10 x 12	120
4			398

CORRIDORS

(1/6 room area)		7,758

LOCKERS

1,000	Lockers	1,000

(a) These lockers should be recessed in the walls of the corridors to conserve space and placed reasonably accessible to the home rooms. The steel locker 12" x 12" x 72" is recommended.

SERVICE BUILDING

No. of Units	Name of Unit	Size	Total Sq. Ft.
1	Maintenance shop and boiler room	40 x 60	2,400

PARKING FOR BICYCLES

100 bicycles		1,000

Provision for bicycle storage should be adjacent to the building and under a cover to protect the bicycles from inclement weather.

PARKING FOR AUTOMOBILES

No. of Units	Name of Unit	Size	Total Sq. Ft.
1	Permanent parking for 300 cars		79,200
1	Temporary parking for 200 cars		52,800
2			132,000

The location of these areas should be considered in light of the school building proper and the recreational areas. The temporary areas should be located adjacent to the athletic field with the permanent area near the main school building, but, if possible, not too great a distance from the fields.

PLAYFIELDS

No. of Units	Name of Unit	Over-all Size	Total Sq. Ft.
1	Football field and running track combination	450 x 210	94,500
1	Baseball field	300 x 300	90,000
4	Softball fields	450 x 450	202,500
4	Basketball courts (outdoor)	200 x 85	17,000
4	Tennis courts	100 x 200	20,000
1	Girls' playfield	300 x 180	54,000
1	Girls' utility field	200 x 150	30,000
2	Softball diamonds (girls)	200 x 350	70,000
2	Volleyball courts	60 x 60	3,600
1	Soccer field	350 x 200	70,000
21			651,600

Total Space Needed in First Increment

MAIN BUILDING

	Sq. Ft.	Total Sq. Ft.
Administration area		2,620
Health suite		972
Toilets		1,800
Cafeteria		9,605
Library		4,820
Custodian's office, etc.		398
Corridors		7,758
Lockers (1,000)		1,000
Classrooms		
2 Arts and crafts	3,000	
4 Commercial & Bus.	4,350	
23 Core-Curriculum	24,840	
3 Home Making	3,000	
4 Shops	10,450	
1 Pupil & Community	910	
37		46,550
Gymnasium		20,756
		96,279

SEPARATE BUILDINGS

Service building	2,400
Music building (3 rooms)	4,280
	102,959

OUTDOOR FIELDS

Recreation fields	651,600
Parking areas	79,200
Auto—permanent	79,200
Auto—temporary	52,800
Bicycles	1,000
	784,600

General Comments

When planning the location of the various units in the first increment, it is imperative to keep in mind the facilities needed in increment number two. By careful planning of the location of various areas it will be possible to arrange them so that the additional facilities may be added to the present facilities. This is especially desirable in the cases of the recreational areas and some of the special classrooms such as science, shops and home making.

Space Provisions Recommended for Second Increment

Estimated increases to be provided in second increment based on an additional 500-750 students. The following provisions are in addition to those listed in the first increment.

ADMINISTRATION AREA*

No. of Units	Name of Unit	Size	Total Sq. Ft.
2	Counselors' rooms	10 x 12	240
1	File room for counselors	10 x 12	120
1	File room for attendance office	12 x 14	168
4			648

HEALTH SUITE*

No. of Units	Name of Unit	Size	Total Sq. Ft.
1	Rest room	10 x 10	100
1	Storage room	6 x 6	36
2			136

TOILET ROOMS

No. of Units	Name of Unit	Size	Total Sq. Ft.
2	Boys' Toilet rooms	15 x 20	600
2	Girls' Toilet rooms	15 x 20	600
4			1,200

CAFETERIA*

No. of Units	Name of Unit	Size	Total Sq. Ft.
1	Storage room	20 x 20	400
1	Dining room (seating 200)		3,000
—			—
2			3,400

* Recommended inclusion with first increment for economy of construction.

COMMERCIAL AND BUSINESS PRACTICE ROOMS

No. of Units	Name of Unit	Size	Total Sq. Ft.
2	Classrooms (typing)	30 x 35	2,100
1	Multiuse classroom	30 x 35	1,050
—			—
3			3,150

CORE-CURRICULUM ROOMS

No. of Units	Name of Unit	Size	Total Sq. Ft.
1	Language arts room	30 x 40	1,200
4	Language arts rooms	30 x 32	3,840
2	Mathematics rooms	30 x 32	1,920
3	Social studies rooms	30 x 32	2,880
1	General science room	30 x 48	1,440
1	Chemistry room	30 x 50	1,500
—			—
12			12,780

HOME MAKING ROOMS

No. of Units	Name of Unit	Size	Total Sq. Ft.
1	Multiuse room	40 x 60	2,400

SHOP AREA

No. of Units	Name of Unit	Size	Total Sq. Ft.
1	Machine shop	50 x 60	3,000
1	General shop	40 x 60	2,400
—			—
2			5,400

LIBRARY

No. of Units	Name of Unit	Size	Total Sq. Ft.
2	Conference rooms	15 x 18	540
1	Book room	20 x 26	520
1	Visual aid storeroom	10 x 12	120
—			—
4			1,180

GYMNASIUM

No. of Units	Name of Unit	Size	Total Sq. Ft.
1	Girls' gym		6,000
2	Special exercise rooms	28 x 32	1,792
1	Showers, lockers and toilets		3,000
	Janitor space		50
—			—
4			10,842

AUDITORIUM AND AUXILIARY UNITS

(Areas for music to be provided in the auditorium)　　　20,000

LITTLE THEATER

(Seating capacity—300)　　　3,250

SERVICE BUILDING

Bus garage and equipment storage　　　1,600

CORRIDORS

(1/6 room area)　　　3,955

LOCKERS

500 Lockers　　　500

CUSTODIANS' OFFICE, STOREROOM, ETC.

　　　300

PARKING

Provide permanent additional parking for 100 cars　　　26,400
Provide temporary additional parking for 200 cars　　　52,800

　　　─────
　　　79,200

PLAYFIELDS

No. of Units	Name of Unit	Size	Total Sq. Ft.
4	Basketball courts	200 x 85	17,000
4	Tennis courts	100 x 200	20,000
2	Softball diamonds (girls & boys)		85,625
2	Volleyball courts	60 x 60	3,600
1	Utility field for archery range	200 x 100	20,000
—			─────
15			659,225

SWIMMING POOL BUILDING

No. of Units	Name of Unit	Size	Total Sq. Ft.
1	Swimming Pool		10,000
1	Lockers, showers, toilets and dressing area		3,000
1	Pool office	12 x 14	168
1	Janitor's office	8 x 10	80
—			─────
4			13,248

(a) Provision should be made for a limited seating arrangement for 100 seating capacity adjacent to the pool.

Total Space Needed in Second Increment

MAIN BUILDING

	Sq. Ft.	Total Sq. Ft.
Administration area	648	
Health suite	136	
Toilets	1,200	
Cafeteria	3,400	
Library	1,180	
Custodians' office, storeroom, etc.	300	
Corridors	3,955	
Lockers (500)	500	

Classrooms

3	Commercial & Bus.	3,150	
12	Core-Curriculum	12,780	
1	Home Making	2,400	
2	Shops	5,400	

	23,730	
		35,049

GYMNASIUM

		10,842

SEPARATE BUILDINGS

Auditorium	20,000
Little Theater	3,250
Service Building	1,600
Swimming Pool	13,248

	83,989

OUTDOOR FIELDS

Recreation fields	659,225

Parking areas

100 auto—permanent	26,400
200 auto—temporary	52,800
100 bicycles	1,000

	739,425

Total Space Provisions for Both Increments

Total classrooms—first increment	40
Total classrooms—second increment	18

	58
Total square feet—first increment—building	102,959
Total square feet—second increment—building	83,989

	186,948
Total square feet—outdoor facilities—first increment	784,600
Total square feet—outdoor facilities—second increment	739,425

	1,524,025

OUTDOOR PLAY AREAS

As in the case of planning other senior high school facilities, it is desirable to attain maximum utilization of playfields through flexibility and multiuse. It is common practice to combine the football and track facilities. A combined playfield 320' x 800' is adequate for these activities.

A second area 700' x 800' will provide two baseball fields, four softball fields, four basketball courts, five tennis courts, and two utility fields. In addition, some eight physical education areas can be laid out in the same area, so that realistic scheduling will make possible physical education programs for a school of one thousand students.

Public toilet facilities should be planned in conjunction with the competitive athletic facilities, though gymnasia facilities will be satisfactory for student use.

The need for up to fifty acres of land for a high school site can be easily justified when total needs are analyzed to accommodate a community school.

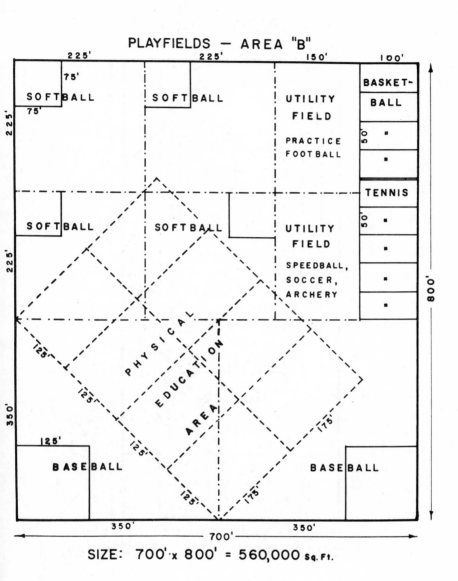

FIGURE 57. Field plan.

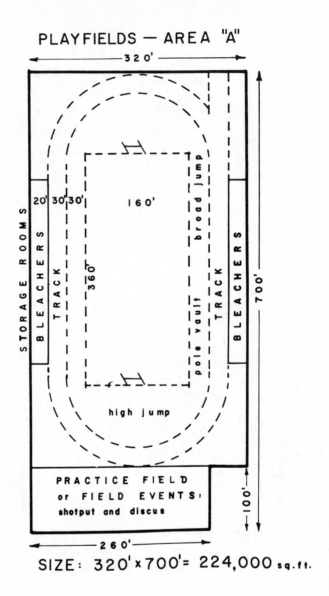

FIGURE 58. Alternate field plan.

BIBLIOGRAPHY

Arce, William Benjamin, "Planning Boys' Gymnasium Facilities for Secondary Schools." Unpublished Ed. D. Dissertation, School of Education, Stanford University, September, 1956.

Ashley, Warren H., "Advantages of the Unit Plan for Secondary Schools," *American School and University*, Volume 27 (1955-56), pp. 219-224.

Becker, J. B., "Essential Construction Features of School Shops," *Industrial Arts and Vocational Education* (March, 1955), pp. 66-68.

Bobbitt, B. G. and Others, "The Los Angeles Plan for Science Rooms," *Clearing House* (October, 1952), p. 71.

Bollinger, Gilroy W., "Suggestions for Planning Industrial Arts Facilities," *American School and University*, Twenty-first Annual Edition. New York: American School Publishing Corporation, 1949, pp. 211-220.

Burris-Meyer, Harold and Cole, Edward C., *Theatre and Auditorium*, Progressive Architectural Library. New York: Reinhold Publishing Corporation, 1949, Chapter 15.

"City High School," *Architectural Forum*, 91:129-31 (October, 1949).

Clift, Thomas W., "High School in Atlanta—Conservative Modern," *Nation's Schools*, 43:31-32 (March, 1949).

Cocking, Walter D., "Secondary School Design Since World War II," *American School and University*, Vol. 27 (1955-56), pp. 185-192.

Conrad, Marion J., "A Technique for Determining the Operating Capacity of Secondary School Buildings." Doctor's thesis, Ohio State University, Columbus, Ohio (1952).

Cowles, Ruth C., "Needed Facilities for a Modern Homemaking Program," *American School and University*, Vol. 27 (1955-56), pp. 273-278.

DeLancey, Opal H., "Twenty-five Suggestions on Planning the One Room Business Department," *Business Teacher*, 1:192 (March, 1950).

Deniston, Ross C., "Planning Art Facilities for Secondary Schools." Unpublished Ed. D. Dissertation, School of Education, Stanford University, September, 1956.

Easton, J. A. G., "Specifications for School Shops," *American School and University*, 22:335 (1950-51).

Emery, Raymond C., "Facilities for Programs of Arts and Crafts in Secondary Schools: A Symposium," *American School and University*, Vol. 27 (1955-56), pp. 289-306.

Engelhardt, M., Nickolaus L. Engelhardt, Jr., and Stanton Leggett, *Planning Secondary School Buildings.* New York: Reinhold Publishing Corporation, 1949.

Engelhardt, Nickolaus L., Jr., "Changes in Secondary School Buildings," *School Executive,* 42:25 (August, 1949).

Erbes, Raymond G., Jr., "Criteria for High School Library Spaces and Facilities," *American School and University,* Vol. 27 (1955-56), pp. 267-272.

Finsterbach, Fred C., "Toward the Ideal General Shop," *Industrial Arts and Vocational Education,* 39:104-106 (March, 1950).

Garinger, Elmer H. and French, John E., "Solution for New Secondary Schools—The Campus Plan," *American School and University,* Vol. 27 (1955-56), pp. 209-214.

Garrison, J. Don, "A High School Designed for the Future," *American School and University,* Vol. 27 (1955-56), pp. 205-208.

Gillies, Harry W., "Planning the School Auditorium to Serve the Community's Needs," *School Executive* (August, 1951), pp. 19-22.

Goldsmith, J. L., "3-D Block Layout and School Shop Planning," *Industrial Arts and Vocational Education* (March, 1955), pp. 69-70.

Gorman, Marie and Herbster, William E., "A High School Library Designed for Youth," *American School and University,* Vol. I, 28th Edition, American School Publishing Corporation, New York, 1956-57, pp. 331-334.

Grassell, E. M., "Tool Storage in the School Shop," *Industrial Arts and Vocational Education* (March, 1955), pp. 91-95.

Griffin, J. D., "DeLuxe Model Gym," *Scholastic Coach* (January, 1950), p. 10.

Hackett, Donald F., "Guides for School Shop Planning," *Industrial Arts and Vocational Education,* Vol. 42, No. 3 (March, 1952).

Hanson, Abel, "Facilities for Art Experience in General Education," *California Journal of Secondary Education,* 23:279 (May, 1948).

Heckler, R. D., "Planning and Equipping the School Lunchroom," *School Executive* (July, 1952), p. 93.

Heid, E. J. and Paulson, G. L., "Industrial-Arts Shop Planning Factors," *Industrial Arts and Vocational Education,* 1955 School Shop Annual (March, 1955), pp. 59-66.

Herrick, John H., McLeary, Ralph D., Clapp, Wilfred F. and Bogner, Walter F., *From School Program to School Plant.* New York: Henry Holt and Co., 1956.

Herrick, John H., "The Development of Educational Specifications in Planning the Secondary School Plant," Bulletin of the National Association of Secondary School Principals, 32:213-19 (March, 1948).

Hipplak, Thomas A., "Planning School Shops," Industrial Arts and Vocational Education, 38:91-95 (March, 1949).

Hurd, Paul DeH., Science Facilities for the Modern High School, Educational Administration Monograph Number 2, School of Education, Stanford University, Stanford, California (1954).

——, "How to Achieve Outstanding High School Facilities," American School and University, American School Publishing Corporation, New York, 1956-57, pp. 317-326.

Irwin, Ruth B., "Make Room for the Speech and Hearing Therapist," School Executive (September, 1949), p. 60.

Jordan, Wayne Noll, "Planning Music Facilities for the Secondary Schools." Unpublished Ed. D. Dissertation, School of Education, Stanford University, September, 1956.

Koopman, G. Robert, "Changing Secondary School Programs and their Implications for Design," American School and University, Vol. 27 (1955-56), pp. 199-204.

Kubik, Betty Martin, "Modern Planning for Business Training: The Hamilton, Ohio, D. E. Room," Business Education World (November, 1953).

Lee, Alta, "Homemaking Suites," School Executive, 68:68-69 (January, 1949).

——, "Space and Equipment for Homemaking Programs," Division of Vocational Education, Misc. No. 9, Federal Security Agency. Washington, D.C.: U.S. Government Printing Office, 1950, p. 8.

McDermott, James R. Jr., "Design the Industrial Arts Laboratory Around Objective," School Executive, 67:29-30 (October, 1947).

Moyle, William D., and Ashley, Warren H., "Development of a Small Campus-Type High School," American School and University, Vol. 27 (1955-56), pp. 235-240.

Munch, Theodore W., "High School Science Facilities," American School Board Journal, 126:52 (March, 1953).

——, and Warren J. Pelton, "A Suggested Plan for a Physical Science Suite," American School Board Journal, 126:52 (March, 1953).

Nichols, John, "Inexcusable Mistakes in Planning School Auditoriums," School Management, Vol. 19 (December, 1949), pp. 6-7.

Planning Manual for Educational Science Laboratories, Kewaunee Mfg. Co., Adrian, Michigan, AIA File No. 35E, Section 5A (1955 Edition).

Planning Tomorrow's Secondary Schools, School Planning Laboratory, School of Education, Stanford University (1954).

Wenger, P. N., "Check List for Planning and Evaluating School Shops," *Industrial Arts and Vocational Education*, School Shop Annual (March, 1953).

Willoughby, G. A., "How to Plan a Functional School Shop," *Industrial Arts and Vocational Education* (March, 1955), pp. 68-69.

CHAPTER 9

PLANNING
THE JUNIOR COLLEGE

During the past twenty-five years American junior colleges have emerged from the role of preparatory institutions to their present status as community colleges. The transition has been gradual; junior colleges vary considerably since they have discarded the idea that their only function was to duplicate the first two years of a liberal arts program. These institutions, because of their newness, are relatively unfettered by tradition—which has made it possible for them to adapt more readily to the needs of the communities. Their purpose and function is fourfold.

(1) The transfer program, in which lower division students are prepared for transfer to upper division status in four-year institu-

tions. With the increasing population growth and overcrowding of many colleges and universities, this function takes on new importance for these two-year colleges.

(2) Terminal education, which includes a general education program which has also emerged to an extent in four-year colleges and universities. The basic effort of such a program is to help people prepare for life. The primary concern of the teacher is with the individual rather than with the course. Another aspect of terminal education is vocational and technical training. Patterns for such training usually depend on the occupational opportunities of the community. Vocational education aims, for the most part, to introduce semiprofessional, subtechnical, and technician training.

(3) Adult education and training—preparation for a new occupation or an advanced course in a particular vocation. An important phase of this program is the teaching of leisure time avocational activities. Another phase is education in parenthood, interpersonal relations, and personality development. Junior colleges also offer courses in elementary English and Americanization procedures.

(4) Community service—forums, lectures, and concerts. Junior colleges also conduct community surveys to discover community needs—surveys whose results prove useful to community agencies and groups.

The junior colleges, uniquely among educational institutions, exemplify the democratic philosophy of education. The base of these institutions is the concept of equal opportunity for all individuals.

The tax-supported junior college has emerged in response to the economic and social demands of our technological civilization. These institutions also give impetus to the spiraling technology. There has been a constant increase in junior college enrollments—from about seventy-five thousand students in 1930 to nearly three quarters of a million students in 1955. This growth is likely to continue.

The planning techniques employed are similar to those used on the elementary and secondary levels. The need to schedule classes in the early part of the day to accommodate students participating in cooperative training programs, the desire of faculty members to have certain specialized facilities, and the inherent demands on an academic as well as a vocational institution, complicate the educational and architectural plan. The following topics are only a few that should receive careful consideration:

1. Present and probable future enrollments.
2. Educational outcomes and general considerations.
3. Discernible trends in junior college education. Indications that future educational patterns would be seriously limited by the kinds of teaching spaces now used.
4. Special orientation requirements. Relationships in connection with other components of the college plant.
5. Internal traffic pattern. Physical areas used by students and instructors.
6. Furniture and equipment.
7. Utilities.
8. Color, decoration, acoustic, and light levels.
9. Specific materials to be stored in the classroom. Departmental storage.
10. Special requirements for unique spaces.

Minimum space requirements should then be determined.

The working program for planning the Contra Costa Junior College gives an indication of the complexity of a well organized procedure:[1]

I. FIRST STAGE
   A. Organization of combined office staff
   B. Work schedule arranged
   C. Preliminary survey work
      1. Relationship of area to county and surrounding area
         (a) Area to be served by college
         (b) Population trends in the area
         (c) Subdivision and building trends
         (d) Present land use
         (e) Prospective land use
         (f) Zoning
         (g) Existing streets and highways
         (h) Future streets and highways
         (i) Impact of traffic and other disturbing influences
      2. Utilities and services
         (a) Water supply
         (b) Sewage disposal
         (c) Power supply
         (d) Policy and fire protection
      3. Scope and function of the college
         (a) Present student enrollment

[1] Drummond J. McCunn, John Carl Warnecke, Frederick L. R. Confer, and Lawrence Livingston, Jr., "Planning Contra Costa Junior College," *American School and University*—1952-53, pages 241-254.

      (b) Future student enrollment
      (c) Educational aims
      (d) Present curriculum and methods of instruction
      (e) Anticipated future curriculum
      (f) Agriculture and other specialized courses
      (g) Sports and other physical education programs
      (h) Student activities and social life
      (i) Maintenance

4. Preliminary development of campus relationships
      (a) Circulation pattern
      (b) Vehicular access
      (c) Parking requirements and areas
      (d) Pedestrian circulation
      (e) Athletic areas
      (f) General study of building types—one-story, two-story, and so forth
      (g) General orientation study; weather
      (h) Topographical studies
      (i) General building locations determined on site, forming a preliminary site utilization plan

II. SECOND STAGE

A. Detailed Master Plan Studies
    1. Scope and function of the College Program (Similar to No. 3 above but in greater detail—in conferences the representatives of the entire faculty)
    2. Description of use to be made of buildings and site facilities by adult education departments and the community
    3. Written report and analysis of the use and functions of the buildings and their relation with other buildings on the campus
    4. Development of schematic plans of all buildings
    5. Development of architectural master plan
    6. Landscape master plan
    7. Mechanical master plans
      (a) Electrical
      (b) Water Supply
      (c) Drainage
      (d) Gas
      (e) Sewer

III. THIRD STAGE

A. Model—existing and final
B. Photographs
C. Architectural drawings
D. Sketches

E. Final schematic plans and elevations
F. Construction budget
G. Written reports
   1. The progressive development of the Master Plan
   2. Recording of all the requirements
   3. Recording of all the discussions
   4. Recommendations of the State Department of School Planning
   5. Description of the general physical aspects of the school, including materials of building construction, design, color, height relations—integration to site
   6. Recommendations for progressive development of the campus
   7. Additional uses of the report

The following total minimum areas are being submitted as an example of the educational planning of one junior college. This information is basic in determining space needs and room designs.

TABLE 8

MINIMUM LAND AREA REQUIREMENTS FOR ADEQUATE FACILITIES TO SERVE A JUNIOR COLLEGE WITH AN ESTIMATED ENROLLMENT OF 2,000-2,500

	I	II	III	IV	V	VI
Type of Facility	No. of Facilities	No. of* Sq. Ft.	Clearance Factor	Total to Nearest 100	Ext. to Nearest 1,000	Total Acres
Academic	34[1]	960[2]	1,440[3]	2,400	82,000	1.88
Art	2	1,920	2,600	4,500	9,000	.21
Science	8	1,920	2,600	4,500	36,000	.83
Homemaking	6	1,920	2,600	4,500	27,000	.62
Music	2	6,000	18,000	24,000	48,000	1.1
Shops	8	5,000	20,000[4]	25,000	200,000	4.6
Men's gym	1	24,800[5]	32,825	58,600	59,000	1.3
Women's gym	1	11,300[6]	20,792	32,100	32,000	.74
Pool	1	5,145[7]	29,725	34,900	35,000	.80
Administration	1	6,000[8]	8,796	8,800	9,000	.21
Auditorium	1	20,140[9]	40,280	60,400	60,000	1.38
Student center	1	25,000[10]	30,000	55,000	55,000	1.2
Library	1	10,000	20,000	30,000	30,000	.68
Office	30	144[11]	211	355	11,000	.25
Parking for 1,000 cars, 125/acre	1					8.0
Maintenance shops, transportation						5.0
Roads—access						5.0
						33.80

* All figures in this and the following tables are approximate and listed here as a guide for the architect.

Outdoor Physical Education Facilities

Type of Facility	No. of Facilities	Area Each in Acres	Total Acres for Facility	Clearance for Area	Total Acres
Stadium	1	4.3	4.3	3.0	7.3
Baseball	1	2.5	2.5	1.0	3.5
Softball	4	1.0	4.0	2.0	6.0
Practice football field ...	1	2.4	2.4	1.6	4.0
Tennis courts	6	.09	.54	.75	1.29
Outdoor basketball	6	.09	.54	.75	1.29
Volleyball	6	.04	.24	.50	.74

Women's Physical Education Facilities:

Hockey field	2	1.0	2.0	1.0	3.0
Softball	4	.5	2.0	2.0	4.0
Outdoor basketball	6	.09	.54	.75	1.29
Tennis courts	6	.09	.54	.75	1.29
Volleyball	6	.04	.24	.50	.74

Total Minimum Acres   68.24

Additional Acres for Landscape gardening and
ornamental horticulture   7.00

Total Acres   75.24

Footnotes to Table 8

1 Assumed 30 students per classroom.

2 Estimated average classroom size. This will vary according to room use.

3 Clearance factor for each facility is determined by multiplying the room size by a weighted factor used for each of the facilities—divide column (3) by column (2).

4 Clearance factor includes fenced shop yards plus area required to isolate the shops from other facilities.

5 Includes a gym floor 80' x 135' = 10,800 sq. ft. plus 5,000 sq. ft. for lockers, showers, toilets, offices and storage —(50 sq. ft. per student—peak load of 100 students); plus 10,000 sq. ft. for seating 1,000 people. This figure does not include sq. ft. considerations for the following:
   1. Visiting team room lockers, showers, toilets.
   2. Apparatus room.
   3. Uniform drying room.
   4. Wrestling room.
   5. Foyer—ticket booth, community rest rooms.
   6. Recreation—reading room.
   7. Heating plant, if other than central.
   8. Swimming pool.
   9. Classroom.
  10. Training room.
  11. Store.
  12. Laundry.

6 Includes a gym floor 60' x 105' = 6,300 sq. ft., plus 5,000 sq. ft. for lockers, showers, toilets, offices and storage—(50 sq. ft. per student—peak load of 100 students). This figure does not include sq. ft. considerations for the following:
   1. Spectator seating.
   2. Special rooms, i.e., correctives, dance, or reading and recreation.
   3. Classroom.
   4. Visiting team room lockers, showers, toilets.

7 Includes a swimming pool 49' x 105'.

8 Includes lobby, general office, recorder, auditor, business manager, vaults, and consultation rooms.

9 Designed to seat approximately 1,500 people. Includes a stage, two dressing rooms, orchestra pit, projection booth, foyer, rest rooms, and storage space.

10 Includes cafeteria, store, student administrative offices, combination dance floor and lounge, newspaper annual offices, and storage.

11 Assumed that office space for approximately thirty staff members will be necessary. Excluded is office space for the gymnasium personnel as well as music, shops, and homemaking.

In this particular project some seventy meetings were held, involving over eighty faculty members and twenty different consultants during a period of twelve months—resulting in thirty educational specification documents each varying from twenty to one hundred pages of printed matter and illustrations.

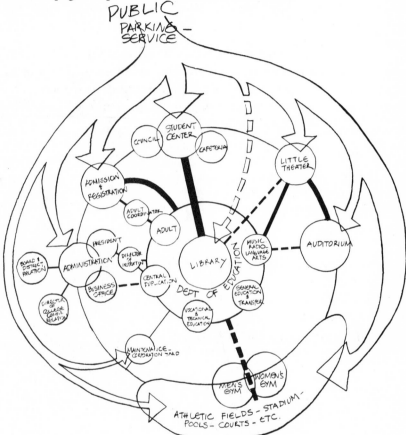

FIGURE 59. Area relationship diagram (*Courtesy J. C. Warnecke, Architect*).

The first draft of the music educational specifications are submitted as a guide to this type of document:

1.1 *Special orientations in relation to other components of the school plant.* Since the college has a growing radio broadcasting station music plays an important part in the offerings of such a station. There are large rehearsal rooms around an elevated monitor room for tape recordings. It is not necessary to have the music department close to the radio station. Most of the music could be taped prior to broadcasting. The auditorium should be close to the music department—many public appearances will be made by performers. Since the auditorium will also serve as a community center it should have a seating capacity of 1,500. An additional room for rehearsing large classes and teaching music appreciation will be necessary.

1.2 *Activities.* Courses in the music department serve two major purposes: to teach professional musicians and music majors and to provide the opportunity for self-expression and recreation. The following courses listed in the school bulletin are offered or will be offered should there be a demand for them:

Courses

Musicianship
Advanced Musicianship
History and Appreciation
Harmony
Advanced Harmony
Advanced History and Appreciation
Counterpoint
Elementary Music Education
Form and Analysis
Instrumentation and Arranging
Composition in Smaller Forms
Piano
Orchestra
Band
Study of the Brass Instruments
Study of Woodwind Instruments
Study of Stringed Instruments
Ensemble (Instrumental)
Dance Band
Men's Glee Club
Women's Chorus
A Cappella Choir
Voice
Vocal Ensemble
Opera Production (summer only)

In addition to these instructional objectives the Music Department serves the public. Program services provide from 45 to 90 appearances by individuals from the music department, with the year's activities culminating with the spring concert. It is probable that such services will increase as the department expands, and as a marching band is formed.

Increasing and sustained interest in classical music means that the music department will be an ever growing one.

1.3 *General considerations and trends*. The music department will require classrooms for lectures coupled with demonstrations on the piano and with recording equipment. The major requirements for the department are for large rehearsal rooms and a band room with minimum space of 28' x 40' with not less than a 16' ceiling. This would also be used for technique instruction and small group rehearsals. A combination orchestra and band room should be provided to seat approximately 150, with 80 fixed side-arm chairs on tiers in a semicircle overlooking the podium. It could also be used as a classroom for some of the lecture courses, such as history and art appreciation. A room 30' x 40' should meet the space needs. A small ensemble rehearsal room will be necessary. This room could double as a small classroom for piano practice and instruction. There would be need for twelve 6' x 8' practice rooms, including two 12' x 12', with windowed doors for private practice. Most of the instruction in the music department is individualized and consequently the spaces, furniture and equipment must be flexible.

1.4 *Internal traffic circulation*. It should be possible for the instructors to move freely between student stations. Doors in rehearsal rooms should be large enough for the passage of a grand piano.

1.5 *Utilities*. Lavatory facilities should be provided in the music building for from 200 to 300 people. In addition there should be separate faculty wash rooms and rest rooms. The storage of delicate instruments requires that the temperature remain uniform. There should also be humidity control. Lighting should be of high quality and of uniform intensity. There should be outlets for recorders, record players, and other materials. An intercommunication system is necessary between the office and the practice rooms. Heating and ventilating should be adequate and quiet.

1.6 Color, decoration, and acoustics. The rooms should be light and cheerful and within the standards of reflectance. There should be nonecho acoustical treatment, but not a deadening treatment. The practice rooms should be sound resistant. Choral rooms and classrooms should be light controlled by means of a rheostat.

1.7 Furniture and equipment. In the classrooms and rehearsal rooms, ruled blackboards 12' x 4' should be provided. In the classrooms a minimum of 32 lineal feet of ruled blackboard will be necessary. The blackboard should be ruled in 1¼" wide lines. These rooms should be equipped with 4' x 4' tackboard sections. The band and orchestra rooms should have a counter along their lengths with a sink and with undercounter storage, and with a sloped front edge so that students can use the counter as a music rack. Movable chairs should be provided throughout the rehearsal rooms, with the exception of 80 fixed seats in the choral room. A podium in each of the rehearsal rooms should be of sufficient size to hold a spinet piano. There should be a projection screen in each classroom and an elevated blackboard.

1.8 Storage. In each rehearsal room there should be a 10' x 14' storage room. Music library shelving should be in excess of 32 linear, with 48 additional linear feet for choral material.

1.9 Special needs. Faculty lavatory facilities should be provided. A small workshop room is necessary for instrument repair, including a counter sink and tool storage. The floor throughout the department should be smooth and made of sound absorbent material —perhaps cork.

BIBLIOGRAPHY

Atkinson, William N., "Current Problems in the Administration of the Junior Colleges," *Junior College Journal* (March, 1953), pp. 389-96.

Badger, Henry G., "Operating Costs in Junior Colleges," *Junior College Journal* XXV (October, 1953), pp. 389-96.

Basler, R., "Consistent and Increasing Adaptability of the Junior College," *Junior College Journal* 25 (April, 1955), pp. 427-9.

Bogue, Jessie P., "Analysis of Junior College Growth," *Junior College Journal* XX (February, 1950), pp. 317-26.

McCunn, Drummond J., John Carl Warnecke, Frederick L. R. Confer and Lawrence Livingston, Jr., "Planning Contra Costa Junior College," *American School and University* (1952-53). pp. 241-254.

Flint, Calvin C., "Factors Relating to Establishment of a Junior College in Santa Cruz County." Doctor's thesis, Stanford: Stanford University, 1952.

Frasier, G. W., "An Introduction to the Study of Education," pp. 426-29. New York: Harper & Bros.

Fretwell, Elbert K., *"Founding Public Junior Colleges: Local Initiative in Six Communities."* New York: Bureau of Publications, Teachers College, Columbia University, 1954.

Henderson, A. D., "Broadened Concept of Function and Scope of Junior Colleges," *Junior College Journal*, 25:479-81 (April, 1955).

Jacobson, P. B. and R. R. Wiegman, "Selected References on the Organization and Administration of Secondary Education; Junior College (cont.)," *School Review*, 63:400 (October, 1955).

MacConnell, James D., and William R. Odell, "A Survey of San Mateo Junior College, San Mateo, California," Stanford, California (March, 1953).

McCallum, William J., "The Financial Support and Control of Public Junior Colleges in the United States." Doctor's thesis, Stanford: Stanford University, 1955.

Roland, L. J., "Professional Preparation of Junior College Administrators," *Junior College Journal*, 24:72-80 (October, 1953).

Starrak, James Abel and Raymond M. Hughes, *The Community College in the United States*. Ames: Iowa State College Press, 1954.

Strayer, George D., and others, *A Report of a Survey of Needs of California in Higher Education* (March, 1948), pp. 5-6.

PART 3

THE PLANT IS
BORN

CHAPTER 10

INTERPRETING
EDUCATIONAL
SPECIFICATIONS

In Chapter II the architect's role was defined as one of management. His ability to coordinate the activities of the many participants and specialists in the preliminary planning and throughout the building, will determine the success of the total project.

PRELIMINARY PLANS

The day to day pressure of school business is so great that important decisions often have to be made with little time for careful study of all phases of each problem. The importance of basic decisions made on the basis of the architect's preliminary sketches cannot be overstressed. Cowgill and Small stated that,

> As much time as possible should generally be given to the study of the design before the preliminary sketches are made. Unfortunately though, most clients expect at least tentative solutions of their problems soon after they have [been] presented . . . to an architect. For this reason, the first preliminary sketches are usually prepared under pressure, within a limited time, and without thorough study. Although the time for the study of the design is limited, no designer should be rushed into presenting a sketch until a reasonable solution is found. To be able to do this within as short a period as is usually expected requires practice in addition to native ability.[1]

School officials should consider these factors in their review of preliminary plans. Preparation time, as well as the experience of the architect is of immeasurable value to lay and professional school people in resolving the problems of this early stage. Basic decisions must be made on all principal phases, such as: the site's selection and its utilization, site preparation, general type of building, space relationships, engineering, development, installation of prime utilities, and basic area allocations. In so far as it is possible all changes in plans should be made before working drawings are begun.

THE SITE

The demands on the use of the site and the architectural problem of locating the building so as to gain the benefits of natural surroundings will necessitate the preparation of small scale plot plans. Such plot plans indicate the site's limitations as well as its opportunities. An example of this procedure follows.

Educators present a difficult site problem to the architect:

I. *The Project.*
   A. Site: The site is a small parcel of property with a 225 foot frontage, increased to 268.56 feet at the back, and 111 feet in depth. It lies across White Oak Way from the existing White Oak 10 classroom structure, built on a 2.93 acre site.
   B. Ultimate utilization of the site: The facilities should house

[1] Clinton H. Cowgill, and Ben John Small, *Architectural Practice* (Reinhold Publishing Corporation: N.Y., 1952), pp. 17-35.

kindergarten and Grade I pupils in indoor-outdoor self-contained classroom units, and a small storeroom for janitorial equipment and supplies.

C. Present project: The Board is in the final stages of acquiring the property. It would like the architect to submit pencil drawings revealing his ideas as to the type of kindergarten and Grade I classroom units possible on the site; ideas as to the kinds of architecture that will blend with neighboring homes.

II. *Function.*

A. Grades to be housed: The unit is scheduled to house three kindergarten units and as many Grade I units as the architect deems possible on the site. The construction is to remedy the overcrowding in the existing school. Heavy preschool population figures indicate that the neighborhood will provide pupils for some time to come.

B. Basic organization of the school: Administrative facilities already exist in the present structure; hence the annex is to have only classroom facilities and a janitorial service closet.

1. Each classroom unit is to be self-contained and to resemble a home with its yard as much as is advisable. Children just entering school will remain with their teacher throughout the official school session.

2. The program in kindergarten and Grade I is primarily one of providing a transition from the family unit to the larger group experience. The teacher, working with a group of 30-35 children, will help them to develop mentally, socially, physically, emotionally.

3. Accommodations will have to be made for class group play, construction, music, and art activities and for quieter organizations—skills and reading periods. . . .

Six alternate layouts were presented by the architect and were scored by the educational team and the architect in terms of harmony with the educational specifications.

The following series of plot plans indicates preliminary thinking by the architect on the solution of this complicated site problem.

Planning housing facilities becomes more complex as the program and plant facilities become more complex. The architectural solutions to junior high school, high school, junior college, and college educational problems require increased skill and ingenuity on the part of the architect and his technical team.

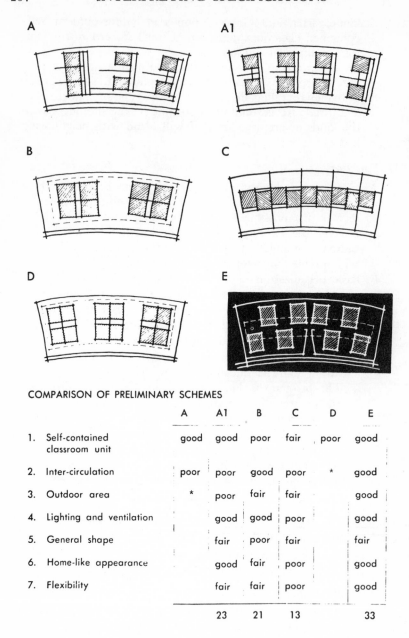

COMPARISON OF PRELIMINARY SCHEMES

		A	A1	B	C	D	E
1.	Self-contained classroom unit	good	good	poor	fair	poor	good
2.	Inter-circulation	poor	poor	good	poor	*	good
3.	Outdoor area	*	poor	fair	fair		good
4.	Lighting and ventilation		good	good	poor		good
5.	General shape		fair	poor	fair		fair
6.	Home-like appearance		good	fair	poor		good
7.	Flexibility		fair	fair	poor		good
		23	21	13			33

Poor........1; Fair........3; Good........5
........Eliminated at this point

FIGURE 60. Preliminary schemes for a classroom (*Courtesy John C. Warnecke and The School Executive*).

FIGURE 61. Kindergarten classroom (*Courtesy John C. Warnecke*).

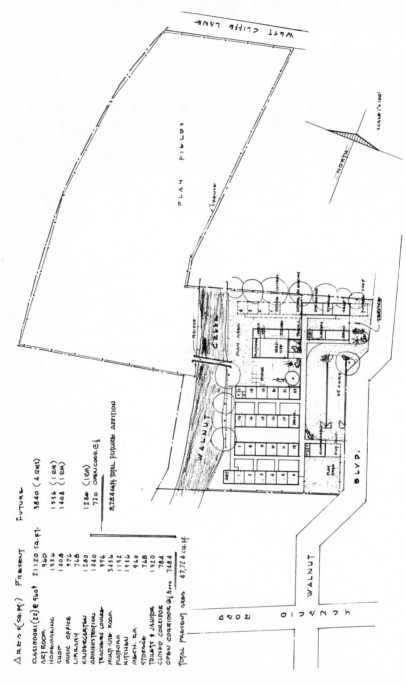

FIGURE 62 . East Central School Plot plans (*Courtesy Walnut Creek* (*Calif.*).
School District).

266

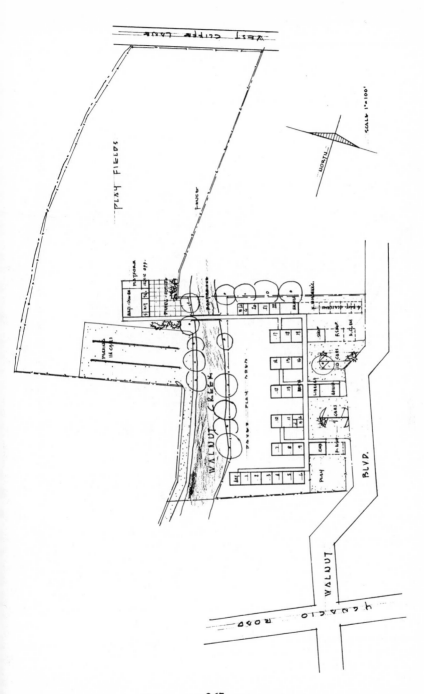

FIGURE 62 (*continued*).

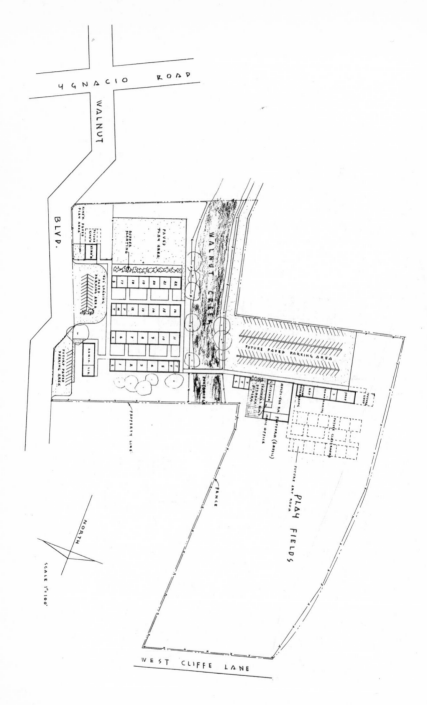

FIGURE 62 (*continued*).

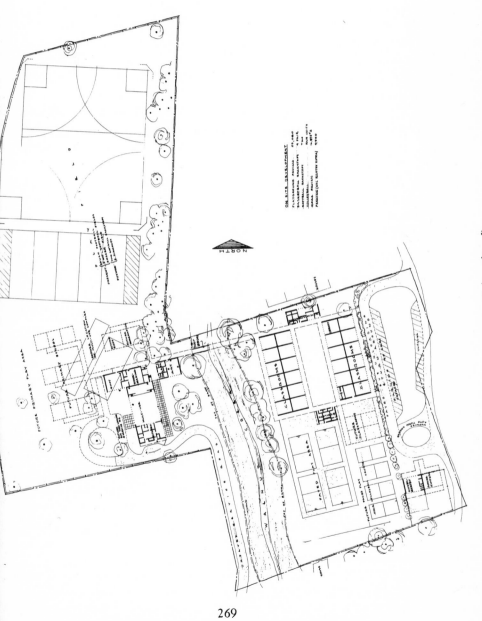

FIGURE 62 (*continued*).

PLANNING MEETINGS

Committee activity should range in groupings and in the specific kinds of activities to be detailed. The architect and/or his representatives participate in the various study groups and read the educational specifications to coordinate demands and to separate problems which require individual treatment. During these meetings he forms a picture of the total project as he assimilates its numerous separate parts. Until all of the project's components can be combined into a homogeneous whole, the architect is not ready to begin the working drawings.

The architect's first impressions at these meetings with the board of education or trustees, the school employees, and of his visits with local citizens, will influence the ultimate design of the school plant. In the area of athletics, for example, the architect can emphasize or de-emphasize its department's design in the proposed plant, depending upon his interpretation of the importance the community places on it.

THE TOTAL PLAN

In these meetings the architect has been working with and assisting specialized lay and professional groups concerned to form an adequate physical environment to accommodate particular areas of concentration. His next job is to design the school plant which will meet the educational needs of the community within the financial limitations designated by the board of trustees.

THE ARCHITECT–CONSULTANT– ADMINISTRATIVE SCHOOL PLANNING ADVISORY COMMITTEE

The architect must first present his work to the administration, its consultants, and its committee members to suggest accommodations for its proposed activities. The advantages and disadvantages of building types and locations on the site can be discussed. The architect presents the results of his thinking and receives suggestions from those with whom he has worked. These are exploratory meetings—all can express themselves. Often such opportunities are not available until after the architect has committed himself to a particular design. These discussions should not dissuade the architect from a design that he thinks will adequately accommodate the indicated activities. Rather, they should assist him in anticipating future agreements and disagreements to this plan.

The architect will learn the tentative cost of site development. He will be informed of the requests of the school staff and of his budget allocation from the board. Often the decision to build the plant in sections is among the proposals submitted to the board. Certain units are basic and must be built first; others could be partially built or added later if certain building and curriculum adjustments are made during the interim. Although the master plan is never out of mind, its time of realization may have to be postponed because of financial difficulties.

THE BOARD

The architect is now in a position to consider all phases of the proposed plant and submit his recommendations to the board. It is advantageous for a representative from the school planning advisory committee as well as the educational consultants to be present at this meeting, for at this meeting basic decisions as to the extent of the structure will be made. The board and architect should carefully consider all proposals and provide satisfactory reasons for approving, expanding, or disallowing the desires of particular groups. This is the time of careful consideration; it is here that the planning committee eliminates injustices and misunderstandings.

After basic decisions are made the architect should be able to proceed with the final stages of his preliminary planning and lay the groundwork for his working drawings. He will have to seek further information from time to time, and present sketches and other visual aids to assist with the final planning.

At the point at which educational consultants, certified and classified personnel, and lay groups think that the planning is finished, the architect begins the arduous and important task of preparing working drawings. The completeness of the educational specifications and his grasp of the total project will determine the rapidity with which he can work and the degree to which the plan meets the educational needs of the community.

The techniques employed by various school districts to bring about desired ends differs greatly. If the project involves a large number of committees, as it does in a high school project, time and money can be saved by scheduling a one or two day conference between the architects, the committee members, and the consultants.

The following memorandum is an example of a report on a one-day planning conference held after the architect had interpreted, to the best of his ability, the desires of the building committee members.

FROM: Educational consultant on proposed senior high school

TO: Chairman, school building advisory committee plant

RE: Status of the plans for the new proposed senior high

It was indeed a pleasure to have an opportunity to work with the members of the School Planning Advisory Committee and with other staff members at the planning conference—and to crystallize our thinking regarding the new school plant. I am preparing this memorandum for you so that you will be able to inform the committee members as well as the superintendent, the board of education, and the architects of our action at the conference and of the status of the program to date.

I think that the meeting was highly successful; that those who participated in the planning activities should be congratulated for their interesting and helpful suggestions, particularly in this different phase of the planning, when so many decisions have to be made. I will discuss the areas considered and report the reactions of the group to the work done to date.

1. *Art*

The plans for spaces were carefully checked; they will need little change.

2. *Business Education*

The business education areas were accepted as planned; only the minor changes previously suggested are being revised by the architect as of this date.

3. *Foreign Language*

The foreign language areas were felt to be well planned; a warning was given by the chairman of the foreign language committee to take all precautions to keep this area free from disturbing sound influences.

4. *Homemaking*

The homemaking committee said that though the necessary facilities were sufficient, much reorganization would have to be done. The architect is now in the process of evaluating these suggestions and will have this material available for us at the next meeting.

5. *Industrial and Agricultural Education*

The chairman of this committee thought that careful consideration should be given to the reorientation of the shops to ease ventilation difficulties and to secure northern lighting. The architect was asked to consider the possibility of breaking the shop into two buildings and orienting individual shops in a way similar to those in the other buildings. The building as it is now planned could not be kept in one piece if it were reoriented since it would extend into the athletic areas. The committee also would like to spend some time with the architect in the near future discussing in more detail the organization within each department. Plans are being made to fill this request.

6. *Language Arts*

The language arts areas were accepted in so far as their space allocation was concerned. It was thought that the library should be redesigned in order to facilitate supervision. The suggestions are now with the architects; perhaps these changes can be made without interfering with contiguous areas.

7. *Mathematics*

The mathematics department is acceptable; suggested changes are minor.

8. *Music*

The music areas were satisfactory to the music committee; with a few exceptions, they will be designed as proposed at the planning conference (See Appendix A).

9. *Physical Education*

The men's physical education committee was quite satisfied with its indoor accommodations, but would like to plan more carefully the outdoor areas. The women's physical education program was considered to be inadequately planned; a request was made by its chairman for another meeting to explore the possibility of rearranging the space. Arrangements are being made for an additional meeting of this group.

10. *Pupil Personnel*

These areas have been placed in the administrative unit; satisfactory plans have been made to accommodate these activities.

11. *Science*

The chairman of the science committee wanted another meeting in regard to the science facilities; also that a meeting be arranged with the coordinator of the curriculum to determine whether or not adequate science facilities are available to house pupils in the new building.

12. *Social Studies*

The social studies plans were accepted with little change.

13. *Administration*

The only question arising with regard to the administrative areas was whether or not the teachers' lounge should be in it. It was thought that since no space was available the teachers' lounge would have to be included in a later addition to the high school.

14. *Mentally Retarded*

The room for mentally retarded children was checked; suggestions were recorded for necessary minor changes in it.

I suggest that provisions be made to meet with the architects and those desiring to discuss their areas. Afterward an afternoon meeting should be scheduled for committee members, administrators, and board members, in which the final room layouts will be presented to each individual group and to the board. After this is done, I think that with the exceptions of the storage and furniture areas all planning will be complete.

The architects have done excellent work in following the arrangements suggested by each department and in complying with the request of the various staff members. During the summer vacation it was impossible to obtain the necessary detailed information from the teachers; however, as a result of this last meeting there is every reason to believe that the plant will be a credit to the community and will meet its educational needs.

The follow-up of this sort of conference determines the plant's success or failure. The following example of a memorandum from the architect to the chairman of the school building advisory committee on a follow-up meeting with members of the school planning committees indicates the architect's effort to meet the educational specifications. This memorandum from the architect is concerned with an interpretation of a joint education and architect committee on planning four areas of a secondary school:

FROM: Chairman, school building advisory committee

TO: J. C. Warnecke, architect

RE: Report on planning conferences of September 2nd.

Library. The revised plans for a square-room reading space were well received; the supplementary rooms were approved for size and juxtaposition, with the exception of the textbook storage room, and the lack of a magazine room. It was recommended that the magazine room be between the textbook storage room and the librarian's office, if the mechanical room could be made smaller and the librarian's office shortened to provide more space. A request was made for high windows on the south wall to leave room for bulletin boards and high shelving space, and to relocate the charging desk nearer the entry door, and to relocate the exit door. All these suggested changes have been made on the revised plans of this date.

English. The plan as submitted was approved; questionable were the arrangements for the corrective speech facilities to be incorporated in the English department instead of in the speech arts facility, and for the sharing of the social sciences lab in the English curriculum. Instead of dividing the latter facility into two small spaces to maintain its identity in district usages, the architect proposed that the spare room in the west portion of the classroom be made available for the language arts curriculum and as teacher workspace, keeping both workspaces down to classroom size and as such available. The foreign language spaces have been put into a quiet zone, one across the court from the other; the journalism and publication rooms have been moved, as was suggested; and the mechanical space reduced to permit the corrective speech and radio speech spaces to be introduced at one end of the language arts curriculum room, as the plan was revised.

Homemaking. The areas and disposition of the spaces were satisfactory, but the detailed arrangement of the cabinet storage spaces was reviewed and specific size and use recommendations were made as noted on the plan submitted on this date.

Physical Education. The rearrangement of the gymnasiums side by side as previously revised was endorsed by the committees, with additional suggestions made regarding the apparatus room access from the boys' side, and the elimination of the end bleachers in the boys' gym in favor of folding chairs for assembly seating. The boys' locker rooms and playground facilities together with the boys' gym were approved.

The girls' gym locker room arrangement has been changed again, in accordance with the revised thinking of the committee. Structural bay modules have been changed in both girls' and boys' locker rooms to permit the girls' revision to be accomplished.

The girls' playfields have been enlarged as requested, the speech arts building shortened, the removal of the corrective speech facilities from the lobby permitting this change.

Thursday, September 8th, has been set for a subsequent meeting of the architect with the science, shop, music, administration, and library committees. On Monday, September 12th, a working session with the School Board has been set at 3:00 p.m., to review the plan to date.

APPROVING THE PLANS

When the plans are completed to the satisfaction of the architect they are submitted to the board of education or trustees for their approval. Although requirements vary from state to state, some type of approval is usually required by the state fire marshal and the state health department. Also the approval of the offices of architecture or education or both are required. Some counties and cities require approval from their planning offices before the project can be open for bids.

BIBLIOGRAPHY

Alexander, William, "Classroom Equipment in the Winnetka Schools," *School Executive*, 69:67-68 (November, 1949).

Bobbitt, B. G. and Others, "The Los Angeles Plan for Science Rooms," *Clearing House*, Vol. 27 (October, 1952), pp. 71-75.

Bollinger, Gilroy W., "Suggestions for Planning Industrial Arts Facilities," *American School and University*, Twenty-first Annual Edition. New York: American School Publishing Corporation, 1949, pp. 211-20.

Burris-Meyer, Harold and Cole, Edward C., *Theatre and Auditoriums*, *Progressive Architecture Library*, Chapter 15. New York: Reinhold Publishing Corporation, 1949.

"Business Teacher Visits the School Amid the Skyscrapers—New York's Central Commercial High School," *Business Teacher*, 1:270-71 (March, 1950).

Cocking, Walter D., "Adequate Facilities for Teachers," *School Executive*, 68:5 (June, 1948).

DeLancey, Opal H., "Twenty-Five Suggestions on Planning the One-Room Business Department," *Business Teacher*, 1:192 (March, 1950).

Finsterbach, Fred C., "Toward the Ideal General Shop," *Industrial Arts and Vocational Education*, 39:104-106 (March, 1950).

Gillies, Harry W., "Planning the School Auditorium to Serve the Community's Needs," *School Executive*, 70:19-22 (August, 1951).

Griffin, J. H., "DeLuxe Model Gym," *The Scholastic Coach*, 19:10-11 (January, 1950).

"Guide for Housing and Layout of School Shops in California," The Department, California State Department of Education (1950), pp. 3-4.

Hackett, Donald F., "Guides for School Shop Planning," *Industrial Arts and Vocational Education*, Vol. 42, No. 3 (March, 1952).

Hancock, T. S., "Pasadena School Administration Building," *American School Board Journal*, 123:46 (October, 1951).

Hanson, Abel, "Facilities for Art Experiences in General Education," *California Journal of Secondary Education*, 23:279 (May, 1948).

Heckler, R. D., "Planning and Equipping the School Lunchroom," *School Executive*, 71:93 (July, 1952).

Irwin, Ruth B., "Make Room for the Speech and Hearing Therapist," *School Executive*, 69:60-2 (September, 1949).

Kubik, Betty Martin, "Modern Planning for Business Training: The Hamilton, Ohio, D. E. Room," *Business Education World* (November, 1953).

Lee, Alta, "Space and Equipment for Homemaking Programs," Division of Vocational Education, Misc. No. 9. Washington, D.C.; U.S. Government Printing Office, 1950, p. 8.

Levin, Sol, "A Half Century of Developments in Classroom Seating," *American School Board Journal*, 121:34-36 (November, 1950).

"Modern Planning for Business Training in Georgia," Georgia Business Association, *Business Education World*, 33:220 (January, 1953).

"Movable Schoolroom Equipment," *American School Board Journal*, 121:36 (December, 1950).

Munch, Theodore W., "High School Science Facilities," *American School Board Journal*, 126:55-57 (January, 1953).

——, and Warren J. Pelton, "A Suggested Plan for a Physical Science Suite," *American School Board Journal*, (126:52) March, 1953.

National Facilities Conference, *A Guide for Planning Facilities for Athletics, Recreation, Physical and Health Education*. Washington, D.C.: American Association for Health, Physical Education and Recreation, National Education Association (1947).

Niemi, Allan L., "Housing School and Community Music Activities," *American School Board Journal*, 125:44-45 (August, 1952).

Perkins, Lawrence B., "Translating Educational Needs into Building Plans," Administrative Planning for School Programs and Plants, Proceedings, Sixteenth Annual Conference for Administrative Officers of Public and Private Schools. Chicago: University of Chicago Press, 1947, pp. 80-87.

Plan and Specification Guide. Prepared jointly by 1951-1952 School Building Committee of California Association of Public School Business Officials and the 1951-52 Education and Research Committee of the California Council of Architects.

Proceedings, Sixteenth Annual Conference for Administrative Officers of Public and Private Schools. Chicago: University of Chicago Press, 1947, pp. 80-87.

"Review of Educational Research School Plant and Equipment," The Association, National Education Association Bulletin (February, 1951), pp. 10-15.

Shaw, Archibald B., "What is a Good Classroom?" *School Executive,* 70:19-22 (July, 1951).

Shear, Bruce, "Physical Facilities for Pupil Personnel Services," *The American School Board Journal,* 120:25-27 (January, 1950).

Thomas, Orpha Mae, "Planning the School Lunchroom," *School Executive,* 72:113-120 (February, 1953).

Van Duzee, Roy P. and others, "Shop Layouts of Various Kinds," *Industrial Arts and Vocational Education,* 37:90-7 (March, 1948).

AREA RELATIONS
FOR MUSIC FACILITIES

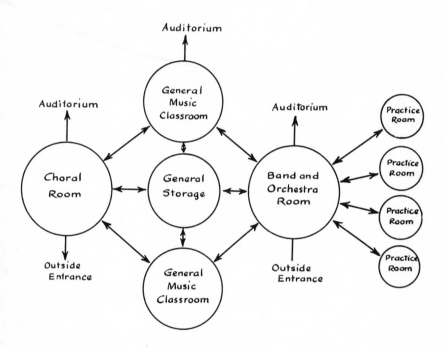

The music committee suggests area relationship and describes activities to be performed.

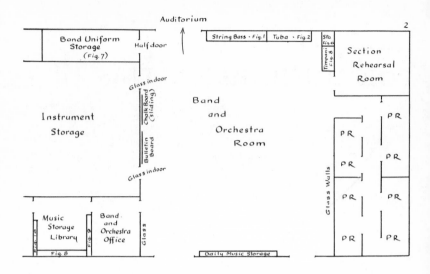

The architect presents rough area sketches as possible solutions.

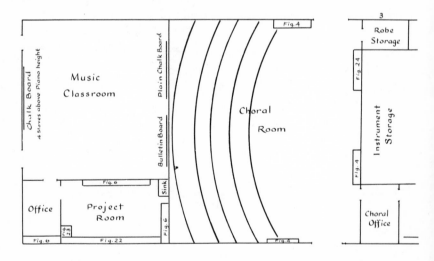

AGREEMENT
DRAWINGS
SPECIFICATIONS
NOTICE TO BIDDERS
LEGALITIES
BID OPENINGS
DISPOSITION OF BIDS
AWARDING CONTRACT
SITE PREPARATION
CONSTRUCTION
SUPERVISION OF CONSTRUCTION
CONSTRUCTION COMPLETED
FINAL INSPECTION
ACCEPTANCE OF BUILDING
FINAL PAYMENTS
SCHOOL BUILDING IN USE

CHAPTER 11

FINAL PLANNING
AND CONSTRUCTION

The final stage of planning is the ultimate construction of the building. Since the construction of a building is an extensive and technical process in and of itself, practically no school district in the United States is in a position to undertake construction with its own resources. This means that private contractors must be secured to do the job. Since building involves, as well, vast outlays of public capital, safeguards must be established to guarantee to the public that the funds are spent wisely, efficiently, and honestly. Although there are still many weaknesses inherent in the procedures for bidding for the construction of schools and other public buildings, yet fairly adequate systems have been established, and in want of better procedures, these should be carefully followed.

281

OPEN COMPETITIVE BIDDING
IS TRADITIONAL

The custom of inviting contractors to participate in open competitive bidding, when public buildings are to be constructed, is a long established American practice. The procedures, open to the public's scrutiny, relieve politicians of suspicions of favoritism. They give assurances to the taxpayers that public funds are being expended with due regard for the savings which result from competitive bidding. They present an opportunity to all qualified contractors to participate in offering proposals.

During the years there have been developed certain accepted procedures of bidding, which are based both on custom and on statute. These will be discussed briefly.

THE CONTRACT DOCUMENTS

The contractor prepares a proposal, often termed a bid, in anticipation of entering into a contractual relationship with the board. The bid, and the resulting contractual relationship, is based upon material considerations. The legal instruments expressing these considerations and relationships are termed the contract documents.

There are three contract documents. They are well identified in the following concise statement, from the professionally recognized authority, *Architectural Practice*, by Cowgill and Small:

> The contract documents consist of the Agreement, the General Conditions of the Contract, the Drawings and Specifications, including all modifications thereof incorporated in the documents before their execution. These form the contract.[1]

Important instruments usually included in the above three classifications, but sometimes treated as individual contract documents, are: the proposal of the bidder, the bid guarantee, the contractor's surety bond, and the advertisement for bids. The three basic contract documents and these other instruments will each receive brief comment.

Contract documents may be prepared and entered into with each contracting firm or with several for a single construction job. The

[1] Clinton H. Cowgill, and Ben J. Small, *Architectural Practice* (New York: Reinhold Publishing Corp., 1949, revised 1951), p. 422.

work may be done under a combined contract with a general contracting firm, which in turn sublets the mechanical and electrical
contracts. The governing board may, however, enter into separate
contracts for the general, mechanical and electrical work. It is
claimed by some that a separate contract for the cabinet work also
will result in savings to the owner.

In areas where the practice is to award separate contracts the
determining factor is usually the size of the job. An arbitrary figure
of one hundred thousand dollars is sometimes established as the
ceiling for the size jobs to be done under a single general contract.
Elliott considers that the practice of using the combined contract
is easier for administration, more economical and presents fewer
problems of work coordination.[2]

THE AGREEMENT

The *Agreement* is the most important of the three basic contract
documents. It should be prepared with great care. All information
from bid proposals or other documents should be secured directly
from the original sources, and the figures in the final form should be
rechecked as a precautionary measure.

The use of the American Institute of Architects' standard forms,
with variations to meet unusual conditions, is accepted practice.
This form is described under six headings in *Architectural Practice*
and is summarized as follows:[3]

(1) Scope of work—refers to drawings and specifications
(2) Time of completion
(3) Contract sum
(4) Progress payments—monthly payments based upon a percentage of the monetary value of the work to date less the aggregate of previous payments
(5) Acceptance of final payments—detailed requirements to be
fulfilled
(6) The contract documents—an enumeration of the documents

There is also available the American Institute of Architects' short
form. This is for small construction projects.[4]

[2] R. T. Elliott, and J. H. Corson, "Segregated vs. General Bids," *American School Board Journal*, vol. 120, No. 1 (January, 1950).
[3] *Op. cit.*, p. 195.
[4] *Ibid.*, p. 196.

THE GENERAL CONDITIONS

The *General Conditions* of the contract are supplementary to the Agreement. They are the detailed definitions and descriptions of the various responsibilities and relationships involved in the construction project. They serve as reference points in establishing responsibility as the work progresses. They have been developed into their present accepted form through years of usage and serve best when properly adapted to the specific job for which they are prepared.

Tyler observes, "The general conditions of the contract is the longest and most thorough of the contract documents."[5] Eifler discusses the general conditions under six main headings:

(1) Definitions and principles
(2) Owner's rights and liabilities
(3) Architect's rights and duties
(4) Contractor's rights and duties
(5) Insurance and bonds
(6) Arbitration[6]

The list of general conditions appearing in *Architectural Practice* has been approved by the American Institute of Architects, the Associated General Contractors of America, and other national associations concerned with construction work. A listing of these conditions here will provide something of an understanding of the breadth of coverage of this important document.[7]

1. Definitions
2. Execution, correlation and intent of documents
3. Detail drawings and instructions
4. ·Copies furnished
5. Show drawings
6. Drawings and specifications on the work
7. Ownership of drawings and models
8. Samples
9. Materials, appliances, employees

[5] James W. Tyler, "Elements in a Satisfactory School Building Contract," *American School Board Journal*, Vol. 128, No. 1 (January, 1954), p. 41.

[6] Carl Eifler, and F. W. Hosler, "A Checking List for the Contract between a Board of Education and a Building Contractor," *Thirty-Third Yearbook of the National Society for the Study of Education* (Bloomington, Ill.: School Publishing Co., 1934), pp. 281-84.

[7] *Op. cit.*, p. 213.

10. Royalties and patents
11. Surveys, permits, and regulations
12. Protection of work and property
13. Inspection of work
14. Superintendence and supervision
15. Changes in the work
16. Claims for extra cost
17. Deductions for uncompleted work
18. Delays and extension of time
19. Correction of work before final payment
20. Correction of work after final payment
21. Owner's right to do work
22. Owner's right to terminate contract
23. Contractor's right to terminate contract
24. Applications for payments
25. Certificates of payments
26. Payments withheld
27. Contractor's liability insurance
28. Owner's liability insurance
29. Fire insurance
30. Guaranty bonds
31. Drawings
32. Liens
33. Assignments
34. Mutual responsibility of contractors
35. Separate contracts
36. Subcontracts
37. Relations of contractor and subcontractor
38. Architect's status
39. Architect's decisions
40. Arbitration
41. Cash allowances
42. Use of premises
43. Cutting, patching and digging
44. Cleaning up

THE DRAWINGS AND SPECIFICATIONS

Drawings and specifications prepared by the architect provide the contractor with the instructions and information from which he constructs the building. They should be accurate, concise, understandable, sufficiently detailed and well organized. They should be prepared according to the highest professional standards.

The National Council on Schoolhouse Construction, recognizing the responsibility of the local school authorities, recommends that they exercise desirable controls through, "carefully worded definitions of what constitutes a complete set of plans and specifications at various stages of their development."[8] They further state that, "Inadequate plans and specifications result in loose irregular bidding, leading to disagreements, delays in construction and extra cost."[9]

The drawings should be prepared with such professional skill that the copies received by the contractor and his workmen will be clear and easily interpreted. There should be sufficient detail to warrant clarity, but superfluous detail should be eliminated.

The specifications are supplementary to the drawings. They explain in words what is left unexpressed in the work of the draftsman. The estimator must rely upon them to discover the kinds and qualities of materials to be used. The workman must find in them the methods he is to use in the details of construction. The supervisor of construction refers to them for testing standards that are required. A concise definition is supplied by Edwards, "Architects' specifications are written instructions distinguishing or limiting and describing in detail construction work to be undertaken."[10]

The importance of high quality specifications is generally recognized. They serve to support high quality drawings, attract the most qualified bidders, and have their own powerful effect on lowering costs. They should be accurate, detailed and well-written. "The conscientious architect of today would no more consider issuing ill-conceived specifications than he would ill-conceived drawings."[11]

THE PROPOSAL OF THE BIDDER

The *proposal of the bidder* is the legal instrument by which a contractor formally advises the board that he proposes to do the

---

[8] National Council on Schoolhouse Construction, *Guide for Planning School Plants* (Nashville, Tenn.: The Association, Peabody College, 1953), p. 20.

[9] *Encyclopedia of Educational Research*, edited by Walter S. Monroe (New York: The Macmillan Co., 1952), p. 1119.

[10] H. Griffith Edwards, *Specifications* (New York: D. Van Nostrand, 1953), p. 3.

[11] Ben J. Small, "Suggestions for Writing Architectural Specifications," *American School and University* (New York: American School Publishing Corp., Vol. 25, 1953-54), p. 181.

work, as described in the drawings and specifications, and that he is qualified and will enter into a contract should his bid be accepted.

The substance of the proposal is that the contractor (1) has examined drawings and specifications and other documents, and has visited the site; (2) agrees to do the work for a certain specified sum; (3) agrees not to withdraw his bid for a specified period after the time set for the bid opening, and guarantees such by enclosing a certified check or bid bond; (4) guarantees to complete the work within a certain number of days; and (5) agrees that the board may reject any and all bids and waive technicalities. Liquidated damages, in a specified amount, for each day of delay in the completion of the project beyond the specified completion date are often included.

THE BID GUARANTEE

The *bid guarantee*, a part of the proposal, and usually a bond or certified check, binds the contractor to enter into a contract with the board should his bid be accepted. The amount is a percentage of the sum bid, usually five or ten per cent, depending upon the accepted usage. The time is usually fifteen or thirty days. The latter is none too long when state or federal approval or both are needed.

THE CONTRACTOR'S SURETY BOND

The *contractor's surety bond*, also called the *performance bond*, is the legal instrument giving protection to the board for the contractor's faithful performance of the work described in the contract documents. It provides for reimbursement of the board for failure of the contractor to fulfill his part of the agreement. A usual clause in the call for bids states:

> The Owner shall have the right, prior to the signing of the Contract, to require the Contractor to furnish bond covering the faithful performance of the Contract, the payment of all obligations arising thereunder, in such form as the owner may prescribe and with such sureties as he may approve. If such bond is required by instructions given previous to the submission of bids, the premium shall be paid by the contractor; if subsequent thereto, it shall be paid by the Owner.[12]

12 Cowgill and Small, *op. cit.*, p. 218.

ADVERTISING FOR BIDS

The purpose of the *advertisement* is to attract a number of qualified bidders. Both the quality and cost of the building are closely related to its effectiveness. Because of its importance to public projects, certain legal requirements have been developed. The chief characteristics of the effective advertisement are: recognition of these legal requirements, inclusive nature of content, clarity of presentation, and careful timing. Each has its own peculiar importance and each contributes to the end result of securing a greater number of qualified contractors.

LEGAL REQUIREMENTS

A knowledge of the details of the *legal requirements* is a prerequisite to any preparation of advertising materials. These requirements are based on the premise that the interests of the public in the expenditure of public funds for construction purposes are best protected by the practice of open competition, and that publicity is required over a sufficiently broad area and period of time to attract proposals from an adequate number of qualified building contractors.

Legal requirements are usually specific, as for instance the use of both a recognized trade journal with wide coverage and a local newspaper, published or distributed in the local district, with the announcement appearing three times, distributed over a period of three consecutive weeks. When state and federal as well as local monies are involved, the statutes and regulations of each must be considered. It is a wise practice to rely upon local legal authorities for detailed information.

CONTENT

The *content* of the advertisement must include all of the pertinent information required by the contractor to enable him to make a decision as to whether or not he shall procure drawings and specifications upon which to make the further decision as to whether or not he shall prepare a proposal.

Details of the content include the following:

1. Name and address of the district inviting bids.
2. Time and place for bids to be submitted.
3. Classification of contractors to which the invitation is being extended—general, mechanical, electrical, or others.
4. Statement of the work to be done and the location of such work.
5. Name and address of the architect from whom drawings, specifications, and contract forms may be obtained.
6. Other locations at which the bid documents may be examined; for examples, the administration office of the school district, contractors' associations, and others.
7. Amount of deposit required for securing the drawings and specifications.
8. Statement of the right of the board to reject all bids and waive technicalities.
9. Name of the representative of the board responsible for inserting the advertisement, usually the clerk, his title and address.

Other information that is sometimes included in the advertisement includes the amounts required for bid and performance bonds, the amounts of insurance necessary, liquidated damages and time limits of the contract. These are included, however, in the *invitation document* given to the contractor with the drawings and specifications. The contractor will often advertise in various building trade journals for subcontractor bids on specific jobs. The contractor must show, with his bid, a list of subcontractors involved, and he usually cannot change subcontractors without penalty.

CLARITY OF PRESENTATION

Clarity of presentation is important. Each statement must be free of ambiguity. For instance, if the proposals are to be opened at a rural school at 8 p.m. but not to be received at the office of the architect in the city until 5 p.m., this must be stated in such way that it will not be misinterpreted by the contractor. The element of ambiguity here arises as to whether the contractor has a choice of delivering his proposal either to the office of the architect or to the meeting in the evening. If a choice is meant, which appears in this case to be logical, then it should be so stated in the advertisement.

TIME OF BID OPENING

The date, day of the week, and hour of the day of the bid opening, are all, in varying degrees, related to the resulting costs of the building. The architect, through his close contact with the building industry, generally will be able to supply favorable information upon which to make decisions. Some of the factors involved are seasonal weather conditions, competition with other building projects for labor and materials, convenience of contractors, and the stability of labor and material markets.

Seasonal weather conditions control the bidding calendar. Contractors, especially in the more northerly climates, are greatly interested in securing jobs during the months of January and February. Although this is not a hard and fast rule, it is definitely a discernible tendency. The contractor securing a job during that period is given time to prepare labor and materials for work during the good weather days ahead.

Competition with other building projects for labor and materials and for the time of the estimators of contracting firms is an important factor. Due consideration must be given to the relative size of competing projects. Contractors usually limit themselves to jobs within certain size limits. For instance, a proposed farm shop building might well be advertised for opening of bids at the same time as several multi-million dollar office and institutional buildings.

The day of the week to be selected is usually Tuesday or Thursday. There are logical reasons to support these choices, quite largely based upon custom and the convenience of the contractor. Tuesday allows him an extra day following the weekend for pencil work and for checking with suppliers of material and labor. Thursday allows two days for those unsuccessful on Tuesday to intensify their estimating efforts in finishing proposals already in process of preparation. Friday is a poor day because of the end-of-the-week letup in effort and the weekend delay.

Illustration 1.—An Example of the Content of an Advertisement for a Specific Project

CHAS. W. & JOHN A. SHAVER, ARCHITECTS
205½ SOUTH SANTA FE
SALINA, KANSAS

BULLETIN #1   Tuesday, June 7

Job #1251-A: East School Bldg., Beatrice, Nebraska
Job #1251-B: West School Bldg., Beatrice, Nebraska
Job #1251-C: Fairview School Bldg., Beatrice, Nebraska
Job #1251-D: South School Bldg., Beatrice, Nebraska

TO THE CONTRACTORS:

As authorized by the School Board, we are starting to issue to the Contractors the plans and specifications for the four (4) above-referenced buildings, for which bids will be received by the School Board, and opened publicly July 8, 1955, 2:00 P.M., C.S.T. at the Little Theatre in the High School building, Beatrice, Nebraska.

Separate plans and specifications are prepared for each of the 4 buildings; and the Contractors may bid on any one building, or on two or more buildings; and may bid on all departments of the work if they choose, or separately on (1) GENERAL CONSTRUCTION, or (2) ELECTRICAL WORK, or (3) PLUMBING, HEATING & VENTILATION.

#1251-A, East School covers approx. 29,003 sq. ft., & has 12 Class R'ms.

#1251-B, West School covers approx. 22,332 sq. ft., & has 8 Class R'ms.

#1251-C, Fairview School covers approx. 28,029 sq. ft., & has 12 Class R'ms.

#1251-D, South School covers approx. 27,711 sq. ft., & has 12 Class R'ms.

All 4 buildings are 1-story, of similar construction, with Class Rooms, Kindergarten, Multi-purpose Room, Hot-Lunch facilities, Offices, Library, Health Room, Toilets, and Boiler Room (Ground Floor); concrete floors on grade; concrete lift-slab roof (alternate on conventional poured-in-place); brick exterior facing and Haydite back-up; masonry interior walls; steel windows, metal door frames; wood doors and misc. millwork; acoustical tile ceilings; pitch-&-gravel roofing. Electric wiring and lighting fixtures. Plumbing for Toilets, Kitchen, and Class Room sinks. Gas-fired hot water heating, with convectors, unit ventilators, air-supply units, and induction units.

Please advise us promptly if you will place a bid on one or more of these buildings so that we can send you the plans and specifications. To assist the Contractors in obtaining quotations on materials we are filing plans and specifications on all 4 buildings at the nine following offices: Lincoln Builders' Bureau, 418 Trust Bldg., Lincoln 8, Nebr.; Hastings Chamber of Commerce, Hastings, Nebr.; Omaha Builders' Exchange, 2565 St. Marys Ave., Omaha 2, Nebr.; Dodge Reports, 404 Sunderland Bldg., Omaha 2, Nebr.; Dodge Reports, 823 Walnut, Kansas City, Mo.; Dodge Reports, Derby Bldg., Wichita, Kansas; Builders' Ass'n., 906 Grand Ave., Kansas

City, Mo.; Construction News, Insurance Bldg., Topeka, Ks.; and Hutchinson Chamber of Commerce, Hutchinson, Kansas. We will notify many material companies where the plans are filed, and give them a list of the bidders, so we suggest you reply promptly to this Bulletin, if you intend to bid, so that your name will be on the list to receive quotations.

When you reply to this Bulletin, please advise which building or buildings you intend to bid, and send us your deposit check in the amount of $40.00 for each set of plans and specifications requested ($160.00 for a set of all 4 bldgs.). The full $40.00 deposit will be returned to bidder for each building on which you submit a bid and return the plans. If a bid is not submitted, and the plans returned, $25.00 of the deposit will be retained by the Architects for each such set, to cover the cost of reproduction and handling.

Anticipating your prompt reply, we are
Cordially yours,
CHAS. W. & JOHN A. SHAVER, ARCHITECTS
By: /s/   Chas. W. Shaver
CWS/hae
CC: Wm. M. Staerkel, Sup't of Schools, & Sec'y of Board, 213 N. 5th, Beatrice, Nebraska
     W. W. Cook, Pres. of School Board, c/o Beatrice National Bank, Beatrice, Nebraska

Illustration 2.—Partial List of Contractors Notified Personally

CHAS. W. & JOHN A. SHAVER, ARCHITECTS
205½ SOUTH SANTA FE
SALINA, KANSAS

Sheet 1 of 3

(4 School Bldgs., Beatrice, Nebr.)
#1251-A, B, C, D.
June 7, 1955

The attached Bulletin #1 sent to the following:

GENERAL CONTRACTORS

E. J. Meinen Constr. Co., Hebron, Nebraska
Korshoj Constr. Co., Blair, Nebraska
Kingery Construction Co., 1941 Y Street, Lincoln 3, Nebraska
Geo. C. Cook Constr. Co., 1740 Vine Street, Lincoln, Nebraska
Ernest Rokahr & Sons Constr. Co., 2241 Y Street, Lincoln, Nebraska
Assenmacher Construction Co., 625 N. 11th St., Lincoln, Nebraska
Olson Construction Co., 410 S. 7th, Lincoln, Nebraska
Westcott & Bowen, 1400 Sunburst Lane, Lincoln, Nebraska

Roberts Construction Co., 1018 Trust Bldg., Lincoln, Nebraska
Wilson Construction Co., Lincoln, Nebraska
Beall Constr. Co., Box 67, College View Sta. 6, Lincoln, Nebraska

PLUMBING AND HEATING CONTRACTORS

Natking & Co., (Pbg. & Htg.), 1400 Furnas St., Lincoln 8, Nebraska
Wentz Pbg. & Htg. Co., Lincoln, Nebraska
American Pbg. & Htg. Co., 1537 P St., Lincoln, Nebraska
Fay W. Smith Pbg. & Htg. Co., 642 West A St., Lincoln, Nebr.
Ace Pbg. & Htg. Co., 2241 Y St., Lincoln, Nebr.
John Anderson Co., (Pbg. & Htg.), 709 S. 24th St., Omaha, Nebr.
J. J. Hanighen Pbg. & Htg. Co., 915 N. 20th St., Omaha, Nebraska
Quality Pbg. & Htg. Co., 1810 Military Ave., Omaha, Nebr.
O'Hara Pbg. & Htg. Co., 802 E. 12th St., Grand Island, Nebr.

ELECTRICAL CONTRACTORS

A. B. C. Electric Co., 2348 N. Street, Lincoln, Nebraska
Commonwealth Elec. Co., Box 2067, Lincoln, Nebraska
Lester & Schenk Elec. Co., N.W. Corner of Square, Fairbury, Nebr.
Stull Electric Co., 513 Fourth Street, Fairbury, Nebr.
Sterling Electric Company, 2429 Farnum St., Omaha, Nebr.
Snyder Elec. Co., Omaha, Nebraska
Dodson Electric Co., Douglas at Saddle Creek Road, Omaha 3, Nebr.
Gus H. Mettenbrink Elec. Co., 221 E. 10th St., Grand Island, Nebr.
Roberts Electric Co., 8 E. 19th St., Kearney, Nebr.

OPENING OF BIDS

Procedure

The procedure for the opening of bids has been established through longe usage. The very essence of the ceremony is openness, fairness, and high ethical standards. It is an ironclad professional and legal rule that no bid be opened before the appointed time, even though it be delivered to the architect or school authorities many hours previously.

The place and time of day shall be those stated in the advertisement. The place is usually the office of the architect or the administration unit of the school district. If it is the former, the time is usually in the afternoon, perhaps 2 o'clock; in the school district, it is usually in the evening, perhaps 8 o'clock.

TABLE 9

BID SUMMARY—HILLSDALE HIGH SCHOOL, SAN MATEO UNION HIGH SCHOOL DISTRICT

BID OPENING
8:00 P.M.
May 26

John Lyon Reid, A.I.A., Architect
1069 Market Street
San Francisco 3, Calif.

General Contractor	Base Bid	Unit Prices		Paving		Alternate Bids					
		No. 1 Forming	No. 2 Conc.	No. 3 Add	Deduct	No. 1 Delete Auditorium	No. 2 Subst. Type X Partitions	No. 3 Subst. Metal Ext. Panels	No. 4 Bus Loading Shelter & Storage Shed	No. 5A Public Address System	No. 5B Reduce Alt. 5A % Audit.
James Barnes Const. Co.	$3,846,000	$4.50	$16.00	25¢	18¢	—125M	—19M	+55M	+16M	+18,000	—2,700
Robert E. McKee	$3,614,600	2.50	30.00	20¢	16¢	—136,500	—26M	+53M	+16,700	+19,300	—2,700
Rothschild, Raffin & Weirick	$3,607,500	2.00	35.00	20¢	14¢	—153M	—29M	+50,500	+13,500	+18,400	—2,700
E. H. Moore	$3,633,000	.74	22.00	20¢	20¢	—160M	—20M	+50M	+13M	+17,520	—3,400
Morris Daley & Parrish Bros.	$3,748,793	1.75	45.00	20¢	14¢	—151,530	—26,955	+50,781	+13,651	+19,311	—2,700
Williams & Burrows	$3,653,600	.85	33.00	19¢	16¢	—143M	—26M	+51M	+15M	+18,000	—2,700
M & K Const. Co.	DID NOT SUBMIT BID										
Monson Bros.	$3,685,000	1.30	45.00	20¢	17¢	—150,800	—27M	+50M	+15,100	+19,000	—2,700

294

The principals involved are members of the board of education, representatives of the administration staff, representatives from the architect's staff and representatives from the firms presenting bids. It is a public meeting and others, including the press, may attend. All of the principals are provided with tabulation sheets listing all of the bidders and with appropriate spaces for any bid figures that will be read. Chart No. I is a reproduction of the tabulation sheet used to record the bids submitted for the construction of the proposed Hillsdale High School.

The meeting is called to order by the chairman of the board or by a designated representative promptly at the hour as advertised. The bids are opened by a representative of the architectural firm or by a representative of the school district. If opened by the former, the district representative rechecks the bid figures and accuracy of the bid bond, and vice versa. Unless all bids are combined with the base bid, the usual order of opening is general, mechanical, electrical. Bid figures should be read clearly and slowly so that all those interested may be able to make correct tabulations. Any request to reread a figure should be treated courteously. When only the base bid is read, the usual procedure is to read the names of subcontractors associated with low base bidder. Should any irregularity appear regarding the bid or the bid bond it should be noted at the time so that all present may receive the information.

FIGURE 63. A bid opening (*Courtesy John C. Warnecke*).

Illustration No. 3.—List of Successful Bidders

CHAS. W. & JOHN A. SHAVER, ARCHITECTS

205½ SOUTH SANTA FE

SALINA, KANSAS

BULLETIN #5   July 12

ELEMENTARY SCHOOL BUILDINGS, BEATRICE, NEBRASKA

Job. No. 1251-A: East School   1251-C: Fairview School
1251-B: West School   1251-D: South School

To: The Contractors who filed a bid on the above-referenced building, and to the construction newspapers and reporting offices.

Bids on the above-referenced buildings were opened July 8, 1955 as scheduled; and the School Board has awarded contracts on all four buildings to the lowest bidders as follows:

Lift-slab operation to Skyhook Lift Slab Corp., 810 Rialto Bldg., Kansas City, Mo.

GENERAL CONSTRUCTION to Johnson Bros. Constr. Co., P.O. Box 457, Salina, Kansas

PBG., HTG. & VENTILATION to Anderson Bros. Pbg. & Htg. Co., P.O. Box 305, Kearney, Nebraska

ELECTRICAL WORK to Crawford Elec. Co., 121 W. 8th St., North Platte, Nebraska

The following base bids were received (on all 4 bldgs., or 1 bldg., as shown):

LIFT-SLAB Operation:

Skyhook Lift Slab Corp., K.C., Mo. .... $ 31,616.00

GENERAL CONSTRUCTION:

Johnson Bros. Constr. Co., Salina, Ks. (4 bldgs.) ..	848,689.00
M. K. Eby Constr. Co., Wichita, Ks. (4 bldgs.)	914,856.00
Frank Quinlan Constr. Co., K.C., Mo. (4 bldgs.) ..	1,086,300.00
Westcott-Bowen Constr. Co., Lincoln, Nebr. (4 bldgs.)	935,687.00
L. R. Foy Constr. Co., Hutchinson, Ks. (4 bldgs.) .	1,095,660.00
Hunter & Lundberg Constr. Co., Manhattan, Ks. (4 bldgs.)	1,013,297.00
Busboom & Rauh, Salina, Kansas (4 bldgs.)	1,055,045.00
Parsons Constr. Co., Omaha, Nebr. (4 bldgs.)	971,500.00
Olson Constr. Co., Lincoln, Nebr. (4 bldgs.)	1,093,068.00
D. C. Bass & Sons Constr. Co., Enid, Okla. (Bldg. #1251-C only) .	254,883.00
Pat Hutson Constr. Co., Fairbury, Nebr. (Bldg. #1251-B only)	213,000.00

PBG., HTG. & VENTILATION:

Anderson Bros.
    Pbg. & Htg. Co., Kearney, Nebr. (4 bldgs.) 169,122.00
Geo. H. Wentz
    Pbg. & Htg. Co., Lincoln, Nebr. (4 bldgs.) 186,333.00
B. & R. Plumbing Co., Beatrice, Nebr. (4 bldgs.) ..   207,365.00
Robertson Pbg. & Htg. Co., Salina, Ks. (4 bldgs.) ..   207,017.00
Natkin & Co., Omaha, Nebraska (4 bldgs.) 208,096.00
Davidson Pbg. Co., Wichita, Ks. (4 bldgs.) 204,066.00
Parry Pbg. Co.,
    Marysville, Ks. (Bldg. #1251-A only) 48,509.00

ELECTRICAL WORK:

Crawford Electric Co.,
    North Platte, Nebr. (4 bldgs.) 47,975.00
Shrake Elec. Co., Topeka, Kansas (4 bldgs.) 66,266.00
Barber & Sebby Elec. Co.,
    Beatrice, Nebr. (4 bldgs.) 58,960.00
Commonwealth Elec. Co.,
    Lincoln, Nebr. (4 bldgs.) 83,000.00
Lester & Schenk Elec. Co.,
    Fairbury, Nebr. (4 bldgs.) 67,127.00
Williamson Elec. Co.,
    Manhattan, Ks. (4 bldgs.) 69,422.00
Behrens Elec. Co., Schuyler, Nebr. (4 bldgs.) 72,063.00
A. B. C. Elec. Co., Lincoln, Nebr. (4 bldgs.) 71,000.00
Erickson Elec. Co.,
    Holdrege, Nebr. (4 bldgs.) 61,897.00
E. W. Elec. Co., Fremont, Nebr. (4 bldgs.) 67,391.00
John G. Cook Elec. Co.,
    Beatrice, Nebr. (Bldg. #1251-D only) 13,178.21
Mason Elec. Co.,
    Lincoln, Nebr. (Bldg. #1251-A only) 15,324.00

To all except the successful bidders, we are returning herewith the Bid Bond submitted with bid; and on behalf of the School Board we want to thank all of the bidders for having submitted their bid.

All except the successful bidders should promptly return the plans and specifications to the Architects; then the deposit check or refundable portion of same will be returned by the Architects. The deposit checks of the successful bidders are being returned herewith.

Cordially yours,
    CHAS. W. & JOHN A. SHAVER, ARCHITECTS
      By: /s/ Chas. W. Shaver
CWS/djb

cc: W. W. Cook, Pres. of School Board
    Wm. M. Staerkel, Sec'y of School Board

DISPOSITION OF THE BIDS

At the conclusion of the opening of all bids it is customary for the chairman to express his appreciation to the contractors for having submitted proposals. This courtesy is important as the preparation of each proposal represents a considerable cost and effort. It is customary, also, for the board to take the bids under advisement rather than to make efforts to arrive at an immediate selection. There should be ample time for careful studies by the architect and the school officials. This ordinarily requires a second meeting.

The bid proposals are important legal documents and as such should receive proper protection for future reference. It should be definitely decided as to who shall have possession of them. It is logical for the architect to assume such responsibility.

INFORMATION TO THE PUBLIC

The general public is entitled to full information regarding the bid opening. Representatives of the press will likely be present at the meeting and secure direct information then. Others interested will contact the architect and the office of the school district. Information requested will usually include the names of the bidders and sums bid, including alternates if any, and action of the board as to disposition.

SELECTION OF THE CONTRACTOR

The selection of the contractor rests within the powers of the local board when only local funds are used. State and federal approvals are necessary when funds from these sources are involved. The selection is determined from a careful study, by the architect and school authorities, of the bids submitted and of the qualifications of the contractors submitting them. *American School Buildings* lists as qualifications for the contractor, "Financial adequacy, suitable construction equipment, competent personnel, size and quality of recently completed projects."[13] These must receive due consideration in the over-all study.

[13] American Association of School Administrators, *American School Buildings*, Twenty-seventh Yearbook (Washington, D.C.: The Association, a department of the National Education Association, 1949), p. 324.

The board further has the power to refuse to accept bids that do not meet the conditions as prescribed. Garber notes that, "Since the Commission would have the right to prescribe the conditions upon which bids would be accepted, it would also have the right to refuse to accept any bids not in substantial conformity therewith."[14]

The prime basis, however, for the selection is the sum bid in relation to those proposed by other contractors. The board usually selects the low bidder. Should it make any other selection it must be for reasons that it is able to defend. Such a decision should be made only after careful deliberation and upon legal advice. Since bonding companies employ fairly rigid standards in the granting of performance bonds, the presentation of such a bond by a contractor is evidence of his having demonstrated his ability to perform adequately in the past. The requirement of the bond further protects the school district in the event that the contractor defaults.

CONCLUDING THE CONTRACTUAL AGREEMENT

The details of concluding the contractual agreement are important because of their legal significance. Three copies each of the agreement, the conditions and the drawings and specifications should be signed by an authorized official from the board and the contracting firm. These copies, when signed, are to be delivered to the board, contractor, and architect.

Prior to the affixing of signatures, each of the documents should be carefully examined as to the accuracy of its content and authenticity. The signatures should be checked as to correct placement. Each of the drawings should be signed. The complete signed sets should each be properly stored in a safe place for future reference.

CONSTRUCTING THE PLANT

After three copies each of the agreement, the conditions, the drawings, and the specifications are signed and delivered to the board, the architect, and the contractor, the architect orders the

---

[14] Lee O. Garber, "Legal Pointers in Letting Building Contracts," *Nation's Schools,* Vol. 53, No. 3 (March, 1954), pp. 53-54.

contractor to proceed with construction. The notice to proceed states an exact starting date and repeats the time allowed for the job. The final drawings and specifications are a *part of the contract,* not a guide. They must be followed with the same precision as any other part of the contract and are subject to interpretation only to the extent of determining "job conditions," "workmanlike construction," "generally accepted practice," and so forth. Any actual deviation must be authorized by the architect, who in most cases will protect himself and the owner by issuing a descriptive "Change Order" whether or not any change in cost is involved.

Illustration No. 4—Architect's Notice to Contractor to Proceed with Construction

JOHN CARL WARNECKE   A.I.A.   ARCHITECT

507 Howard Street
San Francisco 5, California
Telephone Yukon 2-6393
April 2

Mr. Herbert E. Brown
P.O. Box 100
Berkeley, California

Re: Hillcrest Junior High School

Dear Mr. Brown:

Referring to official notification received by us from the Berkeley Board of Education, pertaining to award of contract to you on above mentioned project dated March 22, 1955, we hereby direct you to start work immediately. This project is to be completed on or before April 1, 1956.

Before commencing work the City Building Inspector requires that you file a set of plans with his office. A permit will be issued to you without fee.

As requested in our "Cooperative Procedure Between Architect and the Contractor," which we recently mailed to you, may we remind you to inform us of the person in your organization whom you have designated to act as your representative.

All letters to our office shall be directed to attention of C. H. Arras. Mr. Albert B. Johnson has been designated by the Board of Education to act as Job Inspector.

The following persons in the office of our consulting engineer, G. M. Simonson, are to be consulted regarding mechanical information:

Mr. D. Footer for heating and ventilating work
Mr. Frank Alexander for electrical work

As soon as telephone service has been established at your job office, please inform us of the number.

Very truly yours,

JOHN CARL WARNECKE, A.I.A.

/s/

C. H. Arras

The job commences when all required legal papers have been completed and there is a physical "breaking of the ground," which may take the form of a public ceremony in which certain public or school officials take part. The ground breaking ceremony is a good public relations move, which not only serves to inform the public of the progress of the building program, but also makes possible its wide participation in the beginning of the project. The press and representatives of other communication media should be involved in planning this ceremony in order to insure the fullest possible coverage of the event.

After the ground breaking ceremony, the layout is made on the basis of the services of a professional surveyor. It is common prac-

FIGURE 64. Ground-breaking ceremony (*Courtesy Inglewood Unified School District, Inglewood, Calif.*).

tice to employ the services of the same surveyor who did the initial layout work since he has become familiar with the site and the general needs.

Following this layout, excavation work is done by earth-moving equipment. There are two types of foundation work for which excavation is necessary. The first of these is a pour against dirt and the second is a pour within wooden or metal forms. In either case reinforcing steel is used. These reinforcing bars are installed by tyers. Prior to the actual pouring of concrete all mechanical subcontractors must place any openings for later installation of various kinds of lines.

Also prior to the actual pouring of concrete, soil borings should be taken to determine the nature of the supporting materials and to determine load requirements on the concrete castings. Such borings should be taken before structural design is commenced as they influence it directly. In some cases where questionable conditions exist, borings may even be taken before the site is purchased in an attempt to foresee unusual foundation costs. This information is used in determining the footing designed and the required strength of the concrete. There must be an analysis of the local aggregate, testing of the actual mixes, the adoption of a mixed design (the recipe for the mix which provides for certain proportions of sand, gravel, cement, and so forth).

During the actual pouring of concrete, samples are taken and consistently tested as shown in the sample laboratory certificate, Illustration 5.

During much of the initial work, and preceding some of it, grading and general site preparation is done. In case of a rough or hilly site considerable grading has to be done prior to any excavation and concrete work, but in other cases it is possible to do the two different jobs more or less simultaneously.

After the foundation and initial concrete work is done, the framing is begun. In the particular job from which this sequence was derived construction was frame stucco on slab. In other types of construction, such as brick or reinforced concrete, the steps would be similar. The first framing job is the installation of the mud sills followed by stud walls and ceiling joists and rafters. Two types of sheathing which are commonly used are diagonal sheathing and plywood sheathing, although there are other materials which are readily usable for this purpose.

*Illustration No. 5—A Typical Laboratory Certificate
of Concrete Mix*

LABORATORY CERTIFICATE

JOHN DOE & CO., INC.

Testing Laboratory

Report to:
Jones and Jones, Architects

	Date Received:	Specimen:
Date: March 12, 1955	2-7,14-55	Concrete Cylinders, 6" x 12"

Elmwood Junior High School	Shop Building Slab	Covered Walkway of Shop Building
Mix No. 384	COPY	COPY

	JH-121A	JH-121B	JH-126A	JH-126B
LABORATORY NUMBER	29968	29969	30028	30029
Date Cast	2-2-55	2-2-55	2-8-55	2-8-55
Date Tested	2-9-55	3-2-55	2-15-55	3-8-55
Age at Test	7 days	28 days	7 days	28 days
Slump	6"	6"	4"	4"
Wt. Cylinder, Lbs.				
Dimensions	5⅞" x 12"	5⅞" x 12"	5⅞" x 12"	5⅞" x 12"
Area Sq. In.	27.1	27.1	27.1	27.1
Ult. Strength	46400	92300*	46000	77500*
Ult. Strength Lbs. Sq. In. ..	1712	3405	1697	2859
Fracture	Concentric	Concentric	Concentric	Concentric

* Meets specifications for 28-day test	Fails to meet specifications for 28-day test	No strength requirements given	Cast by our Inspector at job site	Cast by others

2CC—State Division of Architecture
CC—Rivett & Steele, Engineers
CC—Stone & Mortar, Contractors
CC—George Watson, Inspector

Respectfully submitted,
JOHN DOE & CO., INC.
By ——————————

After the sheathing is completed and the roofing applied, paper and wire or other bonding materials are installed before the application of the exterior surface materials, and finally the exterior trim.

Interior walls may be of many different materials. Plaster or a dry wall construction such as plywood or sheetrock are common. After the installation of the interior walls, the interior millwork and trim are installed. This includes such things as special cases, window and door trim, and special equipment such as chalkboard, tackboard and map rail. The flooring is installed last. Again, it may be of many different kinds including clay tile, resilient tile, wood, concrete aggregate, and other kinds.

Mechanical installations which are made by separate trades are installed some time simultaneously with other work but are here treated separately because of the difference in personnel involved. The plumbing would include storm drains and sewer lines as the first installed items. The house sewer lines are usually installed under the slab and consequently must be done prior to the pouring of the slab. House water lines, usually copper, may be installed as overhead lines. Last steps for the plumbers would be the installation of downspouts on the building, and fixtures and trim within the building.

The second mechanical group to be involved is the heating and ventilating contractors. Since some school jobs make use of radiant floor heating, the first task for the heating and ventilating crew is the laying of coils within the slab and the installation of manifolds with which to balance the system. Forced air installations providing for ventilation, heating, and (or) cooling will require a different priority since these installations will often become an integral part of the building framework. The installation of the boiler and controls is made during the regular work sequence.

The third of the mechanical installations is the electrical. The first major job for electricians is the installation of the under slab conduit followed by the framing of conduit and panel boxes. Service transformers are then installed with the last job being the actual wire pulling through the conduit and installation of light fixtures. Electricians also install the clock system, the speaker system, the fire alarm system, and the intercommunication and interbuilding phones.

During the final work stages painters do the exterior and interior painting, and the cleanup crew eliminates the scrap and waste materials. At the same time finish grading is done and landscaping work begun. Final paving is one of the last jobs.

At this time there is a completion inspection, at which time a punch list (consisting of a list of odds and ends yet to be done) is compiled. After this final inspection the board of directors authorizes the job acceptance and the recording of a notice of completion which establishes the legal finish of the job. However, there is a lien or waiting period during which time any claims against the job must be filed. At the end of the lien period final payment is released to the contractors.

One of the most important men on the actual construction job is the building inspector who represents the owner. He is sometimes called the clerk of the works.

THE BUILDING INSPECTOR

Adequate, conscientious, and intelligent inspection is necessary from the ground breaking to the dedication if maximum benefits are to be realized. The importance of adequate inspection cannot be overemphasized. Poor inspection can nullify the efforts of the architect to obtain a sturdy, safe, attractive, and useful building.

The inspector is an employee of the school district but generally acts under the direction of the architect. He is usually required to make periodical verified reports certifying that he has personal knowledge that all work has been performed strictly in accordance with the plans and specifications. Continuous inspection by him means his complete supervision of every part of the work. Concrete or brick work, which can be appraised only as it is placed, will require the constant presence of the inspector. Other types of work which can be completely studied after the work is installed may be carried on while the inspector is not present, but in every case the inspector must personally consider every part of the work.

Since the inspector need not hold a special certificate, the job is subject to pressure groups and local politics. Much could be written about unfortunate happenings that have resulted because of local personal interests being placed ahead of proven competencies when the inspector was selected for a school job. Although it is difficult to arrive at specific training and experience requirements for the job, the following are suggested as minimum:

1. He should be not less than twenty-five years old.
2. He should have had at least three years of experience in construction work of a type similar to that for which he is being assigned.
3. He should have a thorough knowledge of building materials and construction procedures.
4. He should have the ability to read and understand plans and specifications of all sorts.

FIGURE 65. The building inspector (*Courtesy Walnut Creek (Calif.) School District*).

306

The inspector serves as the "eyes" of the school board and the architect to make sure that the design is carried out as planned. He must be alert in inspecting structural phases and must give careful attention to all of the finished work, with particular emphasis on the mechanical and electrical systems.

The inspector must do more than report mistakes. He must be so well acquainted with the plans and specifications that he can anticipate costly and time-consuming mistakes and foresee bottlenecks due to a delayed delivery of material or an improper scheduling of the work. The good inspector is an important member of the team, necessary to insure a smoothly running construction job, a safe and properly constructed building, and an "on schedule" delivery of an urgently needed school.

The inspector, along with the contractor, decides on a percentage of the completion of various jobs on a month-to-month basis. These statements of percentage of completion then go to the architect for certification, thence to the board of education who authorizes payment. From the board the statement goes to the custodian of school funds who draws a warrant for payment to the general contractor. There is always a percentage of each payment withheld until the final acceptance of the plant. The general contractor pays the sub-contractors on a similar basis.

BIBLIOGRAPHY

Barbour, Julius E., "The Selection and Instruction of Public School Custodians in Selected School Systems," Doctor's thesis. Lansing: Michigan State College, 1954. Abstract: Dissertation Abstracts 14:1969-70; No. 11, 1954.

Carpenter, W. W. and Others, Schoolhouse Planning and Construction. Publication No. 5, 1950. Jefferson City, Mo.: Missouri State Department of Education, 1946.

Cowgill, Clinton H. and Ben J. Small, Architectural Practice. New York: Reinhold Printing Co., 1949, revised 1951.

Cyr, Frank W. and Henry H. Linn, Planning Rural Community School Buildings. New York: Bureau of Publications, Teachers College, Columbia University, 1949.

Eifler, Carl and F. W. Hosler, "A Checking List for the Contract between a Board of Education and a Building Contractor," Thirty-Third Yearbook of the National Society for the Study of Education. Bloomington, Illinois: School Publishing Co., 1934, pp. 277-84.

Elliott, R. T. and J. H. Corson, "Segregated vs. General Bids," *American School Board Journal*, Vol. 120, No. 1 (January, 1950).

Garber, Lee O., "Legal Points in Letting Building Contracts," *Nation's Schools*, Vol. 53, No. 3 (March, 1954), pp. 53-54.

Haggard, Francis, "Make No Little Plans," *School Management*, 19:4-6 (June, 1950).

"Letting of Building Contracts by School Districts," *California Schools* (October, 1951).

National Council on Schoolhouse Construction, *Guide for Planning School Plants*. Nashville, Tennessee: George Peabody College for Teachers, 1949.

Nelson, Thomas L., "A Significant School Building Bid Case," *American School Board Journal*, 129:5 (November, 1954), pp. 31-88.

Oregon State Department of Public Instruction, *Manual for School Building Construction*. Salem, Oregon: Superintendent of Public Instruction, 1947.

Parker, William S., "School Building Contracts," *American School Board Journal*, 128:5 (May, 1954), p. 70.

Roach, Stephen F., "School Board Members and Construction Contractor's Bonds," *American School Board Journal*, 128:1 (January, 1954), pp. 58-59.

School Planning Conferences, School Planning Laboratory, School of Education, Stanford University Press, Stanford, California (1952).

Small, Ben J., "Suggestions for Writing Architectural Specifications," *American School and University*. New York: American School Publishing Corporation, Vol. 25, 1953-54, pp. 181-84.

Tyler, James W., "Elements in a Satisfactory School Building Contract," *American School Board Journal*, Vol. 128, No. 1 (January, (1954), pp. 40-41, 92.

Wilson, Russell E., *Flexible Classrooms*. Detroit: Carter Publishing Company, March, 1953.

CHAPTER 12

THE
NEW SCHOOL

Since school officials usually endeavor to provide the best possible facilities for the learning of those who are to live in the newly created school environment, an attempt should be made to acquaint these people—the staff, the students, and the others who use the plant —with the nature of the facilities and school and their operation and maintenance. New inventions and innovations involving existing ideas by architects, engineers, and manufacturers have led to a more scientific approach to the ways of improving the learning environment. With these advancements complex problems arise, since many of the new ideas are complicated and difficult to understand. It follows that a better understanding of the total plant is needed. Maximum performance of all installations will only be realized if those to whom they are entrusted are thoroughly informed as to their function and proper operation.

INFORMATION MUST BE GIVEN
TO PERSONNEL

Among those who need to have more information about the planning of the plant and its operation and maintenance after the construction is completed are the teachers, the administrators and board of trustees, the noncertificated personnel, the students, and the many community groups who use the school facilities. For each of these groups orientation lectures giving specific instructions should be held to explain the use of the plant and its equipment. In addition to this instruction and information, particular consideration should be given to the following aspects of the educational program:

1. The plant plan and program.
2. The school site and the grounds.
3. The school organization, equipment, and facilities.
4. The community-school facilities and their availability to, and use by, groups within the community.
5. The general school facilities.
6. The service facilities.
7. School plant safety.
8. Acoustical, audio-visual, and custodial facilities.
9. Others, as the individual community warrants.

INSERVICE AND ORIENTATION TECHNIQUES

Administrators and Board of Trustees

During the period of construction of the school plant, the chief administrators and the members of the board of trustees are close to the actual construction. They are trusted with the responsibility for a finished structure that meets the requirements set forth in the specifications. However, much of their approval of the construction has been based upon the recommendation of a number of specialists. The end product delivered to the board is often a surprise package, for few people can visualize the completed school plant even though they have been in fairly close contact with its many parts.

Final acceptance of the school plant is accomplished by the board's approval of the job. Inspection of the entire plant, accompanied by the specialists who were responsible for the construction, results in a better understanding by the board of the new plant. This inspection presents an opportunity for the board and the administration to obtain a preview of the total structure and to become informed of the specific advantages and peculiarities of the plant, since they will be asked to comment on these features during the dedication ceremony or on other occasions during which the public seeks information about the plant. Knowledge of certain specifics, such as natural or artificial light control and acoustical treatments, will be of considerable help to the administrator and the board in giving explanations to interested groups as well as in satisfying themselves as to the over-all usability and construction of the plant.

The Faculty

Faculty members probably share a greater responsibility for the wide acceptance or rejection of a school plant than any other group. The new plant will be their home away from home and for some, the only professional home they will ever have. Its objectionable features, if any, should be laid before all who care to listen. Few things bother a teacher more than classroom or overall plant features that hinder his instructional program. Yet when the program is helped there is no one in the entire organization or community who is so lavish with praise for a satisfactory teaching environment than the professional educator.

The new plant will not be a surprise to many of the teachers who have participated in the preparation of its educational specifications. Many architects prepare preliminary isometric sketches to help the professional staff visualize the completed classroom and the general orientation of the building before the final drawings are prepared. However, there is often a wide gap between what the staff members visualize and what they view as they inspect the new plant. Many of the staff members assigned to the plant will have had little if any contact with the building and grounds up to the time of its occupancy. This necessitates an orientation period to insure their full realization and understanding of the plant.

The architect and his team of specialists can assist the staff members greatly if, during this orientation period, they explain in detail specific areas as they affect the learning environment. The number of meetings necessary will vary with the size of the groups. Instruction and orientation can best be presented to groups not exceeding twenty in number. Specifics discussed usually include ventilation, temperature control, natural and artificial lighting control, color and surface reflectancies, furniture, storage spaces, chalkboard care, efficient use of communication systems, and so forth. The staff members should be made to feel at home, and given sufficient competencies in caring for and understanding their new home.

Classified Personnel

Clerks, secretaries, cafeteria workers, bus drivers, and other classified personnel should be given a general orientation to the plant followed by a specific orientation to the areas of the plant with which they will be concerned. Instruction should be similar to that given certificated personnel.

Custodians will have to have detailed and extensive instructions on the total plant. The architect should prepare a mechanical chart for the custodians showing the locations, the operations, and the service mechanisms of the various areas and pieces of equipment. Actual and detailed instruction should be given by the specialists in the area. For example, operation of boilers and heating and ventilating controls should be given by either the factory representative or by representatives from the architect's staff. Drawings showing the location of facilities and controls should be explained to the custodians and should be filed where they can have ready access to them.

Although it is the district's responsibility to provide trained custodians for the operation of the school plant, it is to the advantage of the architect to assure himself that these custodians know how to properly care for the various materials and equipment in the new school. Floors, blackboards, and control systems are examples of items that can be damaged by an inexperienced custodian.

Students

Students should be given an orientation to the building, with an explanation of its multiple facets. This can take the form of a rapid guided tour through the new plant during the early days of its occupancy. Teachers should be prepared to give students instruction in the use and care of the facilities in each classroom. Leaders of the student government should have detailed information about the construction so that they can help other students realize their responsibilities in the care of the plant.

The Community

Probably the only mass formal orientation of the public generally to the new plant will be at the dedication ceremony, at which brochures explaining facets of the plant are distributed on guided tours. The plant can be better explained at open houses and other public gatherings.

Operating manuals are often prepared by the architect to facilitate the orientation of those who must become familiar with the school plant and its intricate operation. Appendix I is a copy of the Operating Manual prepared for Hillsdale High School.

THE DEDICATION

In the dedication of the school it is suggested that the program be devoted to a general overview of the events leading to the need for the new school plant, the relationship of the curriculum to the construction of the building, the location of the classrooms and corridors, the location of the play areas and parking areas, and the actual operation of some of the construction features. The preparation of the program brochure for distribution to the people who assemble for the open house is usually a joint responsibility of the administration and the architect and should stress: (1) the functionalism of the school plant, emphasizing its safety features, ventilation, heating, lighting, design and color, equipment, and furniture, and the cost of its construction; (2) a history of the school district; (3) the statistical needs for the new school; (4) how the new plant fits the need; and (5) the recognition of the citizens who contributed to the events and activities leading to the completion of the plant. It is suggested that (5) be in anecdotal form.

The program itself can be supplemented by using colored slides or a film with a commentary. These visual aids can summarize the situation by covering the following areas: (1) the community and its district (covered by aerial photographs and maps) in which growth has taken place, creating the need for the new plant; (2) statistics of school enrollment, finances, and so forth; (3) the relationships in the design between such areas as classrooms and playgrounds to the curriculum; (4) the construction at different stages —from the time the site is prepared to the completion of the plant; and (5) some of the newer inventions and innovations.

In addition to the board of trustees, administrative staff, leading community citizens, and students, engineers and technicians often attend the ceremony to discuss particular features of the building. These representatives are often spaced throughout the building in areas where they can best demonstrate their particular contribution after the formal ceremonies are completed.

Displays of miniatures and mockups can be used to explain the operations of these devices in a more generalized way. Companies who manufacture and/or install these items welcome an opportunity to appear at such meetings for purposes of improving public relations.

Dedication programs vary with the community. Sample programs are presented in Appendix II.

BIBLIOGRAPHY

American Association of School Administrators, "Public Relations for America's Schools," Twenty-eighth Yearbook. Washington, D.C.: National Education Association, 1950, pp. 11-57, 275-305.

Anderson, Vivienne, "Press Conferences," *School Executive*, Vol. LXIX (March, 1950), p. 39.

Endres, Mary P., "The Organization of Citizens Committees," *School Executive*, Vol. LXX (January, 1952), pp. 56-57.

Grinnell, J. E. and Raymond J. Young, *The School and the Community*. New York: The Ronald Press Company, 1955.

Hymes, James L., *Effective Home-School Relations*, Part II. New York: Prentice-Hall, Inc., 1953.

Mort, Paul R., Administrative Concern with the Community," *School Executive*, Vol. LXXI (February, 1952), pp. 41-43.

Mowrey, Corma, "A Two-Way Process," *Journal of the National Education Association*, Vol. XXXIX (December, 1950), p. 667.

National Society for the Study of Education, "The Community School," Fifty-second Yearbook, Part II. Chicago: University of Chicago Press, 1953.

Olsen, Edward G., *School and Community Programs*, pp. 407-31. New York: Prentice-Hall, Inc., 1949.

Reeder, Ward G., *An Introduction to Public-School Relations*. New York: The Macmillan Co., 1953.

Yeager, William A., *School-Community Relations*. New York: The Dryden Press, Inc., 1951.

OPERATING MANUAL

HILLSDALE HIGH SCHOOL

SAN MATEO UNION HIGH SCHOOL DISTRICT

San Mateo County, California

OPERATING MANUAL

DESIGN AND OPERATION OF

THE SCHOOL PLANT

John Lyon Reid & Partners
Architects—Engineer
San Francisco

___

A. General Description

Hillsdale High School, fourth high school in the San Mateo Union High School District was planned as a complete school for an enrollment of 1750 students. The thirty-five acre site extending along the south side of 31st Avenue from the Alameda de las Pulgas on the east to del Monte Street on the west, slopes toward the Bay to the east. The compact building group encloses approximately five and one third acres, leaving the remaining 29 2/3 acres for athletic and recreational use, and for off-street parking.

The building group is one story high throughout. The elements vary in height according to use and are disposed about a central court with the elements increasing in height as the site slopes down from west to east. Academic areas lie to the west, Shops to the south, Cafeteria and Little Theater to the north, and Auditorium and Gymnasia to the east.

Framed in steel and decked in steel, divided by movable partitions, lighted by rooflights, heated and cooled by mechanical ventilation, interconnected by ramps, Hillsdale High School is the reflection of change and development in secondary education.

B. Basic Design Premise

Two years of preliminary planning led progressively toward adaptability as the major requirement. The Board of Trustees, Superintendent and Faculty, the Educational Consultants and the Stanford University School of Education, the Architects and Engineers, could not fix upon one program for secondary education to which a conventional building could be designed. The unsettling factor was the diversity in secondary educational philosophy. Current practices, trends, predictions, led in many directions. Assurance of any single course was lacking. The excitement of creative, developing education demanded that the building exceed convention.

The Basic Design Premise of the Hillsdale High School therefore is that it shelter with grace the known program of the present, the unknown programs of the future, and the change which is the sure aspect of secondary education.

C. Nature of the Solution

Stemming from the Basic Design Premise were certain guides to solution.

First, The conviction that a known program would not long remain unchanged favored not the tightly-planned, minimum-area type building where one area interlocks with others, but rather a building where rooms and groups of rooms relate to one another with order and consistency.

A modular plan was therefore adopted. Modules of structure, of natural and artificial illumination, of heating and ventilation, and of room division and arrangement, were carefully related each to the others, to permit unlimited plan possibilities.

Second, The anticipated changes of program would require changes in room size and in the relation of one room to another.

Partitions were therefore made non-bearing throughout. Areas where change was most likely, such as English, language, social science, mathematics, science, homemaking, business education, library and administration, were given movable partitions, completely reusable and subject to repeated change.

To permit the relocation of corridors and rooms, opening up or closing off of views, and to permit adding to the structure, an exterior wall system was designed where opaque, insulated panels, translucent or clear glass panels, and glazed or solid doors could be interchanged.

Third, Movable partitions used most advantageously would permit rearrangement in any direction without respect to distance from windows, arrangement of heating units or location of electrical fixtures.

To make room arrangement independent of window walls, an overhead system of natural daylighting was adopted. The alternative of completely artificial illumination was rejected as a less pleasant, more isolating, solution. Completely mechanical ventilation was then adopted with provision both for heating and for cooling. Artificial illumination and heating modules were combined with the natural daylighting module to form, as it were, one modular utility unit fitting within the structural module.

Further steps proceeded, always with close attention to the needs of the initial program, as well as the future programs. Economy was always in mind in the designing. Where desirable features extended to the limit would yield diminishing advantage, a rational limit was sought. The modular control of heating and cooling for example would have perhaps doubled the cost of the distribution system if it had been set upon a 14' x 14' module instead of the efficient and acceptable 28' x

28' module. Artificial illumination on the other hand would cost little if any more on the smaller module and was adjusted thereto.

D. *Description of Certain Features*

* Indicates features applying particularly to academic areas. Some of the features of the solution which depart from usual practice are described in some detail on the following pages.

1. *Rooflights*. Modular units are used, fabricated in one 6' x 6' piece. An aluminum grid holds glass blocks, sealed with lightweight mortar and tar and sulphur compound. The blocks themselves are prismatic blocks special to the purpose. Desirable light is transmitted through the prisms, diffused by the glass fiber filter and distributed by the lower surface of the block. Desirable light is determined as north light and low angle south light. All other light is determined undesirable and is rejected by the carefully adjusted prism surfaces. The result is an even illumination with compensation for low outside brightness coincidental with low angle sun, and sunless days. The prism also results in the elimination of mid-day glare and heat.

*2. *Ventilation*. At the four corners of each 6' x 6' rooflight well there is a 12" x 12" grill. From these grills comes a continuous supply of fresh outside air. This air may come entirely from ducts carrying heated fresh air, entirely from ducts carrying cool, unheated, fresh air, or a mixture of the two. The balance is controlled by thermostats, one for each 28' x 28' bay. Control is automatic but a check on room temperature is available from a panel in the administration for every thermostat location in the building.

*3. *Artificial Illumination*. On four sides of every rooflight well, abutting the ventilation grills at the four corners, are three-tube, egg-crated, fluorescent fixtures. Intensity of illumination can be adjusted by lamping with one, two, or three tubes per fixture, and thereby may be provided restful general lighting, more intense classroom lighting, or high level illumination for special, difficult seeing tasks. Use of the fixtures is minimized, however, by the even, compensated, light from the rooflights. All switches for these fixtures are located above the ceiling and controlled remotely from any desired location. Low voltage control wiring does not require conduit and can be re-strung to new locations as partitions change.

*4. *Public Address System*. The Public Address System wiring is also above the ceiling. Speakers are housed in sound boxes set into the ceiling panels. Location may be easily changed and new speakers added.

*5. *Other Electrical Service.* In addition to the electrical distribution above the ceiling, there is also a complete under floor conduit system. Each 14' x 14' module has four floor boxes which it can tap for power, making new outlets, or outlets in rearranged partitions each to connect. The asphalt tile is laid over the boxes, and their location is marked by a single tile of solid color placed over each box.

*6. *Plumbing Connections.* To permit new and changed locations for plumbing fixtures, water supply is carried overhead and may be brought down at any column. Waste lines are stubbed out at alternate columns in each direction and capped under the asphalt tile; corresponding vents are capped above the ceiling. Thus, all classrooms may be equipped with sinks if desired. Gas can be brought down at any column; vents for ranges, etc. can be up along columns as in the homemaking rooms.

*7. *Ceiling System.* Because the space between ceiling and roof deck is used for utility distribution of many types, a grid system with removable panels is used for the ceiling. Face of panels is fiber board of the desired absorption value, backed with gypsum board both for fireproofness and to prevent transmission of sound into and therefore through the utility space. Access to any utility is available by removing appropriate panels.

*8. *Movable Partitions.* Metal panels with baked enamel finish spanning from floor to ceiling may be rearranged as desired. Interchangeable panels either solid or with various types of glazing, or with doors, are provided in a limited number of widths permitting an unlimited number of room arrangements. A special provision makes it possible to install the partitions at angles. This was desirable in order to improve acoustics and to avoid monotonous repetition. The corridor walls, for example, are zig-zag in plan. This relieves the reverberation tendency in adjoining rooms, avoids the interminable converging perspectives of the usual long corridor, allows doors to be placed in wider points to reduce corridor obstruction, and creates natural conversational areas for the students.

9. *Relation to Outdoors.* While the projection of the Basic Design Premise has resulted in some interior rooms, they are all daylighted. More rooms have a view than not. It is anticipated that a student will spend less than a third of his time in viewless rooms. As he moves from class to class he will, by design, encounter vistas to the surrounding countryside and into landscaped areas; where he will be encouraged to gather with other students.

10. *Swimming Pool.* The swimming pool is located within the central court as a result of wind tunnel tests which favored such a location as best possible for an outdoor pool. Consciously drawn away from the blank-wall, high fence, type of enclosure the pool is a center of interest and an integral part of the landscaping. Bleachers are provided to encourage casual viewing of pool activities.

11. *Auditorium and Little Theater.* These valuable educational facilities have been designed with such economy that their worth will be unquestioned. Each of these areas is essentially one room with the sloping floor scooped from the earth forming the platform, or stage, and providing walkways completely around the room at stage level. Lighting and curtains can be hung in great variation from the ceiling of the platform. Platform and audience can be made very much an entity for concerts, pageants, and experimental drama, or can be separated by curtains for conventional relationships. The choice between no auditorium and the costly theater has been avoided. These are instructional areas, sufficient to instructional purposes, and less costly than many other instructional areas.

12. *Cafeteria.* It is assumed that the cafeteria is also an instructional area. As learning the customs of society can be a pleasant natural experience if properly nurtured, a system of cafeteria service is offered which encourages the maximum use of its facilities. An alcove area is provided for luncheon meetings of student organizations. All food is dispensed within the cafeteria. Four lines are provided. These may be any combination of hot or cold lines. The cold lines can serve the purpose of the "Snack Bar." But while it is made possible for a student to pick up a snack and dash out, he is exposed to the prospect of hot nutritive food at adjoining lines, and to a healthful balanced diet of cold food in his own line. He is also given a glimpse of a pleasant social activity which will, it is hoped, look hospitable.

13. *Fire Protection.* Special research was conducted in cooperation with the State Fire Marshall's Office to make Hillsdale High School as nearly a fire-safe building as possible, and at the same time to avoid fire protection that was costly and restrictive to good planning. The result is a completely incombustible, fire-sprinklered building. Advantage is taken of sprinklering to eliminate all plastering of steel members except in the largest assembly areas, to permit corridor construction to be identical with class room construction, to increase the permissible area of structure, and to reduce the need for fire walls. The considerable cost of the fire-sprinkling was more than regained by savings it made possible in construction. The District has determined that savings in insurance rates will pay for the system in very few years.

E. Cost Analysis

It is the intent of this analysis to state costs clearly and accurately and to leave no question about what is included in each cost quoted. No claim is made that Hillsdale High School is the cheapest high school that could be built and the costs are not selected to enhance favorable costs. The costs do indicate, however, that costs were low compared with much current school construction and that any extra cost for movable partitions, prismatic glass-block rooflights, mechanical ventilation, etc. was more than offset by the savings resulting from a compact plan, repetitive structure and consistent detailing.

The following is a tabulation of pertinent areas and costs with descriptions of items included.

BUILDING AREA: 225,779 sq. ft.
> Includes all enclosed portions of building at full area and all open, roofed areas at one-half full area.'

BUILDING COST:
> For comparative purposes three Building Costs are given including different amounts of equipment.

Building Cost A:
> Total $3,300,360.00
> Per square foot $14.62

Includes complete cost of constructing all of the Building Area as described above complete with the following equipment:
All fixed casework, kitchen equipment, and athletic equipment; visual-aid darkening devices for selected classrooms; 2 shop auto hoists, all shop hoods and paint spray booths; complete fire sprinklering of all enclosed sheltered areas; complete mechanical ventilation under both heating and cooling cycles for all rooms.

Building Cost B:
> Total $3,350,560.00
> Per square foot $14.84

Includes the following equipment which is integral with the design of this building:

Communications: Complete electronic general and selective communication system (public address, phonograph, radio) for all rooms, separate local electronic communication systems for auditorium, little theater, each gymnasium, each locker room, pool and central court; local telephone switchboard serving all rooms.

Theater Equipment: Theater seating for 282 in the Little Theater (folding chairs (N.I.C.) increase audience capacity to 307), for 905 in the Auditorium (folding chairs (N.I.C.) increase audience capacity to 1005); 54' main curtain, valance, borders and back curtain and rotators in Little Theater, 92' main curtain only in Auditorium.

Shop Equipment: Sawdust collection equipment.

Building Cost C:
> Total $3,442,678.00
> Per square foot $15.25

Includes the following equipment in the contract which is customarily purchased by separate contracts:
Movable cabinets, laboratory furniture, movable kitchen equipment and appliances, lockers.

GRADING CONTRACT: $39,000.00

SITE UTILITIES: $96,600.00

Includes separate water mains for sprinkler system and domestic system, sanitary lines, storm sewer on-site and off-site with all catch basins.

POOLS AND SITE WORK: $221,294.95

Include all site improvement outside of building lines and swimming and diving pools.

TOTAL OF ABOVE CONTRACTS: $3,799,573.17

DEDICATION PROGRAMS

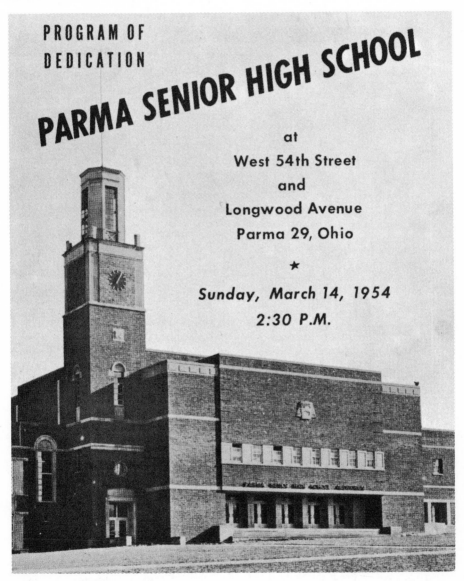

PROGRAM OF
DEDICATION

PARMA SENIOR HIGH SCHOOL

at
West 54th Street
and
Longwood Avenue
Parma 29, Ohio

★

Sunday, March 14, 1954
2:30 P.M.

PROGRAM

Invocation　　-　　　-　　-　　-　　-　　-　　Dr. Holland F. Burr
Pastor, Piedmont Community Church

Introductions　　-　　-　　-　　-　　-　　Mr. Theodore L. Bystrom
Superintendent of Schools

Appreciation of Community Support　　-　　-　　Mr. Roy S. Milligan
Member, Piedmont City Council and
Former President, Piedmont Board of Education

Presentation of School to Principal and Faculty　　Mr. Gordon H. Huber
President, Piedmont Board of Education

Acceptance of School for Faculty　　-　　-　　Mr. Robert G. Brown
Principal, Frank C. Havens School

At the conclusion of the program you are cordially
invited to visit the offices, library and classrooms.

SPECIAL GUESTS

BOARD OF EDUCATION

Mr. Gordon H. Huber　　-　　-　　-　　-　　-　　-　　President

Mr. Russell H. Wilson　　-　　-　　-　　-　　-　　Vice President

Mrs. Margaret R. McIvor　　-　　-　　-　　-　　-　　Secretary

Mr. Robert M. Wells

Mr. Loring Winsor

Mr. Winslow W. Hall　　Chairman, "Piedmonters for Better Schools"

Mr. Carl I. Warnecke　　-　　-　　-　　-　　-　　-　　Architects
Mr. John Carl Warnecke

Mr. John E. Branagh　　-　　-　　-　　-　　-　　-　　Contractors
Mr. Charles Branagh

Mrs. Stanley Cocks　　President, Frank C. Havens School Mothers' Club

Mrs. Kathleen I. Dombrink　　-　　-　　President, Piedmont Parlor,
Native Daughters of the Golden West

From the Frank C. Havens School, Piedmont, California

326

The new Frank C. Havens School replaces an old school built in 1909. Its construction was authorized by a bond issue approved by the voters of Piedmont on April 21, 1953.

The Board of Education's decision to replace the old building was based on the need for making extensive and costly repairs to an outmoded and educationally inadequate building and one which was potentially hazardous in case of a severe earthquake. As time went on it became obvious that additional space would soon be needed to house the growing enrollment.

The architectural firm of Carl I. Warnecke and John C. Warnecke was employed to design a building to meet the needs outlined by the Board of Education. Final plans and specifications, approved by the Board of Education on March 29, 1954, provided for one Kindergarten, eleven classrooms, an administration wing, a library, a cafeteria, and a multi-purpose room. Bids for the construction of the building were opened on April 20, 1954, and the contract for construction was awarded to the firm of John E. Branagh and Son, the low bidder, on May 3, 1954.

COST ANALYSIS

1. Cost of additional property $ 34,900.00

2. Cost of building   391,628.00

     a. Square feet in building   28,900
        (open covered areas taken at $\frac{1}{2}$ area)

     b. Square foot cost $13.55

3. Cost of site work   47,696.00

4. Cost of landscape planting   2,657.00

5. Cost of remodeling existing classroom building   5,300.00

6. Cost of equipment   28,000.00

7. Cost of fees and salaries (architects, inspector, State Division of Architecture, testing and inspecting)   45,949.08

8. Miscellaneous costs (advertising, blue prints, relocating portable building, soil testing, etc.)   2,977.30

        TOTAL $559,107.38

(Courtesy Theodore L. Bystrom, Superintendent of Schools).

P R O G

Presentation of Colors __Conn-Weissenberger Post 587 Am. Legion

Invocation_____ *Reverend James G. Amos*
LUTHERAN CHURCH OF OUR SAVIOR

Washington Junior High Chorus _____*William Stahl*
DIRECTOR
"Deep River," Spiritual
"Ode To The Homeland," Cain

Introduction of Guests _____ *Earl B. Driver*
SUPERINTENDENT OF SCHOOLS, WASHINGTON TOWNSHIP

Remarks _____ *Harold E. Ryder*
SUPERINTENDENT OF SCHOOLS, LUCAS COUNTY

Washington Junior High School Band_____*Vernon Sprague*
DIRECTOR
"Project" — March, Bennett
"Activity" — March, Fillmore

Presentation of Keys by Contractor to Architect__
A. Gideon Spieker

Guided Tours of Building Under Supervis
2:30 P. M. — 7:30 P. M.

From the Washington Jr. High School, Lucas County, O

A M M E

Presentation of Keys by Architect to the Board of Education
Thomas D. McLaughlin, Sr.

Acceptance for the Board of Education __ *Clyde O. Elder, President*

Address—"Public Education, An Expression of Community Living"
Dr. Walter A. Zaugg, College of Education, B. G. S. U.

Whitmer Senior High A Capella Choir _____ *Clyde L. Brown*
DIRECTOR
"O Bone Jesu," Palestrina
"Beautiful Savior," Christiansen

In Appreciation _____ *Homer S. Nightingale*
PRINCIPAL, WASHINGTON JUNIOR HIGH SCHOOL

"Star Spangled Banner"____*Washington Junior High School Band*

Minute of Silent Prayer_____ *In Memoriam of War Heroes*

Benediction _____ *Reverend Robert Kramer*
TRILBY METHODIST CHURCH

•gton Township Parent Teacher Council
30 P. M. — 11:00 P. M.

•rtesy Earl B. Driver, Superintendent of Schools).

INDEX

INDEX